A Concis[illegible]
Sketch of William Penn

Charles Evans

Alpha Editions

This edition published in 2021

ISBN : 9789355899156

Design and Setting By
Alpha Editions
www.alphaedis.com
Email – info@alphaedis.com

BIOGRAPHICAL SKETCH OF WILLIAM PENN.

The following is a brief sketch of the life of one who, though perhaps more widely known as the Proprietor and Founder of Pennsylvania, was also eminent as a minister of the gospel in the Society of Friends, and distinguished for his superior intellectual abilities, his varied culture, and, above all, for his devoted Christian character, exemplified both in adversity and prosperity. It is taken principally from a work entitled "Friends in the Seventeenth Century."

He was the son of William Penn, who, trained to nautical life, had by his genius and courage risen rapidly in the navy, until at the age of twenty-nine he became "Vice-Admiral of the Straits." From the account of his life and public career, given by Granville Penn, a descendant, he appears to have been a man who made self-interest a leading principle of conduct, but who, while eagerly coveting wealth and honor, was never accused of being corrupt as a public servant. His son William was born in London, in 1644, and resided with his mother at Wanstead, in Essex, while his father was absent with the fleet over which he had command.

Owing to information received by Cromwell, through some of the spies kept by him in attendance upon the exiled Charles and his court, that, notwithstanding he had sanctioned the promotion of Admiral Penn, and largely rewarded him by an estate in Ireland, for some losses he had sustained there, he was secretly making overtures to bring the squadron he commanded into the service of the Royalists, he lost favor with the Protector. On his return from an unsuccessful expedition against the Spanish West India Islands, he was deprived of his command and thrown into prison, whence Cromwell generously liberated him at his own humble petition. He then took his family over to Ireland, where he continued to reside for some years, on the estate which Cromwell had had bestowed upon him, and which was near Cork.

In a manuscript written by Thomas Harvey, reciting an account given to him by William Penn, of some of the circumstances of his early life, and which was first published in "The Penns and Peningtons," by M. Webb, it is stated, "That while he was but a child living at Cork with his father, Thomas Loe came thither. When it was rumored a Quaker was come from England, his father proposed to some others to be like the noble Bereans, and hear him before they judged him. He accordingly sent to Thomas Loe to come to his house; where he had a meeting in the family. Though William was very young, he observed what effect T. Loe's preaching had on the hearers. A black servant of his father could not restrain himself from weeping aloud; and little William looking on his father, saw the tears running down his cheeks also. He then thought within himself, 'What if they would all be

Quakers!'" This opportunity he never quite forgot; the remembrance of it still recurring at times. William Penn was then about eleven years of age, and was being educated by a private tutor.

On the retirement of Richard Cromwell from the position for which he had been appointed by his father, Admiral Penn declared for Charles Stuart, and lost no time in going over to the Continent to pay court to him whom he had no doubt would soon be recalled to the throne. Charles employed him in secret service, and rewarded him by the honors of knighthood, and by becoming his debtor for one hundred pounds.

When a little over fifteen years of age, William Penn entered as a "gentleman commoner," at Oxford, where he remained three years, distinguishing himself as a hard and successful student. After the Restoration, the Court set to work to remodel the University, by displacing those who held Puritanical opinions, or who had found favor during the Commonwealth, and installing others, friendly to the re-established church and the lax moral principles then prevailing. Dr. Owen, conspicuous as a scholar and a strict religionist, was ejected to make room for a royalist partisan, and the students became divided into parties, applauding or denouncing the changes made.

There is reason to believe, from observations made by William Penn himself, that throughout his youth he was repeatedly visited by the Day-Spring from on high, convicting him of that which was evil in his ways, and bringing him into serious thoughtfulness. While at college, his associates appear to have been those of a religious cast of character like himself, and who, with him, were greatly influenced by the teaching and advice of Dr. Owen. It so happened that, while much controversy was going on among the scholars relative to religious opinions and practices, Thomas Loe came to Oxford, and held several meetings. To these meetings William Penn and his associates went, and a deep impression was made upon their minds by the powerful preaching of this devoted servant of Christ. They declined being present at what were now the regular "services" of the college, and did not refrain from speaking depreciatingly of what they designated as the "Popish doctrines and usages" re-introduced among them. For this they were lectured and fined. With the ardor and indiscretion of youth, this supposed indignity was highly resented by them. They not only held private meetings for worship and religious exhortation and prayer, but some of them refused to wear the student's gown and cap, and in some instances tore them off of those they met. How far William Penn was implicated in the latter wrong-doing is not known; but his positive refusal to wear the usual garb, his bold denunciation of the doctrine and practices he believed to be wrong, and his courageous defence of the gospel truths he had heard from Thomas Loe, brought upon him the enmity of the Masters in power, and he was expelled the University.

Admiral Penn, who had set his heart upon preparing his son for realizing to the full the ambitious hopes and aims entertained by himself for his family, appears to have been little qualified to understand his son's character, or to rightly estimate the principles that actuated him. His pride was mortified, and, as he thought, his promising schemes were blasted. He received William with anger, and for a time would hardly deign to speak to him. Accustomed to command, and to be obeyed without question, he ordered him to give up his newly-formed views of religious duty, and to hold no further intercourse with those who had shared in his rebellious opinions and course. Enraged on finding that his authority, though seconded by the filial affection of his child, was powerless for removing his religious convictions, he resorted to the use of his cane, followed by solitary confinement in his room, and then banishment from the family.

It was not long, however, before his good sense convinced him that the object he had in view was not to be obtained by severity. He resolved to change his mode of attack, and try if what could not be gained by force might not be brought about by the seductions of a life of gayety and pleasure. Learning that a number of young men, sons of persons considered to be of high families, were about to go on to the Continent and spend some time in study and travelling, he decided to send William with them. Accordingly, furnished with letters that would introduce him into what the world considered the best society, he went to Paris; and, fascinated by the courtly and gay scenes of the company into which he found himself welcomed as an admired guest, he soon caught the worldly spirit that presided over their festivities, and his serious, Quaker-like impressions appeared to pass away, like the morning dew before the burning rays of the sun. He did not, however, allow pleasure to wean him from study. He went to Saumur, and placing himself under the tuition of the learned Moses Amyrault, applied himself to the study of the language and literature of the country, embracing the philosophic basis of divinity. Travelling into Italy, he made himself acquainted with its language, and gratified his taste for the works of the masters in art.

On the breaking out of the war with the Dutch, the Admiral called his son William home, where he arrived after an absence of two years. All trace of the religious seriousness and conscientious restraint that had marked his conduct and manner when he left was gone, and his father was delighted to find his son wearing the carriage and displaying the accomplishments of a self-possessed man of the world. He was at once introduced at Court, and had the opportunity to become acquainted with many who stood high in the brilliant but profligate society that filled the saloons of Whitehall.

William Penn now entered Lincoln's Inn as a student of law, and in 1665, when twenty-one years of age, there seemed every probability of his making an accomplished courtier, and a successful competitor for the honors of this world. Few could enter life with more flattering and apparently better-grounded prospects of attaining to all that would gratify a mind with strong intellectual powers, and naturally ambitious of preferment. His manly form, blooming with health, betokened physical strength and endurance. His disposition, though lively and active, was marked by docility and sweetness. He possessed ready wit, and his good mental abilities had been well developed and trained by careful culture, and strengthened by extensive and profound literary attainments. Men high in power and place smiled upon him. His father enjoyed close intimacy with the Duke of York, heir presumptive to the crown, and eagerly sought to secure for his son the glory and riches of the world, which courted his acceptance.

The Admiral having been appointed by the Duke of York to accompany him in command of the fleet, took William as one of his staff; but after a short absence the latter was sent home with a dispatch to the King. The plague was now spreading in London, and soon the whole aspect of the city was sadly changed. The awful scenes of death that were daily occurring and struck the stoutest hearts with dismay, brought to the sensitive mind of the gay young man conviction of the uncertainty of life, and warning of the necessity to prepare for its sudden termination. The Holy Spirit again broke up his false rest, showed him the emptiness of all worldly grandeur, and wooed him to follow Christ Jesus in the regeneration.

After a cruise of about two months, his father returned, flushed with success in the sanguinary contest in which he had been engaged. He found William again serious, and indisposed to continue the course upon which, but a short time before, he had exultantly entered. The increased honors and emoluments heaped on the victorious sailor by the royal brothers, made him still more fearful lest the foolish whimsies, as he thought them, of his son, would yet disappoint his hopes of the hereditary honors that might be settled upon him. Large accession to his Irish estate, derived from royal bounty as a reward for the service rendered, made it necessary that some one should look after his interest there; and having experienced the good effect, as he considered it, of placing his son within the dazzling circle of gay and fashionable life, he hurried him across the Channel, with letters of introduction to the Duke of Ormond, then Lord Deputy of Ireland.

William found the vice-regal Court comparatively free from the dissipation and loose morals of that which surrounded Charles II., and he soon seemed to enter heartily into the enjoyment it afforded. He joined an expedition sent, under the command of Lord Airan, to quell an insurrection that broke out among the garrison at Carrickfergus, and for a while was so excited by the spirit and enterprise attending active military life, that he became anxious to adopt it as a profession. But his father, when consulted on the subject, decidedly objected, and it was given up.

But He who watches over the workmanship of his hand, and seeks to save that which is lost, was not leaving William Penn to wander in the paths of folly, without the reproofs of instruction, and in mercy, by his witness in the heart, inclining him to accept those reproofs as the way to life; and it was not long before he was brought to a stand, and made to feel that he must then make his election between the life of a votary of this world and that of a self-denying disciple of a crucified Saviour.

Shangarry Castle, the newly-acquired estate of the Admiral, was near to Cork, and when not employed in bringing the place and the affairs connected with it into order, William was often in the town, where he had been well acquainted when a boy. Having one day, while there, gone into the shop of a woman Friend whom he had formerly known, to make a purchase, and finding she did not recognize him, he introduced himself, and entered into conversation with her; recalling to her recollection the meeting held by Thomas Loe at his father's house. Upon her expressing surprise at his memory of the events, he replied, he thought he would never forget them, and that, if he knew where that Friend was, he would go to hear him again, though it was a hundred miles off. She told him he need not go so far, for that Friend was now in Cork, and was to have a meeting the next day. Curious again to hear one who had arrested his attention when a boy, and seriously impressed him by his ministry, when at Oxford, he went to the meeting; and after a time Thomas Loe stood up with the expression, "There is a faith that overcomes the world, and there is a faith that is overcome by the world." It struck deep into the heart of William Penn, who was then made to feel keenly that he had been long striving against or slighting his known duty to his Maker, and allowing the world to overcome the drawing of his heavenly Father's love, to bring him out from the thraldom of sin; and as the preacher with fervid eloquence dwelt on the fruits of such faith, he was thoroughly broken down, and wept much. After the meeting he went with Thomas Loe to a Friend's house, where they had a free conversation, and from that time he became a regular attender of the meetings of Friends. As the Light of Christ shone with more and more clearness upon his soul, he saw how grievously he had departed from the right way of the Lord, and was brought under deep repentance therefor. Convinced of the truth of the doctrines held by Friends, he heartily embraced them, and firmly resolved to live and die by them, whatever sacrifices it might cost him.

Being at a meeting in Cork in 1667, he, with others, was arrested by officers who came to break the meeting up, and was sent to prison: though the Magistrate, who recognized him as the son of the lord of Shangarry Castle, offered to set him at liberty if he would give his word "to keep the peace," which he refused. From the prison he addressed a letter to the Earl of Ossory, giving an account of the arrest and imprisonment of himself and friends, showing their innocence, and pleading the liberty of conscience demanded by the precepts of the gospel. An order was immediately dispatched by the Earl for his release; and as it was soon noised abroad that Admiral Penn's son had turned Quaker, the Earl wrote to his father, communicating the information. Startled and annoyed by the intelligence, the Admiral ordered William to come home immediately, which he did. Josiah Cole, a minister in the Society of Friends, met him at Bristol; accompanied him to London, and being deeply interested for his stability and preservation, went with him to his father's house. Fully as William had adopted the principles of Friends, and many as were the baptisms he had already passed through, he had not yet adopted the plain dress that distinguished them from others; and his father observing this, and that his rapier still hung by his side, hoped that his friend the Earl had been wrongly informed; and he treated him and his friend during the evening with ordinary courtesy, without alluding to the report that had reached him.

Observing, on the next day, that William did not uncover his head when he came into his presence,—in those days men generally wore their hats in the house,—and that he used thee and thou when addressing him, he demanded an explanation. William frankly told him that, having been convinced of the truth of the religion of the Quakers, he was conscientiously scrupulous against taking off his hat as a token of respect, using the plural language, or compliments. An angry altercation on the part of the father, and deeply distressing on the part of the son, succeeded, and was more than once repeated. Finally, the former, finding that neither argument nor threats could shake the latter's firm conviction that to comply with his father's wishes would be to violate his duty to his Lord and Master, told him he might thee and thou whom he pleased, and keep on his hat, except in the presence of the King, the Duke of York, and himself; but to or before these he should not thee or thou, or stand covered; and the son, moved by his father's distress and his own filial affection, asked time for consideration before giving a decisive reply. This was reluctantly granted, though he was forbidden to see any Friend, and William retired, to pour out his soul in prayer for right direction and strength to follow it. At their next interview William told his father that he could not comply with his wishes without violating his duty to his God, and must therefore decline. Irritated at what he considered his son's obstinacy, and foolish determination to sacrifice the worldly honors soliciting his acceptance, for a mere whim, the Admiral upbraided him in no measured terms, and when convinced that he would not be changed, turned him out of doors, with the threat that he would disinherit him. Before leaving his home and family, William assured his father how deeply he was grieved; not so much because of his being driven from his paternal roof and brought to poverty, as because he incurred his displeasure, and was thought by him to be an undutiful child. He then left the house, resigned to make the sacrifice required, and "choosing rather to suffer affliction with the people of God, than to enjoy the pleasures of sin for a season; esteeming the reproach of Christ greater riches than the treasures of Egypt; for he had respect unto the recompense of reward." Friends who knew the circumstances under which William Penn was placed, received him gladly; and his mother, who yearned over the son of her love, and greatly mourned the course pursued towards him, took means to have him supplied with money sufficient to obtain food and raiment, and so managed as to have an occasional interview with him. It was not long after, that, laying aside his rapier and all ornamentation of dress, he appeared in the plain garb of a Quaker.

Some years after, when writing respecting the trials that befell him about this time, he speaks of "the bitter mockings and scornings that fell upon me, the displeasure of my parents, the cruelty and invective of the priests, the strangeness of all my companions, and what a sign and wonder they made of me; but above all, that great cross of resisting and watching against my own vain affections and thoughts."

As he was given up to endure the baptisms necessary for his purification and refinement, his Divine Master brought him up out of the horrible pit, set his feet upon Himself, the Rock of Ages, and made him a partaker of the powers of the world to come; and having thus prepared him for the work, bestowed on him a gift in the ministry of the gospel of life and salvation. He first came forth in this service in 1668, about two years after his convincement under the ministry of Thomas Loe, and in the twenty-fourth year of his age. His uniformly consistent conduct, and careful maintenance of affectionate filial respect toward his exasperated parent, finally won upon him so far that he permitted him to take up his abode in his house; though it was long after he had been so living, before he would have much intercourse with him. But when, sharing in the persecution which Friends were then suffering, his son was cast into prison, it was said he secretly used his influence to obtain his liberty.

In 1668 Thomas Loe was called away from the church militant to enter upon his reward in the church triumphant. When on his death-bed, he said to William Penn, who, with other Friends, was waiting on him, "Bear thy cross and stand faithful to God; then He will give thee an everlasting crown of glory, that shall not be taken from thee. There is no other way which shall prosper than that which the holy men of old walked in. God hath brought immortality to light, and life immortal is felt. Glory! glory! to Him, for He is worthy of it. His love overcomes my heart; nay, my cup runs over; glory be to His Name forever." To George Whitehead he remarked, "The Lord is good to me; this day He hath covered me with glory," and as life was leaving his body, he sang, "Glory, glory to Thee forever!" and so sank to sleep in Jesus.

In 1668 William Penn was imprisoned on account of one of his publications, "The Sandy Foundation Shaken." It resulted from himself and George Whitehead having been unfairly prevented from orally replying to a Calvinistic preacher who had assailed the doctrines of Friends. In this tract he was not so guarded in the language he used, but that he was misunderstood by many, and supposed to be unsound on the fundamental doctrines of the proper divinity and meritorious death and atonement of Christ. The publication attracted general attention, and gave deep offence to some of the Prelates, who either thought it beneath their dignity to enter into argument with a polemic so young, and as they might think, so unskilled in divinity, or, being more in accordance with their practice and the spirit of the times, and more likely to silence their opponent, they applied to the Secretary of State, and induced him to issue a warrant for his arrest; which William Penn hearing of, went and voluntarily gave himself up, and was committed to the Tower. It was evident that William Penn had some bitter enemies, for a letter was picked up near where he had been standing when he surrendered himself, which contained matter of so treasonable a character, that Lord Arlington, the Secretary of State, on receiving and reading it, went immediately to the Tower and had an interview with him, in which he soon satisfied himself that William Penn knew nothing of the note, and was innocent of any conspiracy.

There had been no indictment, no trial, conviction, nor sentence passed upon the prisoner, and yet he was kept in solitary confinement for about eight months; during which time most of his family and friends were forbidden access to him, and the "Bishop of London" sent him word he should either make a public recantation or die in prison. But though thus closely immured as to his body, his spirit was free, and the word of the Lord was not bound. He prepared himself to weary out the malice of his enemies by patience and meekness, and to be resigned to lay down his life within the walls of the Tower, if the sacrifice was called for, rather than violate his conscience.

To occupy his time profitably, and, as far as he had ability, promote the cause of truth and righteousness, he employed his pen; and his thoughts, probably taking their direction and coloring from the afflictive circumstances under which he and many other members of the Society to which he was joined were then placed, he wrote the work, since become so celebrated, "No Cross, No Crown." This treatise is admitted to be of extraordinary merit; not only in a literary point of view, considering the short time and the circumstances under which it was produced, but in the clear and cogent manner in which it presents the sinful indulgences of the great body of the professors of

Christianity, and enforces the self-denying requisitions of the religion of Christ.

Finding that some parts of his "Sandy Foundation Shaken" had been misunderstood or misrepresented, so as to give currency to the charge of his being unsound in relation to the divinity and atonement of Christ, William Penn at once wrote an explanation of what had been misrepresented, and in exposition of his views on these cardinal points of Christian faith. This was entitled, "Innocency with her Open Face." In this work he says, "Let all know, that I pretend to know no other name by which remission, atonement, and salvation can be obtained, but Jesus Christ the Saviour, who is the power and wisdom of God." Asserting his full belief in the divinity of Christ, he observes, "He that is the everlasting Wisdom, the divine Power, the true Light, the only Saviour, the creating Word of all things, whether visible or invisible, and their Upholder by his own power, is without contradiction, God; but all these qualifications and divine properties are, by the concurrent testimony of Scripture, ascribed to the Lord Jesus Christ, therefore without scruple, I call and believe him really to be the mighty God."

In replying to Dr. John Collenges, some years after the publication of "The Sandy Foundation Shaken," who had at that time brought forward exceptions to its doctrines, William Perm again explicitly asserts his full belief in the proper divinity of, and atonement made by, Christ: and in the doctrine of justification as held by Friends at that time and ever since. "I do *heartily believe* that Jesus Christ is the only true and everlasting God, by whom all things were made that are made, in the heavens above or the earth beneath, or the waters under the earth: that He is as omnipotent, so omniscient and omnipresent, therefore God." And in regard to the atonement and justification, he thus writes, "He that would not have me mistaken, on purpose to render his charge against me just, whether it be so or no, may see in *my apology* for 'The Sandy Foundation Shaken,' that I otherwise meant than I am charactered. In short, I say, both as to this and the other point of justification, that Jesus Christ was a *sacrifice for sin*; that He was set forth to be *a propitiation for the sins of the whole world*; to declare God's righteousness, *for the remission of sins that are passed*, etc.; to all that repented and had faith in His Son. Therein the love of God appeared, that He declared His good-will *thereby* to be reconciled; Christ bearing away the sins that are passed, as the scape-goat did of old; not excluding inward work; for till that is begun, none can be benefitted; though it is not the work, but God's free love, that remits and blots out; of which the death of Christ and His sacrificing himself was a most certain declaration and confirmation. In short, *that* declared remission to all who believe and obey, for the sins that are past; which is the *first part* of Christ's work (as it is a king's to pardon a traitor before he advanceth him), and hitherto the acquittance imputes a righteousness—inasmuch as men, *on true repentance*, are imputed as clean of guilt as if they had never sinned—and thus far are justified; but the *completion* of this by the working out of sin inherent, must be by the Power and Spirit of Christ in the heart, destroying the old man and his deeds, and bringing in the new and everlasting righteousness. So that which I wrote against, is such doctrine as extended Christ's death and obedience, *not to the first*, but to the second part of justification; not the pacifying of conscience as to past sin; but to complete salvation without cleansing and purging from all filthiness of flesh and spirit, by the internal operation of his holy power and Spirit."

Notwithstanding William Penn is thus clear and explicit in correcting the misunderstanding of his Christian faith, to which some of his expressions in "The Sandy Foundation Shaken" had given rise, and in his full avowal of his belief in the Deity of Christ, and the atonement made by Him for the sins of mankind; as also in the doctrine of justification by faith in Him; yet those who are anxious to represent Friends as Socinians, or as denying the atonement of Christ, are still so unjust to his unequivocal and widely-published opinions on these points, and so ungenerous to his character and memory, as well as untruthful in their representation of Friends, as to claim him as authority for their disbelief in these fundamental doctrines.

Though he had addressed a communication to Lord Arlington, Secretary of State, on whose warrant he was committed to the Tower, in which he denied the charges brought against him, so far as he had been able to ascertain them; declaring they were the result of ignorance and malice, and requesting that he might have an audience with the King, in order to hear the accusation of his enemies, and have an opportunity to defend himself; or if he could not have access to the King, then to be brought, with his accusers, face to face before him, the Secretary of State, it was disregarded, nor was the rigor of his confinement abated. "Innocency with her Open Face" had, however, produced a change of public feeling towards him; and his father, who could not but respect the consistent firmness and Christian endurance of his son, and who had himself been passing through a severe ordeal from the machinations of his enemies in the House of Commons, visited him in his dungeon, and began to use the influence he continued to hold with the Duke of York and the King, on his behalf. Whether at his instance or not is not known, but Arlington, though declining to give audience to William Penn himself, sent the King's Chaplain, Stillingfleet, to have an interview with him, and ascertain what concessions he would be willing to make to the offended hierarchy. Their conversation appears to have been conducted in a friendly spirit and manner: the Chaplain holding up the brilliant future that would be realized by Penn if he would recant some of his opinions, and dwelling on the favorable disposition of the Duke of York and King towards him. William told him, "The Tower is the worst argument in the world," and that nothing could induce him to violate his conscientious convictions, so there seemed nothing gained. But suddenly and unexpectedly an order came from the King for his release, and he left the gloomy confines of his prison-house without making any concession or accepting a pardon. The discharge was believed to have been the work of the Duke of York, and William ever cherished a grateful feeling towards him for this generous act.

In the year 1670, Friends in England underwent great persecution and suffering on account of their religious principles. The law against Dissenters, that had just expired, had failed in its object, and it was therefore determined to try another method, which enlisted the cupidity of the depraved class as informers, and used the almost unrestrained functions of officials clothed with absolute power to impoverish and harass those who met together for Divine worship in a way differing from the "Church of England," in the hope of rendering such unable to live in their native country. Accordingly a third "Act to prevent and suppress seditious conventicles" was passed by Parliament, and received the royal assent in the Fourth month, 1670.

Persecution now ran riot; and the power being by design placed in the hands of the most profligate and debased, rapine, havoc, and impoverishment were spread over the nation by the graceless informers, abetted by a venal magistracy, eager to share in the plunder.

But the storm, biting and incessant as it was, was no more effective in deterring Friends from assembling for the purpose of worshipping their Almighty Father in Heaven, than that which had been raised under the former "Conventicle Act." Grievously spoiled and cruelly abused as they were, they knew their enemies could truthfully allege nothing against them but that which concerned the law of their God; and in the sincerity of their hearts they made their appeal unto Him, with full confidence that He would extend his fatherly, protecting care over them; would cause the wrath of man to bring Him praise, and when He saw it was enough, would restrain the remainder of wrath, and limit the rage and cruelty of their merciless tormentors. Deprived of the use of their meeting-houses, they assembled as near to them as they could get; and beaten, bruised, imprisoned, and fined, as many of each company were almost sure to be, the next meeting-day found others at the same place, engaged in the performance of the same indispensable duty; ready to encounter, with meekness and patience, the wrath of their persecutors, and to suffer for the maintenance of their rights as men and their obligation as Christians.

Their treatment in London, bad as it was, was thought to be less severe than in many other parts of the Kingdom. Yet in that city, it was a common occurrence for those who attended their meetings for worship, to be beaten with the muskets of the foot-soldiers, and the sabres of the dragoons, until the blood ran down upon the ground; women, sometimes young maidens, were maltreated in the most shameful manner.

On the fourteenth of the Eighth month, 1670, William Penn and William Mead were taken from the meeting held in the street, as near to Grace-church meeting-house as they could get; the former being engaged in ministry at the time. They were brought to trial on the first of the Ninth month, before the Mayor, Samuel Starling; the Recorder, John Howell; several Aldermen, and the Sheriffs. William Mead had formerly been a captain in the Commonwealth's army, but having embraced the truths of the Gospel as held by Friends, he of course gave up all connection with military life, and is mentioned in the indictment as a linen-draper, in London; though it is probable he resided most of his time in Essex, where he had a considerable landed estate. He afterwards married a daughter of Margaret Fell.

The indictment charged that they, with other persons, to the number of three hundred, with force and arms, unlawfully and tumultuously assembled together, on the fifteenth day of August, 1670, and the said William Penn, by agreement made beforehand with William Mead, preached and spoke to the assembly; by reason whereof, a great concourse and tumult of people continued a long time in the street, in contempt of the King and his law, to the great disturbance of his peace, and to the terror of many of his liege people and subjects.

The character of the trial might be judged by the first incident that occurred. Being brought before the Court on the third of the Ninth month, an officer took off their hats on their entrance; whereupon the Mayor angrily ordered him to put them on again; which being done, the Recorder fined them forty marks apiece, for alleged contempt of Court, by appearing before it with their hats on. This trial has become celebrated, not only on account of the ability with which William Penn—then in his twenty-sixth year—defended his cause, and sustained the inalienable rights of Englishmen, but for the inflexible firmness of the jury in maintaining their own rights, and adhering to their conscientious convictions; notwithstanding the iniquitous determination of the Court, to enforce its own will, to convict and punish the prisoners at the bar, and to oblige the jury to become their tools for that purpose.

The indictment was incorrect, even in the statement of the time when the offence was said to have taken place; as it was on the fourteenth of the month, and not on the fifteenth, and therefore it ought to have been quashed by the Court, and the prisoners discharged. The evidence of the three witnesses examined was altogether inconclusive, but William Penn boldly said to the Court, "We confess ourselves to be so far from recanting or declining to vindicate the assembling of ourselves, to preach, pray, or worship the eternal, holy, just God, that we declare to all the world, that we do believe it to be our indispensable duty to meet incessantly on so good an account; nor shall all the powers upon earth be able to divert us from reverencing and adoring the God who made us." He then asked the Court to tell him upon what law the indictment and proceedings were founded. The Recorder answering, the common law, Penn requested him to tell him what law that was; for if it was common, it must be easy to define it. But the Recorder refused to tell him, saying it was *lex non scripta*, and it was not to be expected that he could say at once what it was, for some had been thirty or forty years studying it. Penn observed that Lord Coke had declared that common law was common right, and common right the great chartered privileges confirmed by former Kings. The Recorder, greatly excited, told him he was a troublesome fellow, and it was not to the honor of the Court to suffer him to go on; but Penn calmly insisted that the Court was bound to explain to the prisoners at their bar the law they had violated, and upon which they were being tried; and he told them plainly that, unless they did so, they were violating the chartered rights of Englishmen, and acting upon an arbitrary determination to sacrifice those rights to their own illegal designs. Whereupon the Mayor and Recorder ordered him to be turned into the bail-dock. William Penn,—"These are but so many vain exclamations; is this justice or true judgment? Must I, therefore, be taken away because I plead for the fundamental laws of England?" Then, addressing himself to the jury, he said: "However, this I leave upon your consciences who are of the jury, and my sole judges, that if these ancient fundamental laws which relate to liberty and property, and are not limited to particular persuasions in matters of religion, must not be indispensably maintained and observed, who can say he hath a right to the coat upon his back. Certainly our liberties are openly to be invaded, our children enslaved, our families ruined, and our estates led away in triumph, by every sturdy beggar and malicious informer, as their trophies, but our pretended forfeits for conscience' sake. The Lord of heaven and earth will be judge between us in this matter." The hearing of this emphatic speech was so troublesome to the Recorder, that he cried, "Be silent there!" At which William Penn returned, "I am not to be silent in a cause wherein I am so much concerned, and not only myself, but many ten thousand families besides."

Penn being thrust into the bail-dock, William Mead was called up, and was asked if he was present at the meeting. Which question he refused to answer, on the ground that he could not be required to accuse himself. He then told the jury that the indictment was false in many particulars, and that William Penn was right in demanding the law upon which it was based. It charged him with assembling by force and arms, tumultuously and illegally, which was untrue; and he informed them of Lord Coke's definition of a rout or riot, or unlawful assembly. Here the Recorder interrupted him, and endeavored to cast ridicule on what he had said, by taking off his hat and saying, "I thank you for telling us what the law is." On Mead replying sharply to a taunting speech of Richard Brown, the old and inveterate enemy of Friends, the Mayor told him "he deserved to have his tongue cut out." He, too, was put into the bail-dock, and the Court proceeded to charge the jury. Whereupon William Penn cried out with a loud voice to the jury, to take notice, that it was illegal to charge the jury in the prisoners' absence, and without giving them opportunity to plead their cause. The Recorder ordered him to be put down. William Mead then remonstrating against such "barbarous and unjust proceedings," the Court ordered them both to be put into a filthy, stinking place, called "the hole." After an absence of an hour and a half, eight of the jury came down agreed, but four staid up and would not assent. The Court sent for the four, and menaced them for dissenting. When the jury was all together, the prisoners were brought to the bar, and the verdict demanded. The Foreman said William Penn was guilty of speaking in Grace-church Street. The Court endeavored to extort something more, but the Foreman declared he was not authorized to say anything but what he had given in. The Recorder, highly displeased, told them they might as well say nothing, and they were sent back. They soon returned with a written verdict, signed by all of them, that they found William Penn guilty of speaking or preaching in Grace-church Street, and William Mead not guilty. This so incensed the Court, that they told them they *would* have a verdict they would accept, and that "they should be locked up without meat, drink, fire, or tobacco: you shall not think thus to abuse the Court. We will have a verdict, by the help of God, or you shall starve for it." Against this outrageous infraction of justice and right, William Penn remonstrated, saying: "My jury, who are my judges, ought not to be thus menaced; their verdict should be free, and not compelled; the Bench ought to wait upon them, but not forestall them. I do desire that justice may be done me, and that the arbitrary resolves of the Bench may not be made the measure of my jury's verdict." The Recorder cried out, "Stop that prating fellow's mouth, or put him out of Court." Penn insisted that the agreement of the twelve men was a verdict, and that the Clerk of the Court should record it; and, addressing the jury, he said: "You are Englishmen; mind your privileges; give not away your right!" To which some of them replied, "Nor will we ever do it."

The jury were sent to their room, and the prisoners to jail, the former being deprived of food, drink, and every accommodation. The same verdict was returned the next morning; calling from the Bench upbraiding and threats, similar to those so lavishly bestowed on the jury before: the Recorder, in his passion, going so far as to say, "Till now, I never understood the reason of the policy and prudence of the Spaniards in suffering the Inquisition among them; and certainly, it will never be well with us till something like the Spanish Inquisition be in England." Again the jury was sent back to their room, and the prisoners returned to Newgate; both being so kept for another twenty-four hours; the jury without victuals, drink, or other accommodations. The next morning they were again brought into Court, and the usual question respecting their verdict being put, the Foreman first replied, "You have our written verdict already." The Recorder refusing to allow it to be read, the Clerk repeated the query, "How say you, is William Penn guilty or not guilty?" The Foreman answered: "Not guilty." The same verdict was given in the case of William Mead. The jury being separately questioned, they all made the same reply. The Recorder, exasperated at their decision and firmness, after pouring out his invectives upon them, said: "The Court fines you forty marks a man, and imprisonment till paid."

William Penn now demanded his liberty; but the Mayor said "No, you are in for your fines." "Fines! for what?" replied Penn. "For contempt of Court," was the answer. Penn then declared that, according to the laws, no man could be fined without a trial by jury; but the Mayor ordered him and Mead first to the bail-dock, and then to the jail; where the jury was likewise consigned.

But this noble stand of the jury for law and right was not allowed to terminate in the punishment of these upright men, and the continued gratification of the revenge of the unjust Judges. After ineffectually demanding of the Court their release two or three times, a writ of *habeas corpus* was granted by Judge Vaughan; who, upon hearing the case, decided their fine and imprisonment illegal, and set them free.

The usage of the Courts had not before been reduced to a legal and positive form. It had been the occasional practice of the Bench to impose fines on "inconvenient juries," and had long remained practically an unsettled question, whether a jury had a right so far to exercise its own discretion as to bring in a verdict contrary to the sense of the Court. This important point was now decided; the Judges—there were others associated with Vaughan—adopting the views that it was the special function of the jury to judge of the evidence, and that the Bench, though at liberty to offer suggestions for the consideration of the jurymen, might not lawfully coerce them.

William Penn, anxious to have the cases of himself and his friend reviewed by a Superior Court, wrote to his father, affectionately desiring him not to interfere to have him released. But the old man, who was fast declining, and anxious to have the company and attentions of his son, to whom he was not only reconciled, but on whose filial affection and care he had learned to lean for comfort and support, was not willing to wait the tardy process of law; and therefore paid the fines of both the Friends, and had them set free. The Admiral survived but a few days the liberation of his son; in which time he sent one of his friends to the King and Duke of York, to make his dying request, that, so far as they could, they would hereafter befriend his loved son; which both promised to do. Addressing his son shortly before his death, he said: "Son William, if you and your friends keep to your plain way of preaching, and your plain way of living, you will make an end of the priests to the end of the world." Again—sensible, it is probable, of the wrong he had before committed in his course towards his son—he said, emphatically: "Let nothing in the world tempt you to wrong your conscience. I charge you, do nothing against your conscience; so you will keep peace at home, which will be a feast to you in the day of trouble."

Near the close of this year, William Penn was again arrested at Wheeler Street meeting, by some of the officers of Robinson, Lieutenant of the Tower, who had sent them there for the purpose, and he was taken before him. His examination, as published, shows his Christian courage and firmness, as he exposed the duplicity of Robinson in his profession of friendship for him; and asserted his innocence of the charges made against him. He was sent to Newgate for six months; during which time he drew up an account of the memorable trial at the Old Bailey; also several dissertations which were afterwards published as tracts: one of these was, "The great Case of Liberty of Conscience, once more briefly Debated, and Defended by authority of Scripture, Reason, and Antiquity."

Soon after his release he married Gulielma Maria Springett, daughter of Sir William Springett. She was a pious young woman, of well-educated and amiable manners. After his marriage he settled in Hertfordshire.

In 1677 George Fox, William Penn, Robert Barclay, and some other Friends, went over to Holland on a religious visit, and travelled into Germany. In the course of this journey, William Penn and two other Friends visited Elizabeth, Princess Palatine of the Rhine, at her Court at Herwerden. She was the oldest daughter of Frederick V., Elector Palatine, and at one time King of Bohemia; her mother being the sister of Charles I. of England. She is represented to have been a woman of good natural capacity, well educated, and of amiable disposition and manners; and to have governed her small territory with good judgment and much consideration for the welfare of her subjects. Having been brought under the power of religion, she manifested strong interest in others who were sincere in their religious convictions, and was opposed to interference with liberty of conscience. Having become acquainted with the religious tenets of Friends, by conversation with Robert Barclay and Benjamin Furly, who visited her in 1676, and with women Friends from Amsterdam, she found them to answer to the convictions of Truth on her own mind; and she not only gladly received Friends when they came to see her, but in her letters to several of the more prominent members among them, and to others at the English Court, she unhesitatingly expressed her high estimation of them, and her disapproval of the persecution to which those that held them were subjected.

The Friends named, having requested permission to have a religious opportunity with her, it was readily granted; she having in her family at that time the Countess of Hornes, her intimate friend, and a French lady. Of this interview William Penn thus writes in his journal: "I can truly say it, and that in God's fear, I was very deeply and reverently affected with the sense that was upon my spirit of the great and notable day of the Lord, and the breaking in of his eternal power upon all nations; and of the raising of the slain Witness to judge the world; who is the Treasury of life and peace, of wisdom and glory, to all that receive Him in the hour of his judgments, and abide with Him. The sense of this deep and sure foundation, which God is laying as the hope of eternal life and glory for all to build upon, filled my soul with an holy testimony to them, which in a living sense was followed by my brethren; and so the meeting ended about the eleventh hour."

In the afternoon they held another meeting with them, which was also so remarkably favored, that William Penn says: "Well, let my right hand forget its cunning, and my tongue cleave to the roof of my mouth, when I shall forget the loving-kindness of the Lord, and the sure mercies of our God to us, his travailing servants, that day."

Subsequently, on their return towards Holland, these Friends again stopped at Herwerden, and upon informing the Princess of their arrival, they were again gladly received by her and her friends. A meeting being held with them and some others whom they had invited, the next morning, William Penn states in his journal: "About eight the meeting began, and held till eleven, several persons of the city, as well as those of her own family, being present. The Lord's power very much affected them, and the Countess was twice much broken while we spoke. After the people were gone out of the chamber, it lay upon me from the Lord to speak to them two—the Princess and the Countess—with respect to their particular conditions; occasioned by these words from the Princess, 'I am fully convinced; but oh my sins are great.' While I was speaking, the glorious power of the Lord wonderfully rose, yea, after an awful manner, and had a deep entrance upon their spirits; especially the Countess, so that she was broken to pieces: God hath raised, and I hope fixed, his own testimony in them."

The next day they had a parting interview in the chamber of the Princess, which was equally favored. "Magnified be the name of the Lord; He overshadowed us with His glory. His heavenly, breaking, dissolving power richly flowed among us, and his ministering angel of life was in the midst of us."

During the time of severe suffering through which Friends were passing in Great Britain after the Restoration, as was natural, on finding that redress or abatement of their grievances was almost beyond hope, they seriously entertained a project for finding homes somewhere beyond the reach of their fellow-men, who seemed bent on extirpating them, by the slow process of the cruel punishments inflicted for their religious faith. George Fox, in common with several other prominent members, seriously contemplated the purchase of a tract of land from the Indians in North America; where, not the whole body of Friends in Great Britain, but such as felt themselves free to leave their native land, might emigrate and enjoy the right of worshipping the Almighty according to the dictates of their consciences.

Josiah Cole, while engaged in religious service in America, was commissioned to look out, and enter into treaty for such a resting-place; and at one time he had several interviews with the chiefs of the Susquehanna Indians, in order to treat with them for a part of their territory. Owing to a war coming on between that tribe and another, the proposed purchase fell through.

In 1676 William Penn, as trustee for the creditors of Edward Billinge, one of the proprietors of West Jersey, and afterwards by the purchase of a proprietary right in East Jersey, became concerned in the colonization of that Province. Others were associated with him in the undertaking, among whom were several of his own Society, under whose management a peaceful settlement was effected. A form of government was agreed on for West Jersey, and a declaration of fundamental principles, to be incorporated in it, consented to; among which was the stipulation, "No person to be called in question or molested for his conscience, or for worshipping according to his conscience."

Many Friends of good estates, and highly esteemed for their religious standing and experience, crossed the Atlantic to this land of liberty, and between 1676 and 1681 about fourteen hundred had arrived and settled; principally in the country bordering the eastern shore of the Delaware. These immigrants suffered the privations and hardships incident to beginning civilized life in an unbroken wilderness, surrounded by savages, who were dependent in great measure upon the uncertain supplies of the chase for their own sustenance, and who rarely laid up much in store for future wants. But, by uniform uprightness in all their dealings with these children of the forest, and their Christian kindness towards them, they soon gained their good-will, and, in times of scarcity, excited their sympathy; so that often they were relieved by voluntary offerings of corn and meat from these untutored red men, when it seemed as though otherwise they must have suffered for food.

Proud, in the preface to his "History of Pennsylvania," gives in a note an account of these trials, drawn up by one of the Friends who settled in New Jersey, containing the following passages:

"A providential hand was very visible and remarkable in many instances that might be mentioned, and the Indians were even rendered our benefactors and protectors. Without any carnal weapon, we entered the land and inhabited therein, as safe as if there had been thousands of garrisons; for the Most High preserved us from harm, both of man and beast." "The aforesaid people (Friends) were zealous in performing their religious services; for having at first no meeting-house to keep a public meeting in, they made a tent or covert of sail-cloth to meet under; and after they got some little houses to dwell in, then they kept their meetings in one of them till they could build a meeting-house."

In the course of the business which necessarily claimed his attention in the colonization of the province of New Jersey, William Penn naturally had his thoughts frequently directed towards the settlements of his countrymen on the far-distant shores of America; and having been disappointed in the part he took in English politics, in an unsuccessful effort to procure the election of his friend, Algernon Sidney, to Parliament, his interest in that part of the world increased, as his mind became occupied with the idea of settling a free colony in the pathless wilderness on the other side of the Atlantic; where men should live under an elective government, enact the laws by which they were to be controlled, admit of no master, but all share in equal rights, and rest in the enjoyment of civil and religious liberty. Witnessing the success that attended the removal of Friends to New Jersey, where they were freed from the cruel persecution they had endured while in Great Britain, under which their brethren at home were still suffering grievously, he became desirous to obtain the control of such portion of the yet unappropriated territory over which the King of England claimed the sovereignty, as would enable him to found a colony, and "make a holy experiment"—as he called it—of opening an asylum for the oppressed of every land; where there should be secured equality of political and civil rights, universal liberty of conscience, personal freedom, and a just regard for the rights of property.

Admiral Penn at different times had loaned money to the British government, and to the Duke of York; which the costly profligacy of the Court had prevented being repaid, and, with the interest accruing, it amounted at that time to between sixteen and seventeen thousand pounds sterling. In 1680, William Penn petitioned the King, that in order to cancel the debt, he should grant him the tract of country bounded on the east by the Delaware River, and on the south by Lord Baltimore's Province of Maryland; while the western and northern limits were undefined; though the latter was not to interfere with the Province of New York. But William Penn was by no means popular at the Court. The courtiers despised him for his strict conscientiousness; the clerical party hated him for his Quakerism, and open opposition to their assumed place and power; while the active interest he had taken in promoting the return of Sidney—a known Republican—to Parliament, had given offence to the King and Duke. Private interests and jealousies were enlisted against him, and the agents of Lord Baltimore and Sir John Werden, deputy for the Duke of York, were assiduous in their efforts to thwart him, and defeat his application.

But he was not a man easily turned aside from pursuing that which he thought right to attain. The Earl of Sutherland was his firm friend in the Privy Council, and there were several other persons of note who took warm interest in the success of his colonial project. Penn sought and obtained an interview with the Duke of York, and succeeded in changing his feelings towards himself, and his views relative to the policy of the grant. But perhaps the most cogent argument with the King and Council was, the persistent presentation by one of the latter that, if the grant was withheld, the money due must be forthcoming. There were many vexatious delays and disappointments; but finally the boundaries of the Province being adjusted as was then thought clearly and definitely, and such clauses introduced into the terms of the patent or charter as were deemed necessary to secure the paramount authority of the King, Charles affixed his signature to it on the fourth of the Third month, 1681. William Penn proposed to call his Province New Wales, but the Secretary, who was a Welshman, would not consent to it. He then suggested Sylvania, to which the King prefixed Penn, out of respect to the late Admiral; and though William objected to it, as savoring of vanity in him, it was determined to adhere to that name.

By the Charter, William Penn was made sole and absolute proprietary of the Province; with power, with the assent of the freemen residing therein, to make all necessary laws, provided they were not inconsistent with the laws of England; to grant pardons or reprieves, except in cases of wilful murder or treason, and to enjoy all such duties on imports or exports as the representatives of the people might assess. There was a clause in the Charter, inserted at the solicitation of the Bishop of London, that whenever twenty of the inhabitants should petition the said Bishop for a preacher, he should be permitted to reside in the Province.

His design from the first was to establish a government upon Christian principles. In referring to this subject, he says: "And because I have been somewhat exercised at times, about the nature and end of government among men, it is reasonable to expect that I should endeavor to establish a just and righteous one in this Province, that others may take example by it; truly this my heart desires. For nations want a precedent, and till vice and corrupt manners be impartially rebuked and punished, and till virtue and sobriety be cherished, the wrath of God will hang over nations. I do therefore desire the Lord's wisdom to guide me, and those that may be concerned with me, that we may do the thing that is truly wise and just."

His constant desire, that all his movements might tend to the glory of God, is shown in the spirit which breathes through the following letter, written to Stephen Crisp, on the eve of his departure from England:

"DEAR S. C.:—My dear and lasting love in the Lord's everlasting truth reaches to thee, with whom is my fellowship in the gospel of peace, that is more dear and precious to my soul than all the treasures and pleasures of this world; for when a few years are past, we shall all go the way whence we shall never return: and that we may unweariedly serve the Lord in our day and place, and in the end enjoy a portion with the blessed that are at rest, is the breathing of my soul!

"Stephen! we know one another, and I need not say much to thee; but this I will say, thy parting dwells with me, or rather thy love at my parting. How innocent, how tender, how like the little child that has no guile! The Lord will bless that ground. I have also a letter from thee which comforted me; for many are my trials, yet not more than my supplies from my Heavenly Father, whose glory I seek, and the renown of his blessed name. And truly, Stephen, there is work enough, and here is room to work in. Surely God will come in for a share in this planting work, and that leaven shall leaven the whole lump in time. I do not believe the Lord's providence had run this way towards me, but that he has an heavenly end and service in it. So with Him I leave all, and myself and thee, and his dear people, and blessed name on earth.

"God Almighty, immortal and eternal, be with us, that in the body and out of the body we may be his forever!"

Amid his preparations for the voyage, he addressed to his wife and children, who were to be left behind, a letter fraught with the most earnest solicitude for their well-being every way, and full of the most tender and judicious counsel. It thus concludes: "So, my God, that hath blessed me with His abundant mercies, both of this and the other and blessed life, be with you all, guide you by His counsel, bless you, and bring you to his eternal glory, that you may shine, my dear children, in the firmament of God's power, with the blessed spirits of the just, that celestial family, praising and admiring Him, the God and Father of it, forever. For there is no God like unto Him; the God of Isaac and of Jacob, the God of the prophets, the apostles, and martyrs of Jesus, in whom I live forever.

"So farewell to my thrice dearly beloved wife and children!

"Yours, as God pleaseth, in that which no waters can quench, no time forget, nor distance wear away, but remains forever."

Being now feudal sovereign of so extensive a territory, so far as the act of the King and Council could make him, William Penn published a description of the natural features and resources of the country, and invited those who were disposed to change their place of abode and prepared to emigrate, to resort to Pennsylvania, and under its Christian government and special privileges, secure the blessings of freedom and political equality. He did not disappoint his friends in their expectation of the benign form of government he instituted. It was democratic in its spirit, and its provisions were liberal, and fitted to meet the demands of the broad principles of popular rights, as they were from time to time developed. The article in relation to liberty of conscience deserves to be noticed, as the public declaration of the principles of Friends on that point, where they had the power of government in their own hands.

"Almighty God being the only Lord of Conscience, Father of lights and spirits, and the author as well as object of all Divine knowledge, faith and worship; who only can enlighten the mind, and persuade and convince the understanding of people, in due reverence to his authority over the souls of mankind: It is enacted by the authority aforesaid, (General Assembly met at Chester, Twelve month, fourth, 1682,) that no person now, or at any time hereafter, living in this Province, who shall confess and acknowledge one Almighty God, to be the Creator, upholder and ruler of the world, and professeth him or herself obliged in conscience to live peaceably and justly under the civil government, shall in any wise be molested or prejudiced for his or her conscientious persuasion or practice; nor shall he or she at any time be compelled to frequent or maintain any religious worship, place or ministry whatever, contrary to his or her mind; but shall freely and fully enjoy his or her Christian liberty in that respect, without any interruption or reflection. And if any person shall abuse or deride any other, for his or her different persuasion and practice in matter of religion, such shall be looked upon as a disturber of the peace, and be punished accordingly."

There were no oaths exacted, and no provision made for military defence. He exempted from the penalty of death two hundred crimes for which that punishment was inflicted in England, though life was to be forfeited for wilful murder. With a view of connecting reformation with punishment by imprisonment, prisoners were to be kept at work, and subjected to moral discipline. And it was enacted: "That, as a careless and corrupt administration of justice draws the wrath of God upon Magistrates, so the wildness and looseness of the people provoke the indignation of God against a country; therefore, that all such offences against God as swearing, cursing, lying, profane talking, drunkenness, drinking of healths, obscene words, (and several other scandalous acts particularly named,) treasons, misprisions, duels, murders, felony, sedition, maims, forcible entries, and other violences to the persons and estates of the inhabitants of the Province; all prizes, stage-plays, cards, dice, May-games, gamesters, masques, revels, bull-baitings, cockfightings, bear-baitings, and the like, which excite the people to rudeness, cruelty, and irreligion, shall be respectively discouraged and severely punished, according to the appointment of the Governor and freemen in provincial council and general assembly."

George Fox had repeatedly expressed his Christian solicitude for the colored people held as slaves, at that time, by Friends. He had strongly urged upon all who held them to see to their instruction, especially in the truths of the gospel as recorded in the Scriptures; that after serving for a certain time they should be freed, and that provision should be made for their comfortable enjoyment of old age. William Penn, in the charter he granted to "The Free Society of Traders," inserted the following article, showing how fully he sympathized in this feeling of George Fox, and his desire to promote manumission after a term of service: "Black servants to be free at fourteen years, and, on giving to the Society two-thirds of what they can produce on land allotted to them by the Society, with stock and tools. If they agree not to this, to be servants until they do."

There were about two thousand inhabitants,—exclusive of Indians,—mostly English, Swedes, and Dutch, when William Penn took possession of his Province. The well-known character of the Proprietor, the strong inducements offered by the system of government proposed, and the natural advantages from soil and climate of the newly-opened domain, all acted as powerful incentives to emigrate; not only to men who were struggling hardly and uncertainly at their native home for the means of subsistence, but to others, who, though with sufficient to live comfortably where they were, were anxious to escape from the intolerant oppression of a Court and hierarchy bent on enforcing the alternatives of conformity to certain prescribed dogmas of their own construction, or suffering, if not ruin, by imprisonment or deprivation of estate.

William Penn arrived in Pennsylvania in 1682, and in that year and the two following fifty vessels came into the Delaware River, bringing several thousand emigrants; the most of them from Great Britain, and some from Germany. Nearly all of them were professors with Friends, and many substantial, consistent members, who came under a sense of religious duty, and made the practice of the religion they had embraced the primary object of life. Some had the benefit of a liberal education, while the great body, farmers, mechanics, or tradesmen, had acquired but the rudiments of English school-learning. Many possessed considerable property, paying cash for the land they took up; and generally the others soon found means to make themselves independent.

Those who came first, as was to be expected, had to encounter the difficulties and privations usually attending pioneers in an uncultivated forest. Some, who brought the frames of small houses with them, were not long in obtaining a comfortable shelter; but very many were obliged to content themselves with hastily constructed shanties, under the overarching branches of trees; while some dug caves in the bank of the river, and made out to obtain in them some of the comforts of a home. This was before William Penn came out; but Richard Townsend, who came in the same ship with him, thus speaks of his experience: "At our arrival we found it a wilderness; the chief inhabitants were Indians; there were some Swedes, who received us in a friendly manner; and although there was a great number of us, the good hand of Providence was seen in a particular manner, in that provisions were found for us by the Swedes and Indians, at very reasonable rates; as well as brought from divers other parts, that were inhabited before. Our first concern was to keep up and maintain our religious worship, and in order thereto, we had several meetings in the houses of the inhabitants; and one boarded meeting-house was set up, where the city was to be (near the Delaware); and as we had nothing but love and good-will in our hearts one to another, we had very comfortable meetings from time to time, and, after our meeting was over, we assisted each other in building little houses for our shelter."

The high motives that prompted them to exile themselves from their native land, and the fervent religious concern to be engaged in promoting the spread of the Redeemer's kingdom, which warmed their hearts, enabled them to bear all they had to endure with cheerfulness. One of them thus expresses himself: "Our business in this new land is not so much to build houses, and establish factories, and promote trade and manufactures, that may enrich ourselves (though all these things, in their due place, are not to be neglected), as to erect temples of holiness and righteousness, which God may delight in; to lay such lasting frames and foundations of temperance and virtue as may support the future superstructures of our happiness, both in this and the other world."

In taking possession, and in the settlement of Pennsylvania, it had been a subject of much solicitude and care with William Penn, that the whole conduct of the settlers, in their intercourse with the aborigines, should be so marked with kindness, and with consideration for their rights and national customs, as to secure their good-will, and influence them to live in peace and harmony with the new-comers upon their soil. Before coming over himself he had appointed three Commissioners to see to the necessary arrangements for the reception and settlement of the colonists, to lay out the site for a town, and to treat with the Indians. By these he sent an address to the latter, in which he tells them it is his desire to enjoy the country over which he had been made Governor, "with their love and consent, that we may always live together as neighbors and friends;" and as he had heard that in some places impositions had been practised upon them which had produced animosity and revenge, it was his sincere desire, and should be his practice, and the practice of those he should send, to treat with them justly for their lands, and to make and preserve a firm treaty of peace.

When, after his arrival on the shores of the Delaware, he had met the Colonial Assembly elected by the inhabitants, and the necessary laws were enacted, and had transacted some other business immediately pressing upon him, he gave the necessary attention to select the location of the future city, to which he gave the name of Philadelphia. Afterwards he went on to New York, and visited Friends there and on Long Island and in New Jersey. On his return from this journey, he took the necessary measures to have the chiefs of the tribes of Indians occupying that portion of the Province which was likely to be soon required by the settlers, to meet him in council. The place of meeting was in Shackamaxon, a little north of the city, and on the Delaware River. There, under the wide-spread branches of a noble elm-tree, was held the treaty of friendship and perpetual peace, between the natives, the Governor, and the immigrant Friends, which has become world-renowned as the *Great Indian Treaty*. Made in good faith and honesty by both parties, this treaty was defaced by no oath, and remained unbroken so long as Friends held the reins of power in the government. Under its provisions, there sprung up a confiding intimacy between the red men and the white; and so long as the Christian policy inaugurated by William Penn and his brethren in religious profession was adhered to, there was no case of wrong or misunderstanding occurred, which was not speedily settled and removed by resort to the peaceable and just means provided for in its stipulations.

Thus the benign and peaceable principles of the gospel, as laid down by Christ and His Apostles, and adopted by Friends, were closely adhered to and fully tested in the settlement of Pennsylvania; and the experience of seventy years of uninterrupted peace and prosperity, while the Province was under the control of Friends, conclusively proves how far they exceed all other rules and motives of conduct, however devised by the wisdom of man or enforced by military power. The enlightened and liberal policy of the settlers, together with the simplicity of manners and refinement evinced in their domestic and social economy and general intercourse, contributed to the powerful attraction exerted by the Colony on all who were disposed to escape from the tyrannous exactions and almost continuous commotions agitating and embittering civil society in Europe.

The just and loving manner in which William Penn treated the Indians from the beginning of his intercourse with them, and the peaceable principles not only professed, but continually acted on by the settlers, besides gaining the confidence of the tribe immediately surrounding them, spread their fame to others more distant; so that during the stay of the Proprietor, when on his first visit to his Province, he made treaties of friendship and amity with nearly twenty different tribes. Nor were the expenditures for the land purchased a mere nominal sum, palmed upon the ignorant natives, easily caught with showy goods, and unaccustomed to estimate things at their real value. From the accounts preserved of these bargains and sales, it appears that, during his lifetime, the Proprietor expended over twenty thousand pounds in the purchase of that portion of the soil which was ceded to him by the aborigines; and yet they were not required to abstain from hunting or fishing within its boundaries, and the laws were so framed as to give them the protection of citizens.

The influx of settlers was unprecedented; the forest began to be cleared, and dwellings were put up rapidly. The soil yielded abundantly, and no calamity occurred for years to check the rapid increase of inhabitants, or create doubts and dissatisfaction as to the course they had taken in removing from their native country. New meetings for worship were established, as the new-comers took up lands in the counties contiguous to the city; so that, in 1684, William Penn wrote, there were eighteen in all, and all were brought within the order of church government, as laid down in the discipline then adopted.

Shortly after witnessing the prosperous beginning of his new colony, William Penn returned to England, and for a number of years continued to reside in or near London. He had provided for the affairs of the Province during his absence; but such was his unceasing solicitude for the spiritual welfare of the Friends he was about leaving, that, after he had embarked, he addressed them a letter from the ship, in which he says: "Now you are come to a quiet land, provoke not the Lord to trouble it, and as liberty and authority are with you, and in your hands, let the government be upon His shoulders in all your spirits; that you may rule for Him, under whom the princes of this world will one day esteem it their honor to govern and serve in their places. I cannot but say, when these things come mightily upon my mind, as the apostle did of old, 'What manner of persons ought we to be in all holy conversation and godliness?'

"And thou, Philadelphia, the virgin settlement of this Province, named before thou wert born, what love, what care, what service, and what travail has there been, to bring thee forth and preserve thee from such as would abuse and defile thee.

"Oh that thou mayst be kept from the evil that would overwhelm thee; that, faithful to the God of thy mercies, in the life of righteousness, thou mayst be preserved to the end. My soul prays to God for thee, that thou mayst stand in the day of trial, that thy children may be blessed of the Lord, and thy people saved by His power."

He had been commended by his father, on his death-bed, to the good offices of the then Duke of York. The respect and kind feeling of the Duke for William Penn appeared to have continued after he became King; and a sense of gratitude and Christian interest, in measure, bound the man he had befriended to his royal benefactor. He was almost daily at Court, and as often his interest there was employed on behalf of those with whom he was united in religious fellowship, or of others who solicited his aid; which his kindness of heart prompted him not to refuse. His house in Kensington was daily thronged with persons who sought his mediation to promote their interests, or desired to engage him to present their petitions or addresses to the King. He received all with courtesy, and aided those he could with cheerfulness; and no one ever charged him with making gain of his position or influence. Nevertheless, in this way, it is probable he appeared in cases where greater prudence would have restrained him from interfering. Certainly he made many bitter enemies, who hesitated not to proclaim him to be a Jesuit, a hypocrite, and an enemy to the Protestant interest. Accustomed to calumny as a Friend, and conscious of his innocence, William Penn allowed these slanders to possess the public ear, until they came to be credited by many, who, without any particular prejudice against him, supposed that, like other emissaries of Rome, he was in league with the King in trying to subvert the religion and constitutional liberties of the nation. At length the Secretary for the Plantations, who knew Penn well, and was greatly grieved with the manner in which he was traduced, and fearful of the ultimate result of his persistently declining publicly to defend himself, addressed him by letter; reciting the charges industriously circulated against him, and earnestly requesting he would notice and refute them. To this letter William Penn replied, taking up each accusation separately, and showing their untruth and their absurdity. He did not hesitate to acknowledge the gratitude and kind feeling he entertained toward King James, and that on some occasions, when his opinion had been sought on matters affecting the nation, he had given it; but he declared that, on all such occasions, he had advocated liberty of conscience, and the best interest of Protestant England; and he challenged any one to come forward and show to the contrary. Notwithstanding this explanation of his intimacy at Court, and his positive denial and refutation of the many false stories raised about him, the feeling produced by them was not entirely removed; and in the last month of 1688, as he was walking in Whitehall, he was suddenly summoned to appear before the Lords of the Council. Some of the Council, who were inimical to him, required him to give sureties for his appearance on the first day of the next term of Court. On his appearance there, his case was postponed until the next session; when there appeared to be no accuser or accusation against him, and he was declared clear in open Court.[A]

[A] The aspersion of the character of William Penn, and the charges brought against his conduct while frequenting the Court of James II., by Macaulay in his History of England, have been fully investigated and refuted by several authors, who have shown the serious mistakes of the historian, and the innocence of Penn of the offences imputed to him.

In 1688 James II., finding himself deserted by the nobility, the gentry, and the army, fled to France, and William, Prince of Orange, who had come over with an army on the invitation of some of the leading statesmen of England, was proclaimed king. Notwithstanding the alienation of the kindly feelings of the people, by the impolitic course pursued by James, and their apparent determination to maintain William and Mary on the throne, the self-exiled monarch resolved to continue whatever effort he could make, with the assistance of his friend Louis XIV., to regain the crown of Great Britain. There were many, who had stood high in State and Church, who refused to take the oath of allegiance to the reigning royal pair. These were termed Non-jurors and Jacobites, and intrigues and covert conspiracies were, for a long time, rife among them. Naturally this gave rise to suspicion and distrust on the part of the party in power. From this cause William Penn was subjected to no little trouble; his intimacy with the former king affording ground to prejudice the minds of many against him. He had already been arrested and discharged, there being no specific charge brought against him. But some letters from James having been intercepted, among them was found one addressed to him. He was again brought before the Privy Council, and some of those present saying the circumstances required sureties from him, he urgently requested to be allowed to appear before King William himself. This was granted, and, after a conference of two hours, the king was prepared to acquit him of being implicated in any treasonable correspondence with James. Some of the Council, however, were not satisfied without bail being given to appear at Court. On coming before the Court, he was again discharged. While King William was conducting the campaign in Ireland, where James was at the head of an army, fighting for possession of that island, a conspiracy in favor of the latter was discovered, originating in Scotland. Queen Mary ordered the seizure of many supposed to be hostile to the government, and among them William Penn was again included. How long he was detained does not appear, but, at the Michaelmas term of the Court (1690), he was once more cleared of any complicity with the opponents of the government. For many months he had been making preparations to revisit Pennsylvania, and on his discharge he hastened to have everything ready to embark; but, before he could complete his arrangements, he was again brought into difficulty, more serious than at any time before, on account of his connection with the Court of King James. King William had crossed over to Holland, to be present at a Congress held at the Hague, and his absence emboldened the disaffected to enter into another plot for restoring James, who was then at the Court of Louis XIV. Two of their number started to cross the Channel, and have an interview with their absent sovereign; but the plot was discovered, and these emissaries, with their papers, seized. One of them was hung; the other, in order to save his life, gave testimony against several of the nobility, and implicated William Penn in the conspiracy. A warrant for his arrest was issued, and, on his return from the funeral of George Fox, he narrowly escaped once more being made a prisoner.

In what manner he was said to be connected with the conspiracy, or what was the specific charge brought against him, is nowhere clearly stated; but as Lord Preston—one of the captured messengers—declared he was one of the plotters, and a man of the name of William Fuller swore to the correctness of Preston's statement, the matter assumed a serious aspect. As the origin of the plot was believed to have been among the Catholics, the same misrepresentations of Penn being a Jesuit in disguise were again brought forward, and the passions of the people being much inflamed against the intriguing papists, it was thought a fair trial could not be obtained for him. Under these circumstances, some accounts represent that William Penn voluntarily secluded himself where he could not be easily seen; waiting until a time should arrive when he might have a fair opportunity to clear himself; while others state that, having been examined before the Privy Council, he was ordered to remain a prisoner in his own house, under surveillance. The latter is the more probable, as he could hardly have supposed he could escape the search the government would make for him; especially as he kept up intercourse with his friends. Thus, in the Third month of 1691, he addressed an epistle to the Yearly Meeting in London, in order to remove any unfavorable impression that might have been made in the minds of his brethren by his forced seclusion. In this he says: "My privacy is not because men have sworn truly, but falsely, against me; for wicked men have laid in wait for me, and false witnesses have laid to my charge things that I knew not; who have never sought myself, but the good of all, through great exercises; and have done some good, and would have done more, and hurt to no man; but always desired that truth and righteousness, mercy and peace, might take place among us."

During his retirement he employed his pen diligently, producing several works of much value. The refusal of Friends in Pennsylvania to contribute money for the erection of forts or other military purposes, had given great offence to the home government, and the enemies of Penn took advantage of this, and of the position he was now in, with charges of treason hanging over him, to obtain an order from the King and Council, in the early part of 1692, to annex the government of Pennsylvania to that of New York, then presided over by Colonel Fletcher. Penn remained shut out from the world, and deprived of opportunity to serve the cause of truth and righteousness, and his brethren of the same faith, except by his pen, for more than two years; his character stained in the estimation of some, and his valuable services forgotten by many others, who, perhaps, thought he had indeed fallen to rise no more. But there were men of eminence who had never believed William Penn guilty of the crime laid to his charge, and were awaiting the right opportunity to have justice done to his position and character. Among these was the celebrated John Locke, who esteemed him, not only as a man of exalted virtue and great literary attainment, but as a personal friend. He applied to King William for a pardon; but William Penn was too conscious of innocence, and too fully persuaded that in due time his innocence would be made manifest to the world, to be willing to accept of any release that would imply he had been guilty. In the meantime, Lord Preston, who had made the charge against him, had fled the country, and Fuller, his witness, having been detected in perjury, was, by order of Parliament, tried as an imposter, in the Court of the King's Bench, found guilty, and sentenced to stand in the pillory. Lords Ranelagh, Rochester, and Sidney now waited on the King, and, stating that the name of William Penn had never been found in any of the letters or papers connected with the conspiracy, and that the charge against him rested solely on the accusation of two men who were known to be unworthy of belief, urged upon him the injustice and hardship of his case. The King appears to have heard them patiently, and replied that William Penn was an old acquaintance of his; that he had nothing to allege against him, and that he might follow his business as freely as ever. Afterwards the King gave an order to the principal Secretary of State for his freedom; which was communicated to him in the presence of the Marquis of Winchester. He, however, sought and obtained a hearing before the Privy Council; and, after a full examination of the charges, he was honorably acquitted. The cloud that had long obscured his standing and services was now dispelled, and he returned to his family and friends, to resume the position he had before attained in the church, and in civil society. His wife survived his release but little more than two months.

In 1696 William Penn was married to Hannah, the daughter of Thomas Callowhill, of Bristol,—a sober, religious woman, who survived him several years. Soon after this event he sustained an afflictive bereavement in the death of his eldest son, Springett Penn, in the twenty-first year of his age. He was a pious and amiable young man, of whom, in a touching testimony to his worth, William Penn says, "I lost all that any father can lose in a child."

He had been absent from his colony for many years, though longing to return there, and oversee the working of the government he had instituted, and the growth of the prosperous colony he had been a principal means of planting on the shores of the Delaware. But the various troubles in which he had been involved, and the great loss of pecuniary means that had resulted from his outlay for the Province, and the dishonesty of his agent in Ireland, had so crippled and embarrassed him, that he had been unable to carry out his strong desire to cross the Atlantic, and spend the remainder of life amid the Friends and scenes he pictured eminently propitious to secure comfort and peace. But in 1699, having settled his affairs in England and Ireland, so as not to require his personal oversight, in the Seventh month he embarked with his wife and family for Philadelphia, expecting to end his days in the Province. The voyage, providentially, was a long one; occupying three months; by which delay on the ocean they did not arrive in the city until after the malignant fever, of which so many had died, had passed away.

William Penn brought with him certificates from three meetings of Friends in England: one from "The Second-day's Meeting of Ministering Friends" in London; one from the "Men's Meeting of Friends" in Bristol, where he had resided for some years, and another from "A Monthly Meeting held at Horsham;" all expressing their full unity with and love for him as a member and minister. The reception of these certificates is recorded on the minutes of the Monthly Meeting of Friends, of Philadelphia.

The arrival of the Proprietor, after an absence of fifteen years, was hailed with joy by the people generally, and doubtless he supposed that he could now pass his days in usefulness and tranquillity. But William Penn soon found that troubles beset him on every hand, and that his wise counsels and cherished plans of improvement were thwarted and opposed by a faction bent upon promoting their own selfish schemes and interests.

A circumstance now occurred which separated him from his American possessions forever. A bill had been introduced into Parliament for changing the colonial into regal government. This measure, if adopted, would take the control of the colony out of his hands, and substitute military rule for the mild and pacific government he had established. From a sense of duty, although very reluctantly, he yielded to the request of his friends in England, that he would immediately return thither.

The news of his intended departure was received by the inhabitants with feelings of sincere regret. Perhaps none felt it more deeply than the aborigines. On this occasion, a number of them waited upon him at his residence at Pennsbury. The interview was conducted with great gravity. One of the chiefs, in the course of his remarks, said "that they never first broke their covenants with any people;" striking his hand upon his head, he said "they did not make them there, but"—placing it upon his breast—"they made them *there*."

William Penn sailed for England in the Eighth month, 1701, having been in the Province about two years. On the eve of his departure he presented Philadelphia with a charter, constituting it a city.

The bill to change the form of the colonial government was never passed into a law, but other engagements prevented his return to Pennsylvania. In 1705, in a brief but forcible epistle to Friends, he exhorts them to hold all their meetings in that which set them up, the heavenly power of God. In 1706 he removed with his family to Brentford, about eight miles from London. In 1709 he went forth on a gospel mission through the western parts of England, which was his last journey of this kind. In 1710 he removed to Rushcomb, in Buckinghamshire, where he continued to reside until his death. In 1712 he had three attacks of apoplexy. By these his mental powers were so weakened that he was rendered incapable of transacting business. In this situation he remained for several years, without much bodily suffering, and appeared to enjoy great quietness and sweetness of mind. In the latter part of 1714 he was visited by Thomas Story, who says of him, "that he had a clear sense of truth, was plain, by some very clear sentences he spoke in the life and power of Truth, in an evening meeting we had there; wherein we were greatly comforted, so that I am ready to think this was a sort of sequestration of him from all the concerns of this life, which so much oppressed him, not in judgement but in mercy, that he might not be oppressed thereby to the end."

When visited by two of his friends, in 1716, he still expressed himself sensibly, and at parting thus addressed them: "My love is with you, the Lord preserve you, and remember me in the everlasting covenant."

He continued gradually to grow weaker until the thirtieth of the Fifth month, 1718, when his Divine Master was pleased to summon him from the tribulations of time to the eternal rewards of the righteous.

Thus peacefully passed away one of the most useful men of the age in which he lived: indeed, history makes us acquainted with few so faithfully and fearlessly devoted to the cause of justice, and to the increase of righteousness in the earth. In early life he felt the tendering visitations of the Holy Spirit, and as he submitted thereto, was led in paths of great circumspection and non-conformity to the world, and soon became an object of scorn, reproach, and even bitter persecution. But none of these things moved him; neither did he count his life dear, being mainly desirous that he might bear a faithful testimony to the truth whilst on earth, and finish his course with joy.

Early called to the "ministry of reconciliation," and wisely instructed in the school of Christ, he was enabled, for the good of others, to bring forth out of the heavenly treasury things new and old.

As an author, his many publications are characterized by the forcible manner in which they set forth the spiritual nature of Christ's kingdom, and the necessity of obedience to the teachings of the Holy Spirit. His views of morality and civil government were the fruit of Christian principle, and adapted to all times and all conditions of men. He shows that oaths, whether judicial or profane, are contrary to the doctrine of Christ and His Apostles, and the practice of the primitive Christians, and, in their direct tendency and effects, injurious to morality. He establishes conclusively, that liberty, civil and religious, is the right of all, so far as its exercise does not infringe the rights of others; and he was consequently opposed to all persecution to enforce conformity in religious opinion. In founding his colony of Pennsylvania, he was influenced by the spirit of the gospel, and a desire that its government might be supported without the violation of any Christian precept. His policy grew out of that religion which breathes "Glory to God in the highest, peace on earth, good-will to men;" and the aboriginal inhabitants, by others deemed treacherous and cruel, became the kind friends and faithful allies of his colonists. The pacific principles of the gospel were found in their operation more effectual than munitions of war, to preserve the State in peace and prosperity.

Our narrow limits are insufficient to do justice to the character of William Penn, in setting forth his uprightness, his firmness, his zeal, his diligence, his love of the truth. Whether we consider him as a religious writer, a wise and Christian legislator, or as a faithful and devoted minister of the gospel, we must regard him as a benefactor to mankind. Of such the everlasting memorial is sure: "They that be wise shall shine as the brightness of the firmament, and they that turn many to righteousness as the stars forever and ever."

THE END.

CPSIA information can be obtained
at www.ICGtesting.com
Printed in the USA
LVHW041914090222
710699LV00008B/243

9 789355 899156

Design, Development and Ar
System: An Auto-Cont

MW01674071

Champak Talukdar

CHAPTER 1

Introduction to Research Problem

1.0 Introduction

The nerve conduction study (NCS) is becoming increasingly important in biomedical field for detection of nerve condition. Over the past decades, there has been increasing focus on research devoted to PC based NCS system for developing quick, accurate, reliable, simple and cost effective systems. Generally PC based commercially available NCS machines are used by the neurophysiologists to study nerve related diseases which are expensive, bulky as well as difficult to operate without a specialist. So design and development of an embedded μC based system is the salient concern for the researchers to acquire and study the NCS signal. However, considerable challenges still exists, therefore research pursuit on new measuring techniques and development of appropriate design could provide a viable solution for further analysis. In this research, such areas are investigated which were previously less unexplored than expected.

1.1. Human Nervous System

The human nervous system mainly consists of central nervous system (CNS) and peripheral nervous system (PNS), however PNS is further divided in to autonomic nervous system (ANS) and somatic nervous system (SNS) [70, 26, 47]. The CNS includes brain and spinal cord while PNS is the communication system between the CNS and the rest of the body with their sympathetic and parasympathetic network tools as well as somatic branches. The ANS is a 'self-regulating' system which influences the function of organs outside voluntary control, such as the heart rate, or the functions of the digestive system [5, 12]. However, it is to be mentioned that nerve cell or neuron performs the function of CNS and the PNS. The details of a human nervous system are shown in Fig.1.1. Since the research aims at development of electronic devices for NCS of PNS, the following sections discusses as PNS and neuropathy.

1.1.1 Peripheral Nervous System

PNS consists of nerves and ganglia outside the CNS i.e. brain and spinal cord. The main function of the PNS is to connect the CNS to the limbs and organs, like a relay between the brain and spinal cord as well as the rest of the body [17]. However, PNS is often exposed to toxins and mechanical injuries because it is not protected by the vertebral column and skull unlike CNS. PNS consists of large myelinated unipolar sensory neurons with the cell body off to one side of the single dendritic-axon process. On the other hand multipolar motor neurons are large myelinated neurons that have many dendrites off the cell body and an axon that may branch to affect many effectors. Nerve impulses are transmitted in three steps- i) neurotransmitters released from one neuron binds to the dendrites of the next neuron, ii) initiates genesis of action potentials and iii) it gets propagated down the axons and excites the next neuron when it crossed the threshold. When a neuron sends a sufficiently strong signal to the next neuron, the neuron is excited to a threshold potential. Transporters on the cell membrane sends positive ions into the cell, causing a change in potential, which spreads to down to the axon. This electrical potential is called the action potential [71]. Satellite cells are present in the sensory neuron and schwann cell present in PNS and both have importance in conduction capacity of peripheral nerve fibers. The cells wrap themselves around neurons in the PNS to synthesise the myeline sheath.

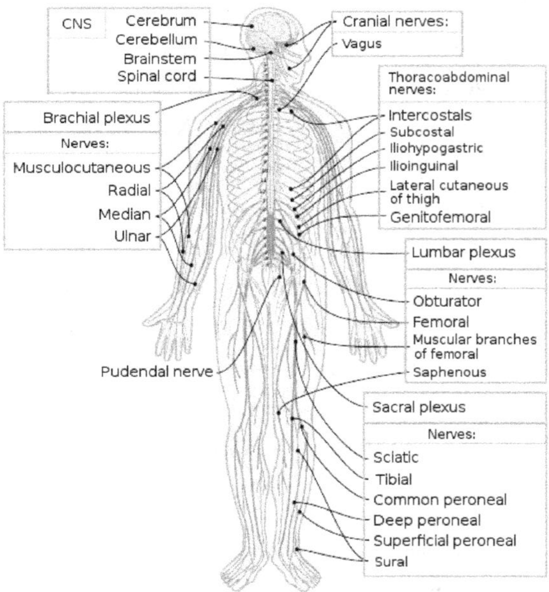

Fig.1.1 Human nervous system [27]

1.2. Neuropathy

Neuropathy refers to disease or any injury conditions that affect the working of nervous system smoothly. Neuropathy involves motor or sensory neurons, affecting fine and broad motor control. Neuropathy may be associated with varying combinations of weakness, autonomic changes and sensory changes like loss of muscle bulk or fasciculation's, a particular fine twitching of muscle etc. may be seen. Symptoms depend on the type of nerves affected (motor, sensory, or autonomic) and where the nerves are located in the body however one or more types of nerves may be affected. Common symptoms associated with damage to the motor nerve are muscle weakness, cramps, and spasms more over loss of balance and coordination may also occur. Sensory symptoms encompass loss of sensation and "positive" phenomena including pain. Damage to the sensory nerve can produce tingling, numbness, and a burning pain. Pain associated with this nerve is described in various ways such as the following: burning, freezing, or electric like, extreme sensitivity to touch etc. [45]. Proper diagnosis of neuropathy can lead to a solution that reduces pain or can at least manage it more effectively.

1.2.1 Types of neuropathy

There are several types of neuropathy which are as follows-

i) **Peripheral Neuropathy:** In peripheral neuropathy, the nerves related to PNS are affected i.e. the nerves of extremities like toes, hand, feet, arms, fingers etc. Physical trauma, repetitive, infection, metabolic problems and exposure to toxins and some drugs can all lead to peripheral neuropathy [81].

ii) **Proximal Neuropathy:** In proximal neuropathy, the damage of nerves related to specially shoulders, thighs, hips or buttocks.

iii) **Cranial Neuropathy:** There are two types of cranial neuropathy i.e. optic neuropathy and auditory neuropathy. The optic neuropathy refers to the dysfunction of the optic nerves that carry signals from the eye retina to the brain, whereas auditory neuropathy refers to malfunctioning of the nerves that carries signals from inner ear to the brain.

iv) **Autonomic Neuropathy:** In this type of neuropathy, the nerves of involuntary nervous system are affected. These nerves control the heart rate, blood pressure circulation, digestion, bowel and bladder function, sexual response and perspiration etc.

Following are most common morphology of neuropathy -

- Carpal tunnel syndrome
- Cubital Tunnel Syndrome
- Central pain syndrome
- Chronic inflammatory demyelinating polyneuropathy
- Guyon Canal Syndrome
- Cumulative trauma disorders
- Spinal disc herniation
- Guillain-Barre syndrome
- Tarsal Tunnel Syndrome
- Ulnar neuropathy
- Locked-In syndrome

1.3 Nerve Conduction Study

Nerve conduction study (NCS) measures how well and fast the nerves can send electrical signals. NCS is a medical diagnostic test commonly used to evaluate the nerve functioning, especially the ability of electrical conduction by the motor and sensory nerves of the human body [73, 7]. Nerve conduction velocity (NCV) is a common measurement made in NCS.

In NCS, the nerve is electrically stimulated by using a stimulating electrode circuit and the electrical impulse travelling from the point of stimulus is measured and recorded with a pair of electrodes that are placed on the skin over the nerve at various locations. The distance between the stimulating and recording electrodes positions are measured as well as the time for the stimulating impulse to travel from stimulating electrode to recording electrodes is also measured [8]. Finally the conduction velocity is measured by dividing the distance i.e. distances between stimulating and recording electrodes by the time [9]. A decreased value of NCV (m/sec) with the standard range of NCV of a healthy subject indicates nerve disease or abnormal pressure on the nerve i.e. neuropathy.

1.3.1 NCS parameters

The NCS signal with different parameters is shown in the Fig. 1.2 -

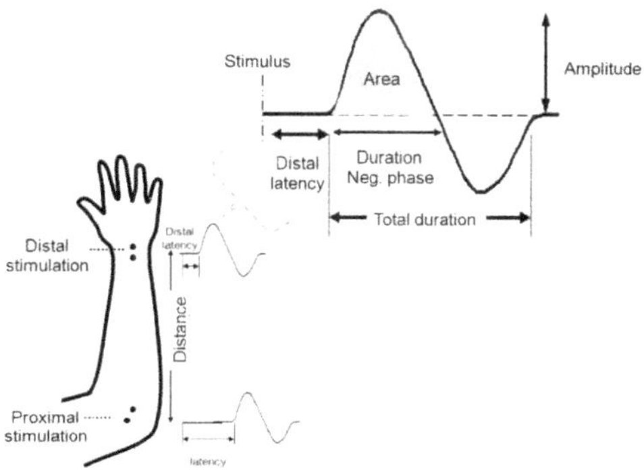

Fig. 1.2 NCS signal with different parameters [88]

The parameters responsible for NCS analysis are-

a) Compound muscle action potential (CMAP)

The CMAP is the summation of all underlying individual muscle fiber action potentials [6]. Furthermore, the height of the evoked response i.e. CMAP is measured from baseline to negative peak [29] as shown in the Fig.1.2. Amplitudes are semi quantitative measure of the number of axons conducting impulses from stimulating to the recording points. CMAP amplitudes are indicative of the efficiency of neuromuscular transmission. Furthermore, the numbers of muscle fibers composition of the recorded muscles generate the action potentials [32, 38]. CMAP is one of the most important parameters of the NCS. If a response is unelicitable i.e., has zero amplitude, then none of the other measurements can be performed [87].

b) Latency

The latency defines the time it takes for the action potential to travel from the stimulation site to the recording site and depends mainly on the conduction time in the peripheral axons. Moreover, if the electrodes are not over the end plates, the latency also includes the conduction time through the muscle fiber to the recording electrodes. There are two types of latencies i.e. distal and proximal based on stimulation site as shown in Fig 1.2.

Distal latency is the onset of a CMAP at the distal site of stimulation and it is measured from the stimulus to the onset of depolarization of the wave response, however, for proximal latency the stimulation site is the proximal position and the mechanism is same as the distal latency [7]. These two latencies are used to calculate the conduction velocity of the nerve. The motor latencies reflect the time required not only for passage of impulses along motor nerves, but also for neuromuscular transmission, and for the initiation of muscle action potentials [38].

c) Duration

This is the time interval during which the evoked response occurs after stimulation, expressed in milliseconds (ms). For CMAPs the duration typically is that period extending from the beginning to the end of the initial negative phase shown in Fig. 1.2. The durations of the CMAPs mainly reflect the relative conduction rates of the impulses as they travel along the various axons between the stimulating and recording points. Duration and amplitude are closely related; as the duration becomes more prolonged (i.e., the response becomes dispersed), the amplitude decreases.

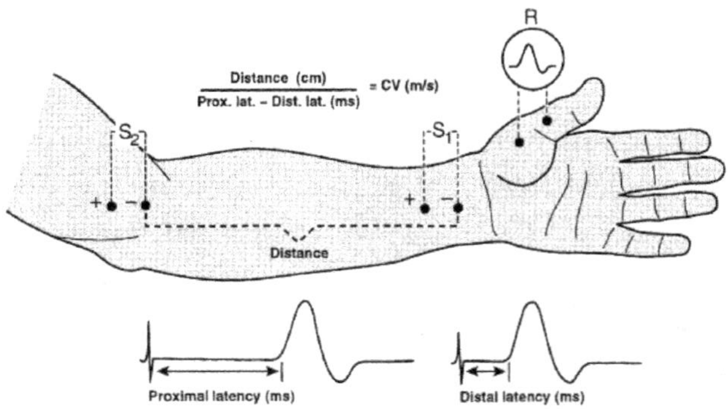

Fig. 1.3 NCV calculation details [32]

d) Conduction Velocity

Conduction velocity (CV) is a measure of the velocity of impulse conduction through the nerves. This parameter is used to detect signs of nerve injury that makes it most important parameter of NCS signal. Most often, CVs are obtained by stimulating the nerve at two points along its course, subtracting the distal latency from the proximal latency, and then dividing that difference by the distance (as determined by surface measurements) between the two stimulating points [7]. Therefore conduction velocity is the rate of conduction which is expressed as the distance travelled per unit of time, in m/sec (Fig. 1.3).

e) Area

Area is a function of both the amplitude and duration of the evoked response, it is measured in mVmsec (motor NCS). Compared to amplitude, it more accurately reflects the number of axons being activated. Nonetheless, it requires more technically sophisticated equipment and it can be compromised, just as the amplitude can be, by such factors as interphase cancellation i.e. when negative and positive phases of different motor unit action potentials overlap, they cancel each other because of temporal dispersion [38].

1.3.2 Types of NCS

There are four types of nerve conduction study techniques-

- Motor nerve conduction study (MNCS)
- Sensory nerve conduction study (SNCS)
- F wave study
- H-reflex study

Motor NCS are performed by applying an electrical stimulation to a peripheral nerve and CMAP responses are recorded from a muscle supplied by that nerve [48]. The size of the CMAP responses i.e. amplitudes are measured as well as latencies are also measured during the test. For motor NCS the amplitudes are measured in millivolt (mV) and latencies are measured in millisecond (ms) [8, 9]. By stimulating in two or more different locations along the same nerve, the NCV across different segments can be determined. NCV calculations are performed using the following formulae [43]-

$$NCV = \frac{distance\ between\ stimulating\ and\ recording\ electrodes\ (cm)}{proximal\ latency - distal\ latency}$$

In sensory NCS an electrical stimulation is applied to a peripheral nerve and CMAP responses are recorded from a purely sensory portion of that nerve, such as on a finger etc. [8]. Similar to MNCS, in SNCS, latencies are also measured in msec, however amplitudes are measured in microvolts (μV) [9]. The sensory NCV is calculated with the same formulae of motor NCV.

F waves are a type of late motor response, when a motor nerve axon is electrically stimulated at any point an action potential is propagated in both directions away from the initial stimulation site [48]. The distally propagated impulse gives rise to the CMAP. The F-wave study evaluates conduction velocity of nerves between the limb and spine, whereas the motor and sensory nerve conduction studies evaluate conduction in the limb itself [86]. The F wave test is very useful for the proximal segments of nerves whether normal NCS cannot able to access it. Therefore F wave test is used for long length of nerves whether MNCS used for shorter nerves so it is a very useful test for the peripheral nerves that sited proximally [48].

H-reflex study uses stimulation of a nerve and recording the reflexive electrical discharge from a muscle in the limb. This also evaluates conduction between the limb and the spinal cord. H reflex is a monosynaptic reflex that evoked by the direct electrical stimulus of large, afferent fibers at low-stimulus intensity [53].

However different types of NCS with the stimulating and recording electrodes positions are shown in Fig.1.4 as follows-

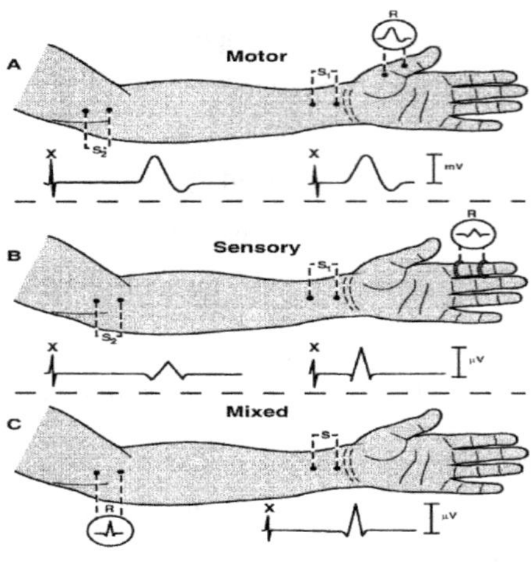

Fig.1.4 Three types of nerve conduction studies performed in the electrodiagnostic laboratory (A) motor, (B) sensory and (C) mixed (motor and sensory) [32]

1.3.3 Motor Nerve Conduction Studies

As already mentioned that, MNCS are performed by applying an electrical stimulation to a nerve and the compound muscle action potential (CMAP) are recorded by surface electrodes overlying a muscle supplied by that nerve. A motor unit is signified as one motor neuron and all of the muscle fibers it innervates. When a motor unit fires, the impulse (known as action potential) is carried down the motor neuron to the muscle. The area where the nerve contacts the muscle is defined as neuromuscular junction or the motor end plate. After the action potential is transmitted across the neuromuscular junction, an action potential is elicited in all of the innervated muscle fibers of that particular motor unit [38]. The total sum of all this electrical activities is known as a motor unit action potential (MUAP). This electrophysiological activity from multiple motor units is the signal typically evaluated. The composition of the motor unit and the number of muscle fibres per motor unit can affect the shape of the motor unit potentials.

The motor axons are evaluated by stimulating and recorded the response that elicits from the innervated muscle. However the main advantage of this arrangement is the magnification effect i.e., activation of a single motor axon causes the near simultaneous initiation of impulses in many individual muscle fibers, the number depending upon the innervations ratio of the recorded muscle [38, 59]. The resulting CMAP amplitudes are of sufficient magnitude which to be measured in millivolts. This recording method, however, also has an inherent disadvantage: the low amplitude or unelicitable CMAPs may be due to other than motor nerve dysfunction because the abnormalities may reside in the neuromuscular junctions, or in the muscle fibers themselves. Motor NCS are valuable diagnostic aids for several reasons. As early as 1961, Lambert listed several reasons for motor NCS which are [38, 39] as follows-

- Provide objective evidence of motor unit abnormalities in patients with suspected hysteria, malingering, or upper motor neuron lesions.
- Identify and localize focal lesions along individual nerves.
- Separate polyneuropathies from both myopathies and motor neuron disease.
- Detect various disorders in neuromuscular transmission and distinguish them from one another.
- Disclose evidence of subclinical PNS disorders, both focal (eg, CTS) and generalized (eg, Charcot-Marie Tooth disease, Type I).

- Reveal some peripheral nerve anomalies, (eg, Martin-Gruber anastomosis).

1.3.4 Factors effecting NCS parameters

There are several factors that can effects the NCS parameters that lead to a false result. Nerve conduction measurements vary with subject to subject as they are dependent upon the individual's age, sex, local temperatures etc. as well as other anthropometric factors such as hand size and height etc. [82, 74, 29]. The ability to predict normal values in the context of an individual's anthropometric characteristics increases the sensitivities and specificities of electrodiagnostic procedures. Following are the factors as follows-

a) Sex

It is to be found that sex is a significant factor in F-wave and H-reflex studies. The median and ulnar sensory amplitudes are higher for female subjects than male subjects as well as females have shorter latency in the upper limbs and longer latency in the lower limbs than males in F wave studies [29]. Female subjects have a negative correlation with the latency of F-wave and H reflex studies [29].

b) Age

It is found that normal subjects with older age have longer latencies, smaller CMAP and slower NCV compared to the younger age subjects [29]. Nerve conduction studies performed on healthy adults reveal that age is negatively associated with the conduction velocities and latencies in the median nerves [7]. In general, conduction velocities for median motor and sensory nerves decrease by 0.8 m/s and 1.3 m/s respectively per decade of aging [7]. Furthermore, age is also an important factor in the H reflex study [29].

c) Skin Resistance

The CMAP signal depends on the skin resistance of the subject which varies with subjects [18, 77]. High resistance of the skin electrode interface reduces the current passing through the skin tissues resulting in ineffective nerve response [47, 61, 90]. The variations of skin-resistance alter the quality and quantitative values of NCS recordings [16].

d) Temperature

In general, the conduction velocities of most motor nerves are positively and linearly associated with body temperature, i.e. low temperatures decrease nerve conduction velocity and higher temperatures increase nerve conduction velocity [74]. The MNCS is reduced by approximately 1 m/s with per degree temperature fall [48].

e) Height and Body Weight

As it is evident, latencies within the Median and Ulnar nerves increases with height of the subjects during motor NCS test [74]. The height is one of the most significant factors in the F wave and H reflex study [29]. Furthermore, weight of a subject is also an important factor, subjects with lower weight have higher median and ulnar sensory amplitude and heavier subjects have slower sural velocity than lighter subjects [29].

e) Hand Factors

Circumference of the index finger appears to be negatively associated with conduction amplitudes in the Median and Ulnar nerves. People with larger wrist ratios have lower Median nerve latencies and faster conduction velocities [82].

1.4 Motivation of the Research Work

The nerve conduction study (NCS) is an essential tool in medical sciences for detection of neuropathy or nerve disease. The conventional NCS is generally performed by Nerve testing machines in the hospitals to know the status of the nerves of the subject. However conventional nerve testing machines are bulky, expensive and not convenient for rapid testing. Furthermore, it is reported that majority of suspected possible neuropathy patients are referred to the hospital for NCS test actually found to be free from neuropathy, so lot of time and money have to be wasted by the patients for going to big hospitals. Therefore, design and development of a microcontroller based NCS setup to conduct NCS test for preliminary neuropathy detection is utmost important to save money and time. Furthermore, it will be helpful to perform the NCS test in remote village hospitals and military applications

1.4.1 Development of NCS setup and Stimulating Circuit

In view of the fact that portable and handheld testing devices are more convenient than desktop PC based devices, there is ample scope for development of an efficient portable and battery operated NCS testing system which will be very helpful for the doctors of remote area hospitals. This will help them to do a rapid and preliminary NCS test to advise the patients for proper follow up.

In this research we aim at development of a microcontroller based NCS testing system with certain special features to overcome the problem of variability of the pulse triggering system with subjects. In order to do the research we have studied the earlier works on portable nerve conduction study devices as explained in the following section on literature review.

Furthermore, the experimental work needs a NCS system connected to a PC with LabVIEW so that the signals can be measured, analysed and interpreted for the sake of experimental research of the handheld NCS system. Therefore we have also developed a custom made PC based NCS system.

Since the commercial PC based system (Neuroperfect-2) in our laboratory don't provide the analog output signal, this system can't be used for analysis of the time domain NCS signals. We have used the commercial system for comparison of the NCS parameters with our custom made PC based system.

Before starting our research, several discussions and deliberations were made with neurophysiologists, GNRC Hospitals about the difficulties and drawbacks of commercial PC based NCS machines.

It was learned that the amount of stimulating current or voltage applied to obtain an ideal NCS signal varies from subject to subject. While applying the stimulating pulse, one has to manually vary the stimulating pulse, one has to manually vary the stimulating current or voltage to obtain the ideal NCS response which is called supramaximal NCS signal, and the ideal stimulating pulse is called supramaximal stimulation. From literature it is found that the supramaximal stimulating voltage depends on the amount of fat of a subject i.e. for a subject with higher body weight requires a higher stimulating voltage [58]. In view of this fact we aim at developing an auto-controlled stimulating circuit that can instantaneously measure representative parameters of the body that depends on the body weight so that the stimulating voltage can be adjusted to obtain the supramaximal NCS signal.

1.4.1.1 Literature Review on PC based NCS System

Development of a PC based acquisition system to acquire biomedical signal in the laboratory environment has significantly facilitated throughout the years that expedite lots of technologies. In recent days, the costs of personal computers are decreases though

performances are increases so these acquisition systems are becoming very adequate and cost effective [23]. In the recent times, the researchers developed many PC based acquisition systems to collect and study the behaviour of the bio-signals and its related problems [19, 78, 91, 24, 30]. Furthermore, in [10, 28, 52, 72, 62] the researcher also developed PC based systems to collect the nerve responses for further analysis.

Banks et al. [10] developed a PC based system to record the peripheral nerve signals that have three sections: the head stage amplifier, the main instrumentation and the DAQ (NI AT-MIO-16-F5). The band-pass filter with a cut off frequency 10 Hz to 10 kHz is used to remove the noise from the recorded signals as well as an anti-aliasing filter for the digitization process.

In [28] Harb and Sawan present a PC based acquisition system to record nerve signal. In this system they have used tripolar cuff electrodes to record the raw bio-signal, then an instrumentation amplifier (INA 103) circuit that have low noise and high CMRR. The amplified signal is filtered by a band pass filter and the signal is stored in the PC by using a DAQ card (DT301) by converting the signal into digital data.

Meister et al. [52] reported a PC based acquisition system for neural signal that consists of a preamplifier, amplifiers, signal processors and a computer with analog and digital interface for communication with the signal processors as well as stores and displays data for on-line study. The analog signal from the preamplifier is inverted, amplified with a gain of 4000 and the signal is filtered by a bandpass filter at 12 dB/octave to a bandwidth of 20-2000 Hz.

Schuettler et al. [72] presented a PC based recording system to record neural signal of frogs. The system consists of hook electrodes, an instrumentation amplifier (gain of 500) and a band pass filter (cut off frequency range 17 Hz to 8.8 kHz). The filtered signal is stored in to a PC by interfacing a 10 bit DAQ card (NI-6062E) with a sampling frequency of 40 kHz.

From the above literature review it is found that PC based bio-signal acquisition systems mostly comprises of a low noise instrumentation amplifier, a filter with appropriate cut off frequency and a DAQ card with a high resolution ADC. The researchers mentioned in [23, 19, 78, 91, 24, 30, 55, 60, 10, 28, 52, 72] developed PC based signal acquisition for analysis of the signals in the PC using software.

Motivated by the above mentioned researchers, we aim at developing a PC based peripheral nerve signal acquisition system that comprises of a nerve stimulator, amplifier, filter and DAQ card. This setup has been used in our research for acquiring signals from subjects for analysis of the NCS dynamics.

1.4.1.2 Literature Review on Noise Analysis of Biomedical Signals and its Removal

It is to be mentioned that, the acquisition of high quality electrical NCS signals like all biomedical signals are very gruelling due to suppression of information by overlapping its profile [65, 49, 68]. The biomedical signals are often contaminated by noise from the sources like power line interference (PLI) and its harmonics [51] as well as due to movement of the recording electrodes [65]. The main reason of PLI is due to the presence of multiple paths in electrical devices from power lines in clinical environments because human body acts like an antenna [50] and one more prominent reason of PLI because of the devices that employ alternating current as a source of power [3]. Moreover low and high frequency noises also corrupt the NCS signals [14, 68] due to movement of subjects along with loose skin electrode contact [4, 11] and electromagnetic interference from surroundings as well as for the electronic components used in the circuits respectively. Therefore, in the past researchers adopted different techniques to remove and analysis the noise profiles from the biomedical signals [3, 49, 69, 57, 80, 36, 54, 67, 22].

Akwei-Sekyere [3] presented a framework to eliminate the power line noise from biomedical signals by using blind source separation and wavelet analysis. This method is simultaneously compared with a 4th order Butterworth band-stop filter, empirical mode decomposition, independent component analysis and a combination of empirical mode decomposition with the independent component analysis.

In [49] Malboubi et al. proposed an efficient adaptive Laguerre filter with fuzzy step size to eliminate the PLI from the EMG signals. The proposed technique uses internal mathematically constructed reference noise for the filter which is independent of the power line information to eliminate the noise.

Seki et al. [69] developed a signal processing method to suppress tremor noise from the surface EMG signal. The proposed filter extracted the attenuation ratio by correlation between last EMG data and one period squared sine wave. Furthermore, the filtered EMG signals designated that essential tremor noise was suppressed during the elbow flexed posture while holding a water-filled bottle, moreover voluntary information was also less affected by the filter.

Nagal et al. [57] implemented an optimization algorithm based on grey wolf optimizer along with gradient based techniques for removal of adaptive noise from EEG signal. The performance of the algorithm is evaluated in terms of statistical analysis like mean value, signal to noise ratio (SNR) in dB and correlation.

Tracery and Krishnamachari [80] developed an algorithm for the estimation and removal of stimulus artefact (SA) from the nerve conduction study signal. In this method, a hardware based model of SA is used and model parameters are estimated from portions of the data which are judged to contain only the artefact.

In [36] Kacar and Sakoglu introduced a general purpose MATLAB-based graphical user interface (GUI) software tool for biomedical signal processing and analysis of functional neuroimaging data. The research includes various signal processing analysis like a) rectification, normalizing and filtering b) statistical analysis: minimum, maximum, mean and standard deviation c) time domain analysis: integral, correlation analysis d) frequency domain analysis: Fourier transform e) multivariate analysis: principal and independent component analysis etc. for the performance evaluation of the system.

Muduli and Mukherjee [54] proposed for incorporation of an improved noise removal or trend-filtering technique for non-invasive FECG signals. The technique is based on improved complete ensemble empirical mode decomposition to analyse and filter out low frequency noises from FECG signals. Furthermore, false detection of intrinsic mode functions is avoided with the combination of both energy and ratio of zero-crossing numbers approaches. The advantage of the proposed method is that the presence of residual noise in different modes is controlled.

Qiu et al. [67] designed an adaptive matched filter via genetic algorithm optimization to remove the functional electrical stimulation from the recorded surface EMG to obtain clean EMG signal. In this method, an adaptive matched filter algorithm based on genetic algorithm (GA-AMF) was designed and its performance was compared with the comb filter for both simulated and real data. The performance was calculated based on the statistical analysis like correlation coefficients, SNR, normalized RMSE and frequency spectrum.

Gowri et al. [22] presented an adaptive filter to remove the noise from the ECG signal based on Least Mean Fourth algorithms that exhibit lower steady state error than the conventional LMS algorithm. The performances of the filter calculate based on the SNR improvement and found to be better performance than the conventional LMS algorithm.

In [65] Philips introduced a new interval-adaptive, time-warped polynomial filter for removing stationary noise from non-stationary biomedical signals. Furthermore an iterative filter adaption algorithm is also presented which does not rely on the computation of the local bandwidth and the performance of the filter is checked based on SNR.

However, there are no comparative noise analysis of NCS signals i.e. for both raw and filtered signals that are acquired with signal processing circuits that are powered by two modes of power supplies i.e. battery and AC/DC converter power supply in the literature survey. Therefore it is to be a great motivation for researchers to analyse the noises of NCS signals by considering the circumstances.

1.4.1.3 Literature Review on Nerve Stimulator

As already mentioned in 1.4.1, there is ample scope for development of an auto-controlled nerve stimulating system to overcome the problem of multiple triggering to get supramaximal stimulation. The system is feedback controlled in nature and therefore we have explored the literature on such systems as discussed below.

In the NCS, stimulator is an essential part which is used to stimulate the nerves so that appropriate recruitment of neurons takes place for supramaximal stimulation. In the recent years, the researchers have studied and developed various kinds of stimulators including voltage and current controlled stimulators that are used to stimulate the nerves to acquire the nerve signals [62, 41, 42, 13, 56, 79, 43, 40].

Pichorim, et al. [62] designed a stimulator for stimulating the nerves with pulse duration of 0.1 ms and with supply voltage of 10-60 V to study the behaviour of nerve signals, however, it is not explored to obtain the variable voltages from the 10 V source of power. The experiment was performed with a fixed supply voltage of 20 V for CMAP and 50 V for SNAP.

Loi et al. [41] developed a biphasic current stimulator for peripheral nerves with programmable and adjustable duration, intensity and frequency by a GUI. The stimulator is designed to generate 0-10 V amplitude (I<10 mA) with pulse duration of up to 100 μs to study the nerve responses. The stimulator circuit has two main blocks: a DAC using LTC2641 and a V/I converter by using an operational amplifier OPA343 with a non-inverting configuration along with a feedback resistor for the electrode impedance.

Luan and Constandinou [42] developed a technique to design charge-metered biphasic voltage mode stimulator that achieves good charge balancing with the help of two small capacitors. The system is divided into two sub-sustems: an analog front-end for the charge sensing and a digital back-end for the charge measuring and control. The stimulus parameters can be programmed and adjusted, the delivered charge quantity is set by a controller, the pulse duration is adjusted by V_{stim} and the inter-phasic delay is defined by a RC network.

Cheng et al. [13] proposed and designed two stimulator circuits that focus the issues of circuit complexity, bulky, expensive and high power consumption. In the first design transformer is used to step up the voltage from 9V to 200 V, however, the design is critical because it needs to handle a pulse current of at least 100 mA as well as the transformer is the bulky and expensive. On the other hand, the second stimulator circuit powered by a 9 V supply or battery is based on zero-voltage switching resonant techniques and in this technique transformer is not needed so no large magnetic components.

Ngamkham et al. [56] presented a constant current-mode biphasic stimulator circuit for a cochlear implant using a single power supply. In the circuit design a double loop negative feedback topology is employed to increase the output impedance without sacrificing voltage headroom. Furthermore, the design circuit is able to generate stimulation output in the range of 10μA to 1.05mA for a wide range of electrode tissue impedances 1 kΩ to 10 kΩ. The feedback used in the system is related to impedance matching.

In [79] Thorsen and Ferrarin designed a voltage controlled current source biphasic neuromuscular stimulator using two coupled transconductance amplifiers in series with pre-charged capacitors to drive the output current instead of transformer coupling. The capacitors are recharged to a high voltage after each stimulation pulse with the help of a switch mode power supply. Furthermore a multiplexer in the output stage is used to provide biphasic stimulation output with a rise-time less than 2 μs.

Lee et al. [43] proposed a 36 V biphasic stimulator and an electrode monitoring circuit to implement in a high voltage 0.35 μm CMOS process. For designing the stimulator, a fast response current mirror and high voltage switch for an input voltage range of approximately twice the gate-source voltage limit of high voltage is proposed. The performance of the stimulator in terms of settling time is around 3.6 μs in worst condition and maximum current efficiency is about 96%. Furthermore the mismatch between the anodic and cathodic output of the stimulator is less than 1.65%.

In [40], Liu et al. proposed a dual-mode stimulator circuit which is able to function in both current-mode and voltage-mode depending upon stimulus charge required for the application. The functioning mode of the stimulator depends on a current feedback path, i.e. if feedback path is not used in the circuit the stimulator effectively works as a standard current-mode and when feedback path is used the circuit work as a voltage-mode stimulator. The dynamically controlled bias current maintains the output impedance of the proposed circuit high, independent of the stimulus current and the load voltage. The feedback used in the system is for the changeover of mode of operation.

It is to be mentioned that current stimulator design requires lots of circuit components that make it more complex for laboratory usage as well as it is very difficult task to control the amount of charge delivered [42]. From the literature review it is found that voltage controlled stimulators are more convenient and less complex. Therefore in this research we aim at development of a voltage controlled stimulator with less circuit complexity. In the literature [62, 41, 42, 13, 56, 79, 43, 40], the nerve stimulators are all open loop systems in terms of control of the stimulating voltage or current. However, we aim at developing an auto-controlled stimulator to tune the stimulating voltage depending upon the skin condition of the subject's i.e. amount of fat below epidermis and dermis layers.

1.4.1.4 Literature Review on Auto-controlled Nerve Stimulator

Researchers have recently tried to develop auto-controlled nerve stimulators using feedback path to control the stimulating amplitudes. We have explored the literature on such devices as discussed below-

Jing et al. [35] present an intelligent biofeedback system based on the pattern recognition of physiological signals i.e. galvanic skin response as well as EMG and electroacupuncture which imitates the traditional Chinese medical acupuncture. The

system is able to make diagnoses and judgements automatically using EMG feedback and control the output of intelligent acupuncture that is used to speed up and treat anxiety disorder as well as some other diseases.

In [92] Zeng et al. designed a biofeedback based transcutaneous electrical nerve stimulation and pattern recognition of surface electromyography (sEMG) signals for rehabilitation treatment. In the system firstly, sEMG signals are acquired and stored in a PC via a DAQ card and secondly, auto-regressive and wavelet transform methods are used to extract the features from the raw sEMG signals. Furthermore, the features are feed to the SVM classifier and by applying spectral analysis mean and median frequency variables are obtained. In the final stage, electrical stimulation of muscle is controlled according to the classification results and level of fatigue.

Im et al. [33] proposed a technique for biofeedback electrical stimulation by extracting meaningful parameters from EMG signals for the rehabilitation treatment. In this technique, EMG signals are acquired with or without electrical stimulation and meaningful parameters i.e. zero-crossing, turns/second and median frequency are extracted and analysed to evaluate the effectiveness of with or without electrical stimulation. The researchers found that both zero-crossing and turns/second are decrease due to increase of muscle fatigue and reduced with electrical stimulation. Therefore the parameters zero-crossing and turns/second can be used as biofeedback parameters for electrical stimulation because the parameters are used to evaluate the muscle strength and fatigue.

Ward et al. [84] designed a biofeedback based autonomous neural control system to control the stimulus delivery that uses the degree of measured nerve activation level as biofeedback parameter to overcome the limitations i.e. efficacy and precludes of open loop mechanism of a fixed stimulus. In real time, the system systematically decodes the evoked compound nerve action potential responses to develop a subject specific nerve activation profile that describes the strength amount of stimulation required for responding each neuron population in the nerve.

In [1] Alejandro et al. developed a biofeedback based system where electrical stimulation is used as feedback. To evaluate the system, the researchers use electrical stimulation as biofeedback for the EMG controlled prosthetic hand user to interact with the environment in order to develop an extended proprioception control. To study the effects a functional magnetic resonance imaging system is used to detect the activation on the brain due to the hand movements as well as the tactile feedback offered by the electrical stimulation.

Arieta et al. [2] proposed a biofeedback based system by using functional electrical stimulation as biofeedback parameter for the EMG controlled prosthetic hand user to interact with the environment in order to develop an extended control. For this purpose, the researchers measured the reaction to different kinds of stimulation i.e. surface and interferential stimulation and checked their effects on the EMG acquisition process to determine the best approach to provide tactile feedback in the prosthetic application.

Lee et al. [44] developed a foot pressure biofeedback proprioceptive neuromuscular facilitation system for which sub-threshold electrical stimulation and visual-auditory as biofeedback parameter for improving balance control and foot sensory compensation in below-knee amputees. In the experiment the researchers found that the proposed proprioceptive biofeedback implementations are effective in order to improve static and dynamic balance control in below-knee amputees.

In the research discussed in [35, 92, 33, 84, 1, 2, 44] all refer to biofeedback stimulation for rehabilitation applications. In [35] EMG biofeedback is used to optimize electroacupuncture for diagnosis of anxiety disorders. In [92, 33, 84, 1, 2, 44], the researchers developed nerve stimulating systems for optimizing the stimulation by using various biofeedback's such as sEMG in [92], EMG [33, 1, 2], nerve activation level [84] and auditory [44]. However, none of the literature explores skin parameters as biofeedback to control the stimulating voltage or current for nerve conduction study applications. Motivated by this necessity, this research also aims at development of an auto-controlled biofeedback nerve stimulator circuit based on skin resistance of the subjects.

1.4.1.5 Literature Review on Impedance Analysis

Peripheral nerves are immensely complex biological systems; therefore understanding of their response to stretch is pivotal to preferable recognition of physiological and pathological states [21]. Moreover, their mechanical reactions are deterministically related to the nature of the external stimulus for which theoretical and computational tools are used to explore the behaviour [21, 85]. Modeling of biomedical phenomena is an important tool for technological and clinical developments [31], furthermore, a well-organized statistical analysis is necessary to validate the models in order to obtain correct model for better prediction and accuracy as well as it helps to identify the problem from the collected data source [37, 25, 89]. A number of productive modeling techniques of biomedical signals were developed to study the behaviour and responses of the phenomena as well as statistical analysis were carried out to validate the models in the past [15, 31, 64, 66, 76, 85, 20, 63].

Dabrowski et al. [15] studied the neuron equivalent circuit, i.e. electrical circuit components in RC circuit that used to resemble neuron components. In the study, membrane of neuron is considered as capacitor because of its ability to store and separate charge, and ion channels are represented with resistors because ion channels allow current to flow in and out of the cell as more ion channels are open more ions are able to flow. Furthermore, concentration gradient of neuron is the external to internal ratio of an ion concentration for which this phenomenon is represented with a battery in the RC circuit. Finally, the validation of the model was tested by using statistical analysis on the basis of mean, standard deviation and pi test.

Hope et al. [31] presented a model for the evaluation of the viability by using electrical impedance tomography (EIT) with a nerve cuff to record neural activity in peripheral nerves for the controlling of a robotic prosthetic. In this modeling, estimation of anisotropic impedance of intra-fascicle tissue was produced that allows the researchers to evaluate potential EIT electrode drive and measurement patterns. Furthermore a testing was carried out by using pseudo-experimental data synthesised to replicate real operating conditions of nerves.

In [64], Puanhvuan et al. proposed a multi regression model for nerve location prediction to estimate the probe-to-nerve distance across various impedances of the mock material. In this method, input features are extracted from CMAP responses, the impedance of the target area and the stimulus current and used in the model. The tissue impedance is calculated from the estimated resistance and capacitance of the tissue equivalent circuit.

Puanhvuan et al. [66] presented a modeling method for the estimation of nerve function. In this method multi-CMAP responses are acquired with various stimulus intensities, the amplitude of multi-CMAP responses are represented as output data and the varied stimulus intensities are represented as input data in the modeling technique. Shifts in mathematical model parameters reflect changes in nerve function. Furthermore, a support vector machine analysis was employed for classification of healthy and severed nerves.

Tarotin et al. [76] developed a model of impedance changes in unmyelinated nerve fibres that allowed optimisation of EIT parameters. The activity of the fibres was modelled by using either Hodgkin-Huxley squid giant axon or mammalian C-fibre model. The impedance changes during action potential propagation were simulated under various conditions by using these models. Finally the model provides an optimized method of EIT for unmyelinated nerves by predicting the important parameters of injected current and the optimal size and position of the electrodes for analysing the biophysical explanation of the simulated impedance changes.

In [85], Wesselink et al. presented a fibre model to describe the electrical behaviour of human myelinated sensory nerve fibres that encompasses a mathematical description of the kinetics of the nodal membrane as well as non-linear fibre geometry. In the modeling, the response of human myelinated sensory nerve fibres to spinal cord stimulation was calculated, and it is initiated the development of a fibre model based on electrophysiological and morphometric data for human sensory nerve fibres. The characteristics like action potential shape, propagation velocity and strength-duration behaviour deliver a good fit with the experimental data. Furthermore, the model performs better prediction of the threshold voltages in spinal cord stimulation.

Dominique and Ferron [20] developed a model for peripheral nerves to improve selective stimulation, it is used to reproduce any internal physical configuration of a nerve bundle from the peripheral system and it allows building any other type of nerves. Furthermore, validity of the model was proved by the simulation data and confirmation of feasibility of performing selective activation of fibres depending on frequency variability was allowed.

Parez-Orive and Durand [63] implemented a finite-element computer model of a multifasciculated nerve with different cuff electrodes to simulate the recordings. The main purpose of the modeling is to determine the effects of nerve reshaping and other cuff design parameters on the fascicular recording selectivity of a nerve cuff. The parameters such as electrode configuration, length of the electrode and number of recording positions that affect the recording selectivity were quantified by using a selectivity index. Moreover, the model included the inhomogeneous and anisotropic properties of peripheral nerves.

In the literature review discussed above, it was found that a good number of researches have been conducted for modeling biomedical systems. Concisely, the modeling techniques discussed above are- RC circuit model of a neuron [15], impedance model of intra-fascicle tissue [31], probe to nerve impedance model of frog nerve [64], linear straight line model equation between input pulse and CMAP of frequency nerve [66], impedance change model in impedance tomography [76] and geometrical nerve model [85, 20]. Since experimental output data in NCS test is very strongly correlated with the nerve conditions provided the input pulse is constant for a particular test, there is ample scope for exploring system identification to model the nerve. Several statistical based system identification algorithms are popular for modeling black box or grey box models. In this research we propose a technique to estimate the transfer function model of the nerve using measured input-output data. Furthermore, we foresee that there is a definite relationship between the model parameters i.e. electrical parameters (resistance and capacitance) with the NCS parameters such as CMAP, latency and conduction velocity of a subject. Therefore, we propose a technique for correlating the model with NCV parameters experimentally.

1. 5 Objectives

The objective of the research work is threefold:

1. Design and development of a PC based experimental setup for NCS.
2. Design and development of a microcontroller based biofeedback auto-controlled neurostimulator.
3. Modeling and Impedance Analysis of NCS signals by system identification.

1.6 Thesis Outline

The research work carried out has been organized into five chapters.

Chapter 1 gives a brief overview on the research work and a comprehensive literature review. In this chapter, an overview of human nervous system mainly peripheral nervous system, types of neuropathy and detail process of nerve conduction study is discussed. Literature review presented describes the state-of-the-art methodologies adopted by various research groups for the development bio-signal acquisition and analysis of the responses. The motivation, objectives, and methodologies adopted in this research work are discussed briefly.

Chapter 2 presents a PC based NCS experimental setup for acquisition of nerve signal in the laboratory based environment to study the nerve responses for further analysis. The setup development includes design of a conventional voltage controlled stimulator and a signal processing circuit to acquire the nerve signals, further, a DAQ card is used to store real time nerve signals in a PC. The performance of the simulator circuit is evaluated by calculating the factors like power consumption, voltage regulation, ripple factor and dynamic response of the circuit. This chapter also discusses the noises and its removal which are present in the NCS signals. Furthermore, it describes the noise analysis with statistical and frequency analysis of raw and filter nerve signals acquired with both power supply modes i.e. DC power supply from AC mains and battery.

Chapter 3 presents the detail design and development a biofeedback based auto-controlled stimulator depending on skin resistance in order to acquire supramaximal responses of the subjects without repeated trials. This chapter also discusses the online measurement of new subjects and results are analysed and validated extensively.

Chapter 4 presents a modeling technique of peripheral nerves of healthy subjects based on impedance analysis. The modeling technique adopts stimulus impulse as input and corresponding CMAP response as output and evaluated the transfer functions by using system identification technique (SIT) in the MATLAB environment to study nerve electrical model. Then, some approximate Randle's circuits were considered and manually evaluated the transfer functions for all those circuits. Moreover, similarity pattern was checked of the SIT generated transfer functions with the evaluated transfer functions of Randle's circuits on the basis of order of S-domain and R-C coefficients. In the next step, by solving the transfer functions, a data set of R-C values are obtained for nerve electrical model. Further, this chapter describes the data set of the 44 subjects in terms of three response parameters- CMAP, latency and NCV. Furthermore, different models are estimated using regression analysis by considering R-C values as input and response parameters as output by employing the data of 30 subject's out of 44 subjects. The remaining data of 14 subjects were used to validate the performances of the models. The chapter extensively describes the validation of the models by using two statistical analysis techniques- linear and support vector regressions in terms of R^2 and RMSE.

Chapter 5 summarizes the conclusion of the research highlighting the major achievements, shortcomings and future scope of this research work.

Bibliography

[1] Alejandro, H.A., Kato, R., Yokoi, H., Arai, T., and Ohnishi, T. An fMRI study on the effects of electrical stimulation as biofeedback. In *2006 IEEE/RSJ International Conference on Intelligent Robots and Systems*, pages 4336-4342, Beijing, China, 2006.

[2] Arieta, A.H., Yokoi, H., Arai, T., and Wenwei, Y. FES as biofeedback for an EMG controlled prosthetic hand. In *TENCON 2005-2005 IEEE Region 10 Conference*, pages 1-6, Melbourne, Australia, 2005.

[3] Akwei-Sekyere, S., Powerline noise elimination in biomedical signals via blind source separation and wavelet analysis. *PeerJ*, 3: 1086-1110, 2015.

[4] Almalchy, M.T., Ciobanu, V., and Popescu, N. Noise Removal from ECG Signal Based on Filtering Techniques. In *2019 22nd International Conference on Control Systems and Computer Science* (CSCS-2019), pages 176-181, Bucharest, Romania, 2019.

[5] Aminoff, M.J. *Aminoff's Electrodiagnosis in Clinical Neurology: Expert Consult-Online and Print*, Elsevier Health Sciences. 2012.

[6] Ahn, S.W., Yoon, B.N., Kim, J.E., Seok, J.M., Kim, K.K., Lim, Y.M., Kwon, K.H., Park, K.D., Suh, B.C., and Korean Society of Clinical Neurophysiology Education Committee. Nerve conduction studies: basic principal and clinical usefulness. *Annals of Clinical Neurophysiology*, 20 (2): 71-78, 2018.

[7] Barthakur, M., Hazarika, A., and Bhuyan, M. A computer-assisted technique for nerve conduction study in early detection of peripheral neuropathy using ANN. *International Journal of Electronics and Communication Engineering Technology*, 4 (5): 47-65, 2013.

[8] Barthakur, M., Hazarika, A., and Bhuyan, M. Classification of peripheral neuropathy by using ANN based nerve conduction study (NCS) protocol. *International Journal on Communication* 5 (1): 31-41, 2014.

[9] Barthakur, M., Hazarika, A., and Bhuyan, M. (2014, May). Rule based fuzzy approach for peripheral motor neuropathy (PMN) diagnosis based on NCS data.

In *International Conference on Recent Advances and Innovations in Engineering* (ICRAIE-2014), pages 1-9, Jaipur, India, 2014.

[10] Banks, D. J., W. Balachandran, P. R. Richards, and D. Ewins. Instrumentation to evaluate neural signal recording properties of micromachined microelectrodes inserted in invertebrate nerve. *Physiological measurement,* 23 (2), 437-448, 2002.

[11] Bortolan, G., Christov, I., Simova, I., and Dotsinsky, I. Noise processing in exercise ECG stress test for the analysis and the clinical characterization of QRS and T wave alternans. *Biomedical Signal Processing and Control*, 18 (1): 378-385, 2015.

[12] Binnie, C.D. *Clinical neurophysiology: EEG, paediatric neurophysiology, special techniques and applications*, Elsevier Health Sciences, 2003.

[13] Cheng, K.E., Lu, Y., Tong, K.Y., Rad, A.B., Chow, D.H., and Sutanto, D. Development of a circuit for functional electrical stimulation. *IEEE Transactions on neural systems and rehabilitation engineering*, 12 (1): 43-47, 2004.

[14] Chang, C.H., Ko, H.J., and Chang, K.M. Cancellation of high-frequency noise in ECG signals using adaptive filter without external reference. In *2010 3rd International Conference on Biomedical Engineering and Informatics*, volume 2, pages 787-790, Yantai, China, 2010.

[15] Dabrowski, K.M., Castaño, D.J., and Tartar, J.L. Basic neuron model electrical equivalent circuit: an undergraduate laboratory exercise. *Journal of Undergraduate Neuroscience Education*, 12 (1): 49-52, 2013.

[16] de Talhouet, H., and Webster, J.G. The origin of skin-stretch-caused motion artifacts under electrodes. *Physiological Measurement*, 17 (2): 81-93, 1996.

[17] Dorland, W.A.N., *Dorland's illustrated medical dictionary*, Philadelphia: Saunders, 1994.

[18] Dorgan, S.J., and Reilly, R.B. A model for human skin impedance during surface functional neuromuscular stimulation. *IEEE transactions on rehabilitation engineering*, 7 (3): 341-348, 1999.

[19] Dunseath, W.R., and Kelly, E.F. Multichannel PC-based data-acquisition system for high-resolution EEG. *IEEE Transactions on Biomedical Engineering*, 42(12): 1212-1217, 1995.

[20] Dominique, P., and Ferron, M.S. Modeling Peripheral Nerve to improve Selective Stimulation. In *10th Annual Conference of the International FES Society*, pages 1-3, Montreal, Canada, 2005.

[21] Giannessi, E., Stornelli, M.R., and Sergi, P.N. A unified approach to model peripheral nerves across different animal species. *PeerJ*, 5: 1-22, 2017.

[22] Gowri, T., Swomya, I., Rahman, Z.U., and Dodda, R.K.R. Adaptive Powerline Interference Removal from Cardiac Signals Using Leaky Based Normalized Higher Order Filtering Techniques. In *2013 1st International Conference on Artificial Intelligence, Modelling and Simulation*, pages 294-298, Kota Kinabalu, Malaysia, 2013.

[23] Grinstead, B., and Parten, M.E. Biomedical signal acquisition using" Labview". In *Proceedings. 11th IEEE Symposium on Computer-Based Medical Systems*, pages 157-161, Lubbock, USA, 1998.

[24] Gupta, R., Bera, J. N., and Mitra, M. Development of an embedded system and MATLAB-based GUI for online acquisition and analysis of ECG signal. *Measurement*, 43 (9): 1119-1126, 2010.

[25] Harimurti, R., Yamasari, Y., and Asto, B.I.G.P. Predicting student's psychomotor domain on the vocational senior high school using linear regression. In *2018 International Conference on Information and Communications Technology* (ICOIACT-2018), pages 448-453, Yogyakarta, Indonesia, 2018.

[26] Hubbard, J. *The peripheral nervous system*, Springer Science & Business Media. 2012

[27] https://en.wikipedia.org/wiki/File:Nervous_system_diagram-en.svg

[28] Harb, A., and Sawan, M. Low-power CMOS implantable nerve signal analog processing circuit. In *7th IEEE International Conference on Electronics, Circuits and Systems* (ICECS- 2000), volume 2, pages 911-914, Jounieh, Lebanon, 2000.

[29] Huang, C.R., Chang, W.N., Chang, H.W., Tsai, N.W., and Lu, C.H. Effects of age, gender, height, and weight on late responses and nerve conduction study parameters. *Acta Neurol Taiwan*, 18 (4): 242-249. 2009.

[30] Hemmsen, M.C., Nikolov, S.I., Pedersen, M.M., Pihl, M.J., Enevoldsen, M.S., Hansen, J.M., and Jensen, J.A. Implementation of a versatile research data

acquisition system using a commercially available medical ultrasound scanner. *IEEE transactions on ultrasonics, ferroelectrics, and frequency control*, 59 (7): 1487-1499, 2012.

[31] Hope, J., Vanholsbeeck, F., and McDaid, A. A model of electrical impedance tomography on peripheral nerves for a neural-prosthetic control interface. *Physiological Measurement*, 1-17, 2018.

[32] Isley, M.R., Kranss, G.L., Levin, K.H., Litt, B., Shields, R.W., and Wilbourn, A.J. Electromyography/electroencephalography. In Redford, Washington, pages 15-30, SpaceLabs Medical, 1993.

[33] Im, J.J., Rho, D.H., Jeon, Y.J., Lee, N.B., and Chung, J.I. Extraction of parameters from EMG signals for the biofeedback electrical stimulation. In *Proceedings of the Second Joint 24th Annual Conference and the Annual Fall Meeting of the Biomedical Engineering Society*, volume 1, pages 133-134, Houston, USA, 2002.

[34] Jamal, M.Z. Signal acquisition using surface EMG and circuit design considerations for robotic prosthesis. In *Computational Intelligence in Electromyography Analysis-A Perspective on Current Applications and Future Challenges*, volume 18, pages 427-448. InTech, 2012.

[35] Jing, J., Zhang, W., Wang, Y., and Yuan, S. An intelligent biofeedback system based on pattern recognition and electroacupuncture imitating traditional Chinese medical acupuncture. In *2006 6th World Congress on Intelligent Control and Automation*, volume 2, pages 9454-9458, Dalian, China, 2006.

[36] Kaçar, S., and Sakoğlu, Ü. Design of a novel biomedical signal processing and analysis tool for functional neuroimaging. *Computer Methods and Programs in Biomedicine*, 125 (1): 46-57, 2016.

[37] Kavitha, S., Varuna, S., and Ramya, R. A comparative analysis on linear regression and support vector regression. In *2016 Online International Conference on Green Engineering and Technologies* (IC-GET-2016), pages 1-5, Coimbatore, India, 2016.

[38] Katirji, B. The clinical electromyography examination: An overview. *Neurologic clinics*, 20 (2): 291-303, 2002.

[39] Lambert, E.H. Diagnostic value of electrical stimulation of motor nerves. *Electroencephalogr Clin Neurophysiol*, 22: 9-16, 1962.

[40] Liu, X., Demosthenous, A., and Donaldson, N. A dual-mode neural stimulator capable of delivering constant current in current-mode and high stimulus charge in semi-voltage-mode. In *Proceedings of 2010 IEEE International Symposium on Circuits and Systems*, pages 2075-2078, Paris, France, 2010.

[41] Loi, D., Carboni, C., Angius, G., Angotzi, G.N., Barbaro, M., Raffo, L., Raspopovic, S., and Navarro, X. Peripheral neural activity recording and stimulation system. *IEEE transactions on biomedical circuits and systems*, 5 (4): 368-379, 2011.

[42] Luan, S., and Constandinou, T. G. A charge-metering method for voltage-mode neural stimulation. *Journal of neuroscience methods*, 224 (1): 39-47, 2014.

[43] Lee, E.K., Dai, R., Reeves, N., and Yun, X. A 36V biphasic stimulator with electrode monitoring circuit. In *2012 IEEE International Symposium on Circuits and Systems* (ISCAS-2012), pages 1087-1090, Seoul, South Korea, 2012.

[44] Lee, M.Y., Lin, C.F., and Soon, K.S. Design of a new biofeedback proprioceptive neuromuscular facilitation system for below-knee amputees. *Biomedical Engineering: Applications. Basis and Communications*, 18 (4): 190-197, 2006.

[45] Lunn, M.P., Hughes, R.A., and Wiffen, P.J. Duloxetine for treating painful neuropathy, chronic pain or fibromyalgia. *Cochrane Database of Systematic Reviews*, 1: 1-125, 2014.

[46] Massó, N., Rey, F., Romero, D., Gual, G., Costa, L., and Germán, A. Surface electromyography applications in the sport. *Apunts Med Esport*, 45 (165): 121-130, 2010.

[47] Mishra, U. K., and Kalita, J. *Clinical Neurophysiology*. Elsevier Health Sciences, 3rd edition, India, 2014.

[48] Mallik, A., and Weir, A.I. Nerve conduction studies: essentials and pitfalls in practice. *Journal of Neurology, Neurosurgery & Psychiatry*, 76 (2): 23-31, 2005.

[49] Malboubi, M., Razzazi, F., Sh, M.A., and Davari, A. Power line noise elimination from EMG signals using adaptive Laguerre filter with fuzzy step size. In *2010 17th Iranian Conference of Biomedical Engineering* (ICBME-2010), pages 1-4, Isfahan, Iran, 2010.

[50] Malboubi, M., Razzazi, F., and Aliyari, S.M. Elimination of power line noise from EMG signals using an efficient adaptive Laguerre filter. In *ICSES 2010*

International Conference on Signals and Electronic Circuits, pages 49-52, Gliwice, Poland, 2010.

[51] Mewett, D.T., Nazeran, H., and Reynolds, K.J. Removing power line noise from recorded EMG. In *2001 Conference Proceedings of the 23rd Annual International Conference of the IEEE Engineering in Medicine and Biology Society*, pages 2190-2193, Istanbul, Turkey, 2001.

[52] Meister, M., Pine, J., and Baylor, D.A. Multi-neuronal signals from the retina: acquisition and analysis. *Journal of neuroscience methods*, 51 (1): 95-106, 1994.

[53] Miller, R.G., and Kuntz, N.L. Nerve conduction studies in infants and children. *Journal of child neurology*, 1(1): 19-26, 1986.

[54] Muduli, P.R., and Mukherjee, A. Noise-assisted trend-filtering of fetal-electrocardiogram signals. In *2016 IEEE EMBS Conference on Biomedical Engineering and Sciences* (IECBES-2016), pages 465-469, Kuala Lumpur, Malaysia, 2016.

[55] Ng, K.A., Yuan, C., Rusly, A., Do, A.T., Zhao, B., Liu, S.C., Peh, W.Y.X., Thow, X.Y., Voges, K., Lee, S., and Gammad, G.G.L. A wireless multi-channel peripheral nerve signal acquisition system-on-chip. *IEEE Journal of Solid-State Circuits*, 54 (8): 2266-2280, 2019.

[56] Ngamkham, W., van Dongen, M.N., and Serdijn, W.A. Biphasic stimulator circuit for a wide range of electrode-tissue impedance dedicated to cochlear implants. In *2012 IEEE International Symposium on Circuits and Systems* (ISCAS-2012), pages 1083-1086, Seoul, South Korea, 2012.

[57] Nagal, R., Kumar, P., and Bansal, P. Optimization of Adaptive Noise Canceller with Grey Wolf Optimizer for EEG/ERP Signal Noise Cancellation. In *2019 6th International Conference on Signal Processing and Integrated Networks* (SPIN-2019), pages 670-675, Noida, India, 2019.

[58] Novakova, L., Ruzicka, E., Jech, R., Serranova, T., Dusek, P. and Urgosik, D. Increase in body weight is a non-motor side effect of deep brain stimulation of the subthalamic nucleus in Parkinson's disease. *Neuroendocrinology Letters, 28* (1): 21-26, 2007.

[59] Oh, Shin J. *Clinical electromyography: nerve conduction studies*. Lippincott Williams & Wilkins, 3rd edition, USA, 2003.

[60] Pancholi, S., and Agarwal, R. Development of low cost EMG data acquisition system for Arm Activities Recognition. In *2016 International Conference on Advances in Computing, Communications and Informatics* (ICACCI), pages 2465-2469, Jaipur, India, 2016.

[61] Peckham, P.H., and Knutson, J.S. Functional electrical stimulation for neuromuscular applications. *Annu. Rev. Biomed. Eng.*, 7: 327-360, 2005.

[62] Pichorim, S.F., Vollmann, W., Pellanda, U.V., and Malca, S.T. Nerve Conduction Velocity Measurement: A didactic example. In *Congreso Argentino de Bioingeniaria*, pages 1-4, 2009.

[63] Perez-Orive, J., and Durund, D.M. Modeling study of peripheral nerve recording selectivity. *IEEE Transactions on Rehabilitation Engineering*, 8 (3): 320-329, 2000.

[64] Puanhvuan, D., Chumnanvej, S., and Wongsawat, Y. Electrical stimulation-based nerve location prediction for cranial nerve VII localization in acoustic neuroma surgery. *Brain and behavior*, 8 (6): 1-12, 2018.

[65] Philips, W. Adaptive noise removal from biomedical signals using warped polynomials. *IEEE transactions on biomedical engineering*, 43 (5): 480-492, 1996.

[66] Puanhvuan, D., Chumnanvej, S., and Wongsawat, Y. Peripheral nerve function estimation by linear model of multi-CMAP responses for surgical intervention in acoustic neuroma surgery. *Physiological Reports*, 5 (23): 1-10, 2017.

[67] Qiu, S., Feng, J., Xu, R., Xu, J., Wang, K., He, F., Qi, H., Zhao, X., Zhou, P., Zhang, L., and Ming, D. A stimulus artifact removal technique for SEMG signal processing during functional electrical stimulation. *IEEE Transactions on Biomedical Engineering*, 62 (8): 1959-1968, 2015.

[68] Satija, U., Ramkumar, B., and Manikandan, M.S. A review of signal processing techniques for electrocardiogram signal quality assessment. *IEEE reviews in biomedical engineering*, 11 (1): 36-52, 2018.

[69] Seki, M., Matsumoto, Y., Ando, T., Kobayashi, Y., Iijima, H., Nagaoka, M., and Fujie, M.G. Filtering Essential Tremor noise on surface EMG based on squared sine wave approximation. In *2011 Annual International Conference of the IEEE*

Engineering in Medicine and Biology Society, pages 7487-7491, Boston, USA, 2011.

[70] Standring, S., Ellis, H., Healy, J., Johnson, D., Williams, A., Collins, P., and Wigley, C. Gray's anatomy: the anatomical basis of clinical practice. *American journal of neuroradiology*, 26 (10): 2703-2704, 2005.

[71] Schmidt, R.F., Dudel, J., Jaenig, W., and Zimmermann, M. *Fundamentals of neurophysiology*, Springer Science & Business Media, 2012.

[72] Schuettler, M., Seetohul, V., Taylor, J., and Donaldson, N. Velocity-selective recording from frog nerve using a multi-contact cuff electrode. In *2006 International Conference of the IEEE Engineering in Medicine and Biology Society*, pages 2962-2965, New York, USA, 2006.

[73] Swen, W.A., Jacobs, J.W., Bussemaker, F.E., De Waard, J.W.. and Bijlsma, J.W. Carpal tunnel sonography by the rheumatologist versus nerve conduction study by the neurologist. *The Journal of rheumatology*, 28 (1): 62-69, 2001.

[74] Stetson, D.S., Albers, J.W., Silverstein, B.A., and Wolfe, R.A. Effects of age, sex, and anthropometric factors on nerve conduction measures. *Muscle & Nerve: Official Journal of the American Association of Electrodiagnostic Medicine*, 15 (10): 1095-1104, 1992.

[75] Soulier, F., Rossel, O., Bernard, S., Cathébras, G., and Guiraud, D. Design of nerve signal biosensor. In *2009 Joint IEEE North-East Workshop on Circuits and Systems and TAISA Conference*, pages 1-4, Toulouse, France, 2009.

[76] Tarotin, I., Aristovich, K., and Holder, D. Model of impedance changes in unmyelinated nerve fibers. *IEEE Transactions on Biomedical Engineering*, 66 (2): 471-484, 2018.

[77] Taji, B., Chan, A.D., and Shirmohammadi, S. Effect of pressure on skin-electrode impedance in wearable biomedical measurement devices. *IEEE Transactions on Instrumentation and Measurement*, 67 (8): 1900-1912, 2018.

[78] Thie, J., Klistorner, A., and Graham, S.L. Biomedical signal acquisition with streaming wireless communication for recording evoked potentials. *Documenta Ophthalmologica*, 125 (2): 149-159, 2012.

[79] Thorsen, R., and Ferrarin, M. Battery powered neuromuscular stimulator circuit for use during simultaneous recording of myoelectric signals. *Medical engineering & physics*, 31 (8): 1032-1037, 2009.

[80] Tracey, B.H., and Krishnamachari, S. Automated removal of stimulus artifact in nerve conduction studies. In *2006 International Conference of the IEEE Engineering in Medicine and Biology Society*, pages 6360-6363, New York, USA, 2006.

[81] Torpy, J.M., Kincaid, J.L., and Glass, R.M. Peripheral Neuropathy. *The Journal of the American Medical Association*, 299 (9): 1096-1096, 2008.

[82] Thanakiatpinyo, T., and Srisawasdi, G. Effect of hand size on the stimulation intensities required for median and ulnar sensory nerve conduction studies. *Archives of physical medicine and rehabilitation,* 94 (5): 925-929, 2013.

[83] Ugalde, H.M.R., Ojeda, D., Le Rolle, V., Andreu, D., Guiraud, D., Bonnet, J.L., Henry, C., Karam, N., Hagege, A., Mabo, P., and Carrault, G. Model-based design and experimental validation of control modules for neuromodulation devices. *IEEE Transactions on Biomedical Engineering*, 63 (7): 1551-1558, 2015.

[84] Ward, M.P., Qing, K.Y., Otto, K.J., Worth, R.M., John, S.W., and Irazoqui, P.P. A flexible platform for biofeedback-driven control and personalization of electrical nerve stimulation therapy. *IEEE Transactions on Neural Systems and Rehabilitation Engineering*, 23 (3): 475-484, 2014.

[85] Wesselink, W.A., Holsheimer, J., and Boom, H.B.K. A model of the electrical behaviour of myelinated sensory nerve fibres based on human data. *Medical & biological engineering & computing*, 37 (2): 228-235, 1999.

[86] Wilbourn, A.J. Nerve conduction studies: types, components, abnormalities, and value in localization. *Neurologic clinics*, 20 (2): 305-338, 2002.

[87] Wilbourn, A.J. Sensory nerve conduction studies. *Journal of Clinical Neurophysiology: Official Publication of the American Electroencephalographic Society*, 11 (6): 584-601, 1994.

[88] Wu, Y., Martínez, M.Á.M., and Balaguer, P.O. Overview of the Application of EMG Recording in the Diagnosis and Approach of Neurological Disorders. In *Electrodiagnosis in New Frontiers of Clinical Research*, pages 1-24. Intech Open, 2013.

[89] Yang, Y. Prediction and analysis of aero-material consumption based on multivariate linear regression model. In *2018 IEEE 3rd International Conference on Cloud Computing and Big Data Analysis* (ICCCBDA-2018), pages 628-632, Chengdu, China, 2018.

[90] Yang, B., and Dong, Y. A Portable Dual-Parameter Tester for Assessing Electrical Properties of Human Skin Surface. *IEEE Sensors Journal*, 16 (2): 426-435, 2015.

[91] Zefeng, Y., Fang, L., Yibiao, R., Yaowen, C., and Zhun, F. Design of a multichannel biomedical signal acquisition system based on Cortex-M4 processor. In *2015 IEEE International Conference on Cyber Technology in Automation, Control, and Intelligent Systems* (CYBER-2015), pages 1023-1027, Shenyang, China, 2015.

[92] Zeng, D., Hu, Y., He, Q., Leng, B., Wang, H., Zou, H., and Wu, W. Study of intelligent bio-feedback therapy system based on transcutaneous electrical nerve stimulation and surface EMG signals. In *2013 IEEE International Conference on Information and Automation* (ICIA-2013), pages 374-378, Yinchuan, China, 2013.

CHAPTER 2

Experimental Setup for NCS Development

2.0 Introduction

Nerve conduction study (NCS) measures how well and fast the nerves can send electrical signals. In NCS test, a set of surface electrodes are placed over the skin overlying the nerve for stimulation and recording. A stimulus voltage or current with millisecond duration is applied by a stimulator over the nerve and it triggers a wave of membrane for which depolarization terminates at a neuromuscular junction. The muscle evoked response is termed as compound muscle action potential (CMAP) in motor NCS [3]. This CMAP is detected with surface electrodes over the nerve at a site away from the point of stimulation and the delay in propagation of the CMAP is called latency. Typically the range of CMAP for motor nerve is 5-10 mV [32].

As mentioned in chapter 1, the acquisition and analysis of biomedical signal has significantly advanced over the years that facilitated lots of technologies. Now a days, with availability in low cost and high performances of the personal computer (PC) , PC based signal acquisition and analysing systems are becoming very efficient and cost effective [9]. Many PC based biomedical signal acquisition systems designed earlier to collect and study the signals and its related issues [6, 37, 41 10, 13]. In [6, 37], acquisition systems were developed for EEG signals including electrodes, signal conditioning circuits with amplifiers and filters, digital control circuitry and PC. Similarly, the authors in [41, 10] also developed the acquisition systems for ECG signals that consisting of electrodes, signal conditioning circuits, ADC and PC. Furthermore, researcher also developed several PC based data acquisition system [27, 34, 2, 14, 26, 36] to collect the nerve responses for further analysis. In [27], a wireless multichannel acquisition system was developed for peripheral nerve signal and CMOS technology was implemented for the design of signal conditioning circuit. An implantable system [34] was developed to acquire nerve signal including electrode, low noise preamplifier, variable gain instrumentation amplifier, ADC and PC. In [2], a system was developed for the recording of peripheral nerve signal that consists of head stage amplifier, filter unit, DAQ card and PC. In the similar pattern, some acquisition systems [14, 26, 35] are also developed to acquire and store the nerve signal that includes electrodes, amplifier, and filter unit to process the signal and further it stores in a PC through DAQ card.

However, as mentioned earlier in the chapter-1, nerve signal data sets in public domain for research purposes are not available unlike ECG and EEG signals. Therefore, this chapter aims to design and develop a PC based data acquisition system to collect the real time nerve signals in the laboratory environment with simple circuit design without compromise the quality of performance. In this work, a conventional voltage controlled stimulator is designed for stimulating the nerve artificially and a set of surface electrodes are used to acquire the corresponding nerve signal from the muscles connected to that nerve. Furthermore, a signal conditioning circuit consists of amplifier and filter units is developed to process the raw nerve signal. In the next level, the signal conditioning circuit as well as stimulator circuit are connected to PC through a DAQ card to store the nerve signals for further analysis. The block diagram of the developed PC based acquisition system for NCS study is shown in the Fig. 2.1.

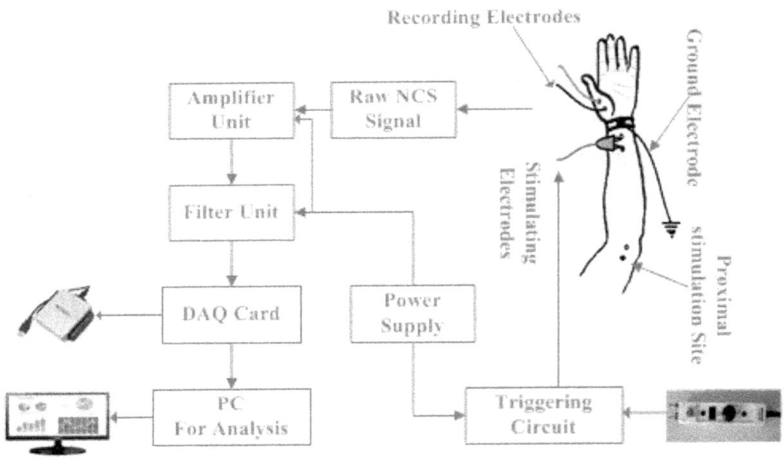

Fig. 2.1 NCS signal acquisition block

Fig. 2.1 shows the nerve stimulation, recording and acquisition system that employs all the required components like stimulator for stimulating the nerve, electrodes to detect the signal, signal conditioning circuit to amplify and filter the raw nerve signal to a suitable form and collected the signals in PC through DAQ card for further analysis. Therefore we have designed and developed a PC based NCS setup to study the real time signals.

2.1 PC Based Nerve Testing Machine

PC based NCS machines are complex and costly. It generally consists of two parts, one is hardware part and another is PC based software part. The hardware portion contains amplifier, filter circuit, ADC etc. It is connected with PC, power supply, electrode box through cable. The NCS signals received from the electrodes are amplified by an amplifier, digitized by an ADC and then applied to the PC for display and measurement of the NCV parameters such as amplitude, latency (both distal and proximal latency), duration etc.

Some PC based Nerve testing machines available in the market are-

- Neuroperfect EMG/NCV Test Machine (EMG-2000)
- Nicolet Viking Quest Console
- Dantec Keypoint laptop
- Cadwell Sierra Wedge
- XLTEK NeuroMax 640
- Cadwell Sierra LT EMG/NCV Test Machine
- Cadwell Sierra 6200a (EMG/NCV/EP)
- TECA TD50

2.1.1 Neuroperfect EMG/NCV Test Machine (EMG-2000)

Neuroperfect plus EMG/NCV/EP systems (Fig. 2.2) with 2-4 channels can be directly connected to USB port and no external power supply is required. Operating system: Windows XP / Vista. Weight: approximately 3 kg (without computer). Auto marking feature is available in the measurement of latency, amplitude and velocity. System perform EMG Recruitment, Insertional, Spontaneous, MUPA, MNCS, SNCV, H-reflex, F-waves, RNS, Evoked Potential, VEP< BAE, SSEP, P-300 and SSR Tests etc. [7]. The front and back panels of the Neuroperfect EMG/NCV Test Machine with specific markings of the parts are shown in the Fig 2.3 and Fig. 2.4 respectively.

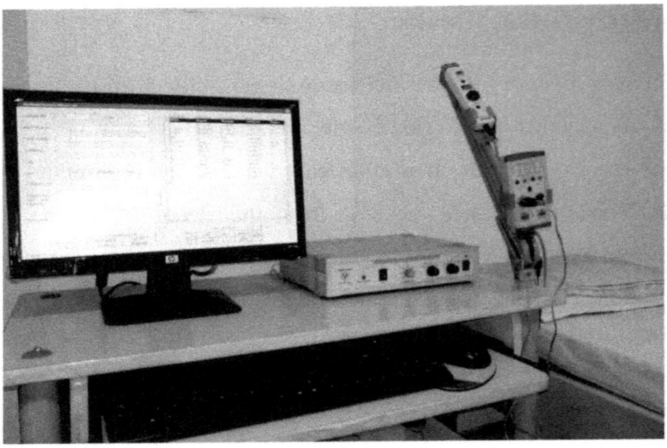

Fig. 2.2 Neuroperfect EMG/NCV test machine (EMG-2000)

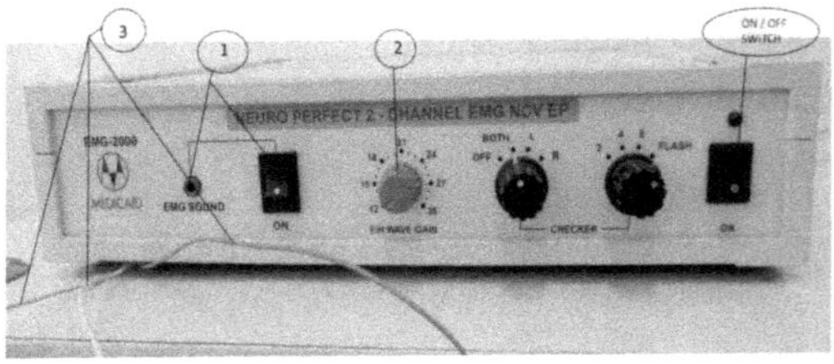

Fig. 2.3 EMG/NCV machine (EMG-2000) front panel (1) EMG sound (Port & ON/OFF Switch): to listen EMG sound as well (2) F/H wave gain: to adjust the F-wave and H-reflex gain (3) output wires: green is ground and white gives the output signal (EMG/NCV) to any external device

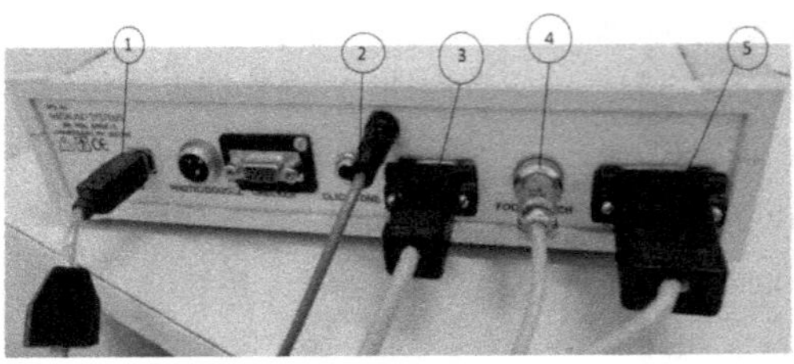

Fig. 2.4 EMG/NCV achine (EMG-2000) back panel (1) USB connector port: USB data cable connects the machine to CPU, it derives it power from CPU itself (2) Ground: it gives the ground reference to the machine (3) Stimulation output: it produces square pulse which is produced at probe (4) Foot switch: it connects to the foot switch which is used as stimulating probe (5) Electrode box: it goes into the electrode box and the nerve output through this port as input to the EMG-2000 machine.

2.1.2. Essential Components and Materials Required in NCS Test

As mentioned earlier, to conduct NCS test a number of components are required like electrodes, stimulator, signal conditioning circuit, DAQ and PC as well as skin preparation materials are required even before conducting the test. The detail descriptions of the components and materials are discussed as follows.

(a) Surface Disc and Ground Electrodes

In NCS test three types of electrodes are used for recording the signal i.e. active, reference and ground. The action potential is measured between active and reference electrodes and the ground electrode act as zero reference point. Typically Ag/AgCl disc surface electrodes are used for its stable electrode polarization potential [23]. Before attaching electrodes to the skin, skin was cleaned by abrading with cleansing jelly to dissolve skin oils and shaving hairs from recording site. The electrode paste is rubbed gently on the skin and then applied for stable contact [5]. Moreover, Surface electrodes Fig.2.5 (a), provide a non-invasive technique for measurement and detection of bio signals [16]. These electrodes usually comprise of Silver/ Silver Chloride disc in one end and a jack on its other side which can directly plug into the jack of the electrode holder. These electrodes are used for variety of tests: Motor Nerve Conduction Velocity (MNCV), Sensory Nerve Conduction Velocity (SNCV), Visual Evoked potential (VEP), Brain's Auditory Evoked Response), F-wave, H-reflex etc.

(a) **(b)**

Fig. 2.5 Electrodes (a) surface disc electrodes (b) ground electrode

These electrodes are mainly used for Motor Nerve Conduction Velocity (MNCV) test. Furthermore, a single wire ground electrode, Fig. 2.5 (b) is used to ground the body of the subject during the NCV/EMG test.

(b) Ring Electrodes: These ring shaped electrodes (Fig.2.6) are specially used for performing SNCV (Sensory Nerve Conduction Velocity).

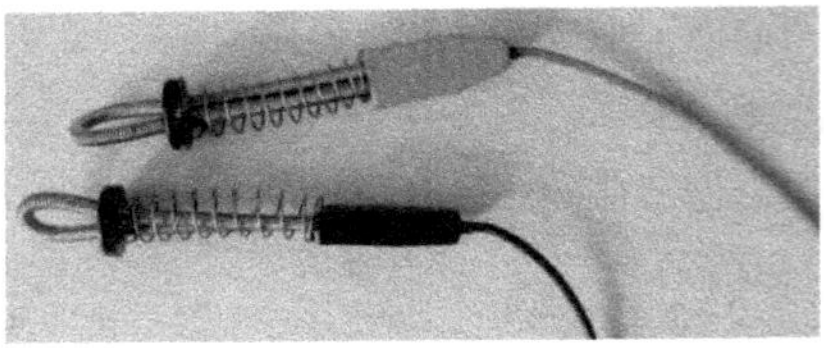

Fig. 2.6 Ring electrode

(c) Electrical stimulator: The hand held stimulator (Fig.2.7) usually consists of two metallic points (Anode & Cathode) which is used to stimulate the nerve of a subject under investigation. One can adjust the intensity and polarity of the stimulations and deliver the required stimulation to the various nerves of a human body.

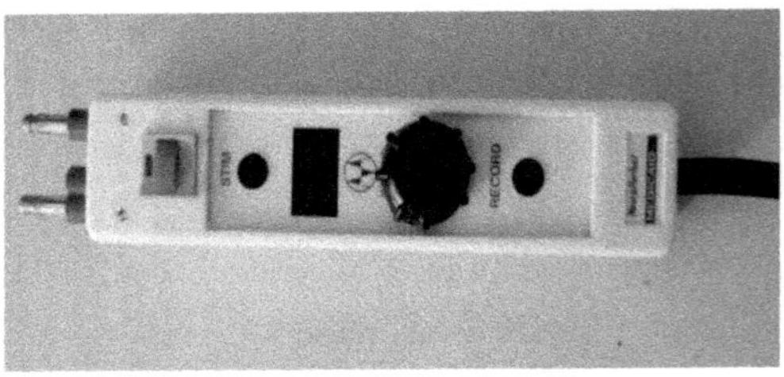

Fig. 2.7 Stimulator probe (Courtesy: Neuroperfect-2 NCV machine)

(d) Conductive Cream gel and paste: The gel and paste, Fig. 2.8 (a-b) are used to minimize the contact resistance at the surface of the skin so that a signal of maximum amplitude can be picked up from that surface. Furthermore a tape, Fig. 2.8 (c) is used to fix the recording electrodes with skin properly so that due to displacement of the electrodes the nerve signal is not interrupted.

(a) (b) (c)

Fig. 2.8 (a) Electrode gel, (b) paste and (c) tape

2.1.3 Motor NCV Test using Neuroperfect-2 NCV Machine (EMG2000)

Before attaching the surface electrodes during NCS test skin preparation of the subject is very essential [16]. For good quality of bio signals, the skin's impedance is reduced by removing the hair from the location for hairy subjects where surface electrodes are to be placed. It is necessary to clean the skin with alcohol in order to eliminate any wetness or sweat on the skin. Furthermore an abrasive gel is used over the skin of the electrodes location so that no moisture is present in the skin [22].

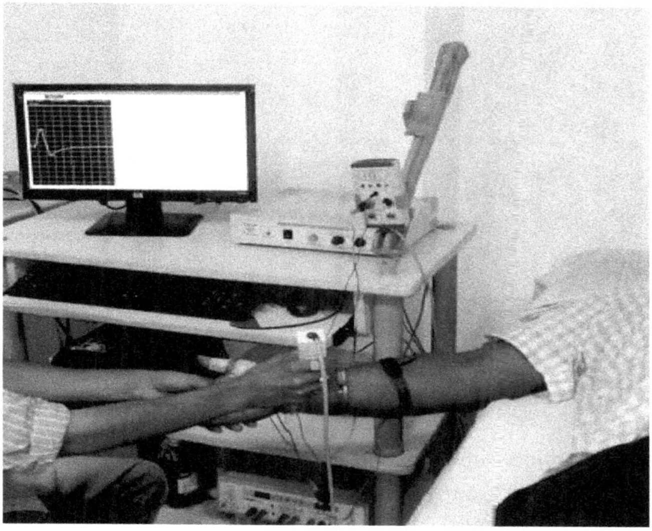

Fig.2.9 MNCV test in neuroperfect-2 machine

This test is done on median motor nerve at wrist position (i.e. stimulating position). The testing setup is shown in the Fig.2.9 and the result is shown in Fig.2.10.

2.2 Design and Development of a Voltage Controlled Stimulator

NCS requires an appropriate stimulator to be applied over the nerve underlying the skin during signal acquisition [24, 17]. Two typical stimulators-current and voltage are usually used in the NCS. However, current controlled stimulator design requires lots of circuit components that makes it more complex for laboratory usage and it is very difficult task to control the amount of charge delivered [20]. Therefore, this chapter explains design and development of a conventional voltage controlled stimulator that is more convenient in terms of circuit design as compared to current controlled stimulator to conduct NCS for the laboratory based experiment. The Fig. 2.11 shows the circuit diagram of the proposed voltage controlled stimulator.

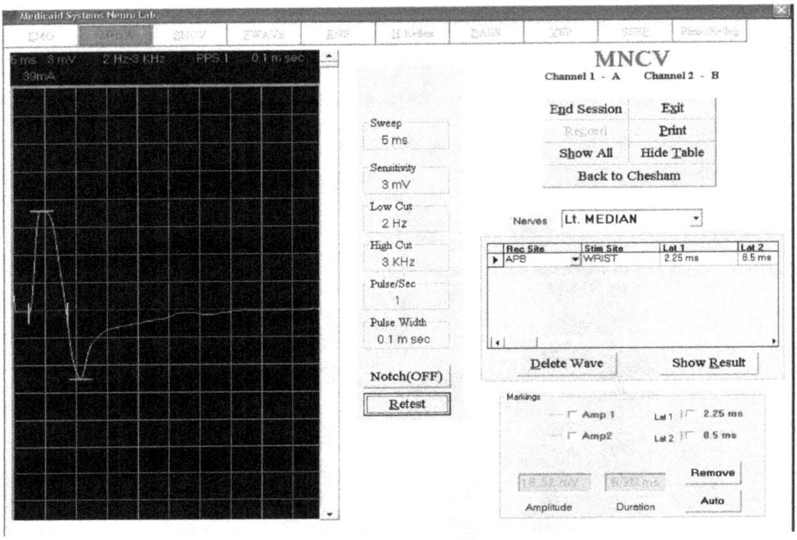

Fig. 2.10 MNCV test result in neuroperfect-2 software

This study aims at developing a voltage controlled nerve stimulator using 9 V Lithium-ion battery (EBL6F22 9V 600 mAh) for properly stimulating the nerve for NCS study. The oscillator circuit Fig. 2.11 (a), is powered by the two 9 V batteries, and is designed to generate sustainable and stabilized sinusoidal oscillation with a frequency 7.23 kHz. The output of the oscillator is fed to the 8-stage voltage multiplier circuit Fig. 2.11 (b), which increases the operating voltage range up to 70 V that will be applied across electrodes to get proper stimulation. The obtained voltage is applied to a voltage divider circuit Fig. 2.11 (d), in order to control the voltage multiplier output as per the requirement. The capacitor (C_8) is associated with the voltage divider circuit to store the charge for a particular level of adjusted voltage. The timer circuit Fig. 2.11 (c), is designed to generate the pulse duration of the stimulator around 110 ms [23]. The Fig. 2.11 (e) is the electrode system unit, the stimulating electrodes are placed over the skin of the subjects for the injection of generated voltage pulse by pressing the puss button switch (SW). The switching transistor is used for discharging the adjusted voltage to the subject through the electrodes which are connected across the collector resistor (R_c). The R_c is placed parallel to the body between the electrodes in order to ensure the final resistance is low enough to reduce the duration of an unavoidable stimulation artefact to suitable values [32].

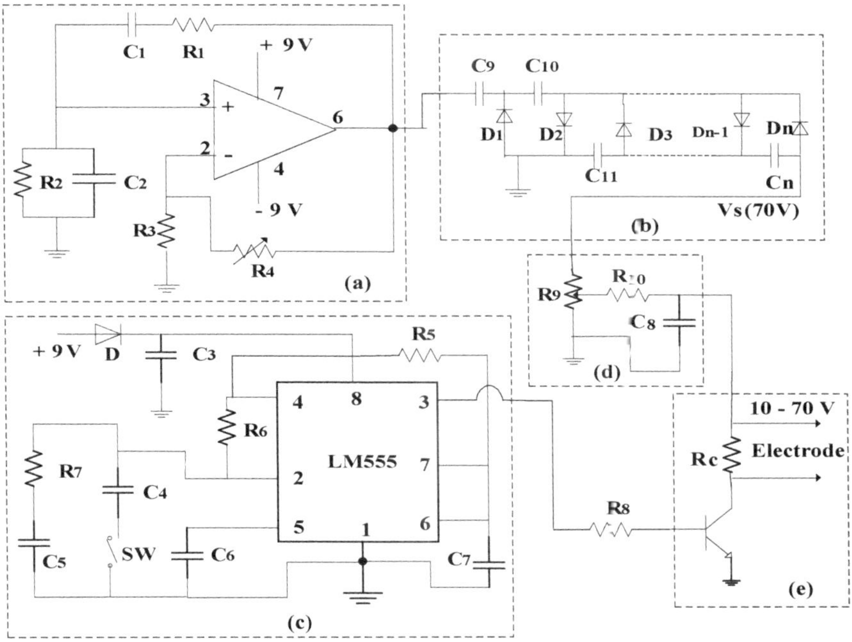

Fig. 2.11 Voltage controlled stimulator circuit (a) Oscillator circuit (b) Voltage multiplier circuit (c) Timer circuit (d) Voltage controller circuit (e) Electrode system with switching transistor

The proposed stimulator design is simple and could be easily tuned the pulse duration and applied voltage according to the requirement during the NCS of the laboratory based experiment. Fig. 2.12 shows the PCB layout and Fig. 2.13 shows the fabricated stimulator for the circuit of Fig. 2.11.

2.2.1. Oscillator Circuit

The oscillator circuit used in the triggering circuit Fig. 2.11 (a) is a Wien bridge Oscillator implemented using an Op Amp 741. The Wien bridge oscillator is a two-stage

RC couple amplifier circuit. It has good stability at resonant frequency, low distortion and easy to tune.

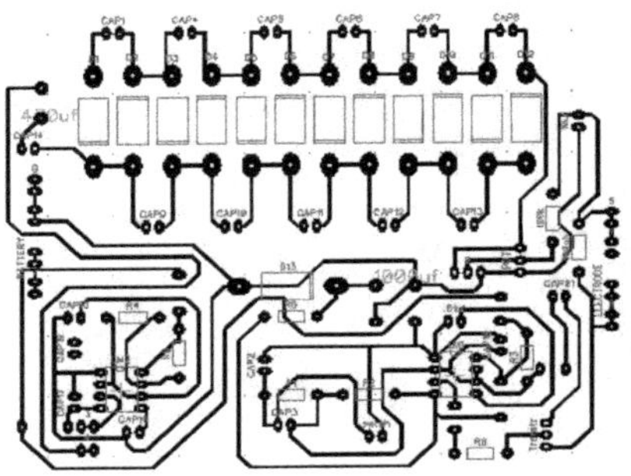

Fig 2.12 Stimulator circuit design in DIPTRACE software (copper side)

Fig 2.13 Stimulator circuit developed in hardware (component side)

The Wien bridge oscillator (Fig. 2.14) uses a feedback circuit, consisting of a series RC circuit connected with a parallel RC circuit of the same component. It produces a phase delay or phase advance circuit depending upon the frequency. At resonant frequency (f_r), the phase shift is zero degree.

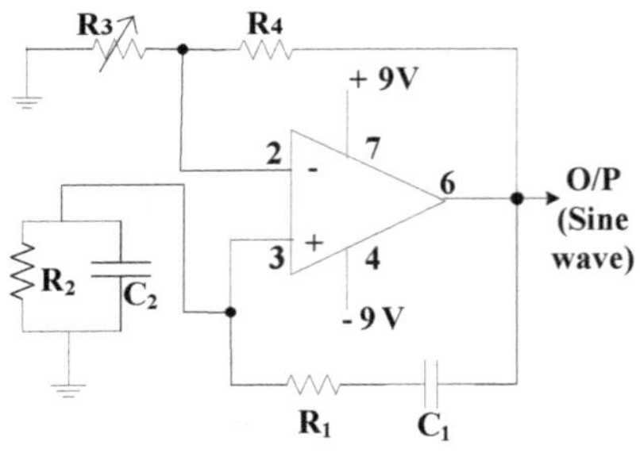

Fig. 2.14 Wien bridge oscillator

To stabilize the amplitude, Barkhausen criterion has to be satisfied. The criterion states that magnitude of overall gain around the loop should be unity with phase shift of either zero or multiple of 360^0.

$$\text{i.e. } \left(|A\beta| = 1\right) \text{ or } \left(|A\beta| = e^{i\Phi} = 1\right) \tag{2.1}$$

$$\text{where, } \Phi = 2n\pi; n = 0, 2, \ldots$$

The oscillator circuit of Fig. 2.14 is composed of an RC network forming a high pass filter (R_1C_1) connected to a low pass filter (R_2C_2) producing second-order frequency dependent band pass filter at the selected frequency, f_r. At low frequencies the reactance of the series capacitor (C_1) is very high so acts like an open circuit, blocking any input voltage signal, V_{in} resulting in virtually no output signal, V_{out}. Likewise, at high frequencies, the reactance of the parallel capacitor (C_2) becomes very low, so this parallel connected capacitor acts like a short circuit across the output, so again there is no output signal.

So there must be a frequency point between these two extremes of C_1 being open-circuited and C_2 being short-circuited where the output voltage, V_{out} reaches its maximum value. The frequency value of the input waveform at which this happens is called the oscillators *resonant frequency* (f_r). This resonant frequency is given by-

$$f_r = \frac{1}{2\pi RC} \tag{2.2}$$

$$\text{where, } R_1 = R_2 = R \text{ and } C_1 = C_2 = C$$

Assuming $R_1 = R_2 = R = 10\ \text{k}\Omega$ and $C_1 = C_2 = C = 2.2$ nF, the value of resonant frequency is calculated as-

$$f_r = 7.23\ \text{kHz} \tag{2.3}$$

At this resonant frequency, the circuit reactance equals to its resistance

i.e. $X_{circuit} = R_{circuit}$ and the phase difference between the input and output equals zero.

For sinusoidal oscillations to begin, the voltage gain of the Wien bridge must be equal to or greater than 3 $(A_v \geq 3)$ [11]. The resistances R_3 and R_4 are used for used for the voltage gain of the oscillator circuit. For a non-inverting op-amp configuration, this value is set by the feedback resistor network of R_3 and R_4 which is calculated as follows-

$$A_v = \frac{V_{out}}{V_{in}} \tag{2.4}$$

$$=1+\frac{R_4}{R_3}=3 \text{ or more}$$

Taking, R_3= 47 kΩ, then the value of R_4 is 94 kΩ. Again, a gain value of 3 is the minimum requirement to ensure oscillations. For practical considerations, if we assume a gain value of 3.1, then the calculations are as follows-

$$1+\frac{R_f}{R_i}=3.1 \tag{2.5}$$

Now, if we assume R_3 = 47 kΩ, then R_4 = 98.7 kΩ, which is tuned by a precision potentiometer.

2.2.2 Voltage Multiplier Circuit (VMC)

A VMC is a special type of diode rectifier circuit (Fig. 2.11 (b)) which can potentially produce an output voltage many times greater than the applied input voltage. However, it is different from a rectifier in the sense that a rectifier is limited by the peak value of its sinusoidal input voltage but a voltage multiplier circuit can effectively multiply this input peak voltage to give a DC output equal to some odd or even multiple of the peak voltage value of the AC input voltage.

2.2.2.1 Voltage Doubler Circuit (VDC)

A voltage doubler circuit (Fig. 2.15) has a voltage multiplication factor of two. The circuit consists of only two diodes, two capacitors and an oscillating AC input voltage. This simple diode-capacitor pump circuit gives a DC output voltage equal to the peak-to-peak value of the sinusoidal input.

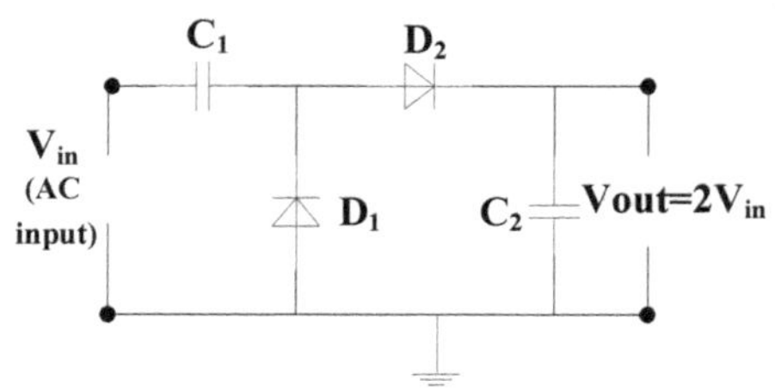

Fig. 2.15 Voltage doubler circuit

The operation of a VDC is as follows- during the negative half cycle of the sinusoidal input waveform, diode D_1 is forward biased and conducts charging up the pump capacitor C_1 to the peak value of the input voltage, V_{in}. Because there is no return path for capacitor C_1 to discharge, it remains fully charged acting as a storage device in series with the voltage supply. At the same time, diode D_2 conducts via D_1 charging up capacitor C_2.

Again, during the positive half cycle, diode D_1 is reverse biased blocking the discharging of C_1 while diode D_2 is forward biased charging up capacitor C_2. But because there is a voltage across capacitor C_1 already equal to the peak input voltage, capacitor C_2 charges to twice the peak voltage value of the input signal.

In other words, on the negative half-cycle, D_1 charges C_1 to V_p and on the positive half-cycle D_2 ads the AC peak voltage to V_p on C_1 and transfers it all to C_2. The voltage across capacitor, C_2 discharges through the load ready for the next half cycle. Then the voltage across capacitor C_2 can be calculated as $V_{out} = 2V_p$ where V_p is the peak value of the input voltage.

Therefore, the oscillator circuit Fig. 2.11 (a), is powered by the two 9 V batteries, and is designed to generate sustainable and stabilized sinusoidal oscillation with a frequency 7.23 kHz. The output of the oscillator is fed to the 8-stage voltage multiplier circuit Fig. 2.11 (b), which increases the operating voltage range up to 70 V with some voltage drop that will be applied across electrodes to get proper stimulation. The obtained voltage is applied to a voltage divider circuit Fig. 2.11 (d), in order to control the voltage multiplier output as per the requirement. The capacitor (C_8) is associated with the voltage divider circuit to store the charge for a particular level of adjusted voltage.

2.2.3 Timer Circuit

The timer circuit shown in Fig. 2.11 (c) is basically a monostable multivibrator circuit designed with a 555 timer IC. The monostable multivibrator (Fig. 2.16) has one stable state and it switches to unstable state for a predetermined time period when it is triggered. The time period is determined by the RC time constant in the circuit.

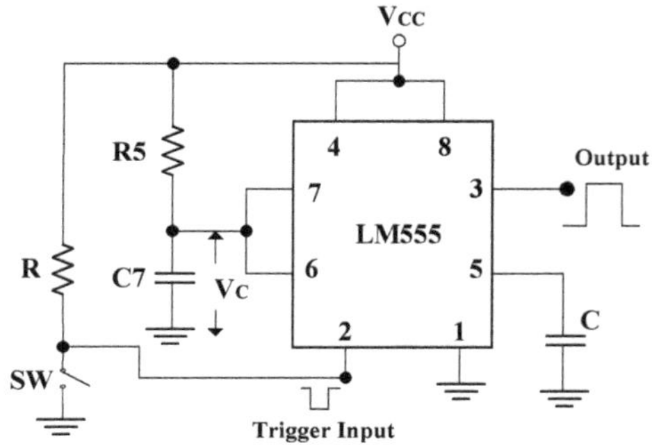

Fig. 2.16 Monostable multivibrator circuit

When a negative pulse just below the reference voltage $\left(\frac{1}{3}V_{cc}\right)$ is applied to the trigger input (pin 2), the output goes high and capacitor (C_7) starts charging through resistor (R_5). However, as the C_7 voltage becomes greater than $\frac{2}{3}V_{cc}$, output goes low and C_7 starts discharging through the discharge pin 7 of 555 timer as shown in Fig. 2.17.

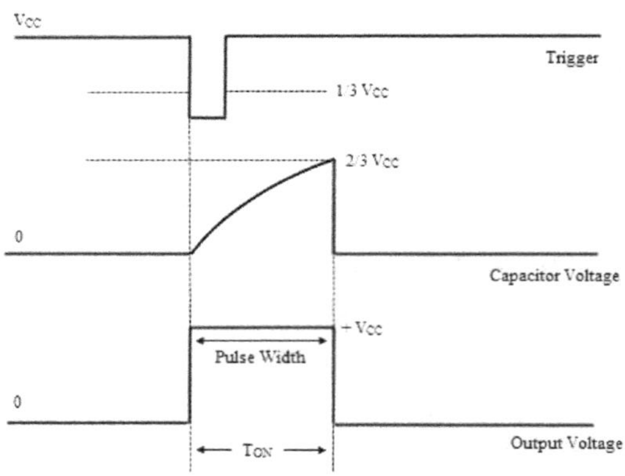

Fig. 2.17 Waveforms of monostable multivibrator operation

Time period of the unstable state or the output pulse width is determined by the expression-

$$T_{ON} = 1.1\ R_5 C_7 \tag{2.6}$$

The Eq. (2.6) is used to determine the pulse duration of the stimulator circuit (Fig. 2.11).

Suppose, for a pulse of approximately 100 ms duration, let us assume that the value of capacitor used is C = 0.1μF.Then the value of R can be obtained by using Eq. (2.6) as-

$$100\times10^{-3}=1.1\times R\times0.1\times10^{-6}$$

$$i.e.R=\frac{100\times10^{-3}}{1.1\times0.1\times10^{-6}}$$

$$=909.09\ \text{k}\Omega$$

Finally, by using this technique, the pulse duration of the timer circuit i.e. stimulation impulse duration of the stimulator circuit is adjusted.

2.2.4 Voltage Controller Circuit (VCC)

The VCC (Fig. 2.11 (d)) is used to control the voltage multiplier output according to the requirement of the application. The VCC output is produced around 70 V dc which is controlled by R_9 (variable resistor) and R_{10} to obtain the desired voltage range 10 V to 70 V across the electrodes. The capacitor (C_8) is connected to the resistor unit to store the adjusted voltage charge, to be applied across the electrodes.

2.2.5 Electrode System with Switching Transistor

A switching transistor (TIP 122, medium powered NPN transistor) is connected in series with the stimulating electrodes as shown in Fig. 2.11 (e), used for discharging the applied voltage to the subject through the electrodes that are connected across the collector resistor (R_c). The R_c is placed parallel to the body between the electrodes in order to ensure the final resistance is low enough to reduce the duration of an unavoidable stimulation artefact to suitable values.

However, as the puss button switch (SW) is pressed ON, the output of the timer circuit produces a predetermined pulse width which is applied to the base resistor (R_b) of the switching transistor and the transistor goes to the saturation state. It will remain in saturation for the time equal to the duration of the pulse, and allows the adjusted voltage (form the controller circuit, Fig. 2.11 (d) for stimulation across the R_c to be discharged through the stimulating electrodes. After that the switching transistor goes back to its prior cut off state until next pulse form timer circuit is applied to its R_b .

2.3 Signal Conditioning Circuit (SSC)

With use of stimulating voltage, the acquired raw signal is processed through SCC. Signal processing is an important requirement due to its inherent low amplitude and high noise profiles [3, 9, 36]. Basic objective of this design is to amplify as well as filtering the raw NCS signal. The SCC includes an instrumentation amplifier Fig. 2.18 (a) by using INA128P with gain ($A_v = 1 + \frac{50k\Omega}{R_g}$), R_g is the gain control resistance that amplifies the recorded CMAP signal. The cascade noise removal circuit employs OPA2604AP to design high-pass and low-pass filter in the frequency range of 2 Hz-10 kHz [32, 17]. The two stage second order filter has roll-off of 12 dB/Octave and consequently, the order of complete noise reduction circuit becomes 4th order butter worth band pass filter as shown in Fig. 2.18 (b-e) and its frequency response plot is shown in Fig. 2.19.

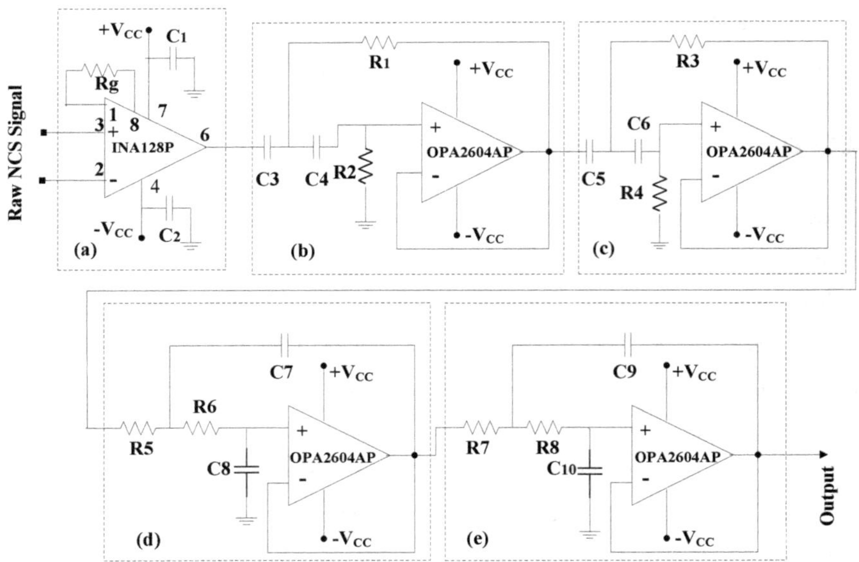

Fig. 2. 18 Schematic circuit of signal conditioning unit that includes (a) instrumentation amplifier, (b-c) high pass filter and (d-e) low pass filter.

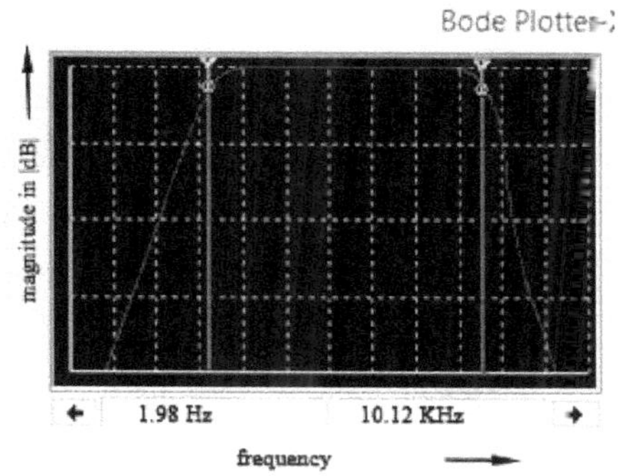

Fig. 2.19 Frequency response plot of the designed band pass filter

2.3.1 Amplification

For amplification stage, an instrumentation amplifier (INA 128P) is used with a closed-loop gain block with differential input and a single ended output with respect to reference terminal. Most of the electronic circuitry which are made for detection and measurement of the bio signals such as EMG, ECG, CMAP, and EEG has widely used instrumentation amplifiers. Instrumentation amplifiers has very high common mode rejection ratio (CMRR) and high input impedance so it makes easy to extract signals from the noisiest and poorest source as in case of bio signals [18] as well as it prevents loading effect. It also has low output impedance, low bias current and low noise.

2.3.1.1 INA 128P

INA128P is a low power, general purpose instrumentation amplifier. It has excellent accuracy and current feedback input circuitry that provides wide bandwidth even at high gain [15].

2.3.2 Filter

The nerve signal contains both high and low frequency noise as like as other biological signals. So an active butter worth band pass filter is used to minimize the noises from the signal. This filter circuit is the combination of high pass filter (HPF) and low pass filter (LPF). Butterworth filter configuration is used because it has a flat pass band as well as stop band characteristic. For the filter circuit OPA2604AP operational amplifier is used.

2.3.2.1 OPA 2604AP

The OPA2604 is a dual, FET-input operational amplifier designed for enhanced AC performance. Very low distortion, low noise and wide bandwidth provide superior performance in high quality audio and other applications requiring excellent dynamic performance [28]. It is also used in data acquisition, active filters, spectral analysis equipment etc.

Some special features of OPA2604AP [28]:

- Low Distortion: 0.0003% at 1kHz
- Low Noise: $10nV/\sqrt{Hz}$
- High Slew Rate: 25V/μs
- Wide Gain-Bandwidth: 20MHz
- Unity-Gain Stable
- Wide Supply Range : ±4.5 to ±24V

2.3.2.2 High Pass Filter

The low frequency components of CMAP signal has several types of noises with different characteristics [23]. As a result, the HPF designing is more complicated than LPF design. The cut off frequency of the butter worth high pass filter is set at 2 Hz [23, 12] with unity gain mode.

First order high pass filter cut-off frequency equation,

$$f_c = \frac{1}{2\pi RC} \qquad (2.7)$$

Pass band gain = 1

When R=169 kΩ, C=470nF, f_c = 2 Hz.

The first order filter has a roll-off rate of -6dB/Octave. Better roll-off rate increase the performance of a filter [11]. A 4th order high pass filter is used which is constructed by cascading two second order high pass filter. It has a roll-off rate of -24dB/Octave (Fig.2.18 (b-c)).

Second order high pass filter cut-off frequency,

$$f_c = \frac{1}{2\pi\sqrt{R_1 R_2 C_1 C_2}} \tag{2.8}$$

By using Eq. 2.8 the cut-off frequency of the 4th order high pass filter is set to 2 Hz.

2.3.2.3 Low Pass Filter

In bio-medical signal, the high frequency noise components are introduced by surrounding electronic components and radio interference. Butter worth low pass filter with 10 KHz cut-off frequency is used at the output of the high pass filter to suppress frequencies beyond 10 KHz [23, 11].

The cut-off frequency of first order low pass filter is set by using Eq. (2.8). As mentioned earlier, first order filter has a roll-off rate off -6dB/Octave. So for better performance, fourth order butter worth low pass filter is used by cascading two second order butter worth low pass filter because fourth order filter has roll-off rate of -24dB/Octave (Fig.2.18 (d-e)).

The cut-off frequency of fourth order butter worth low pass filter is set at 10 KHz by using cut-off frequency Eq. (2.8).

After design of the acquisition circuit, it is developed in PCB as shown in Fig. 2.20 (copper side) and in Fig. 2.21 (top side). The complete hardware based experimental set up is shown in Fig. 2.22.

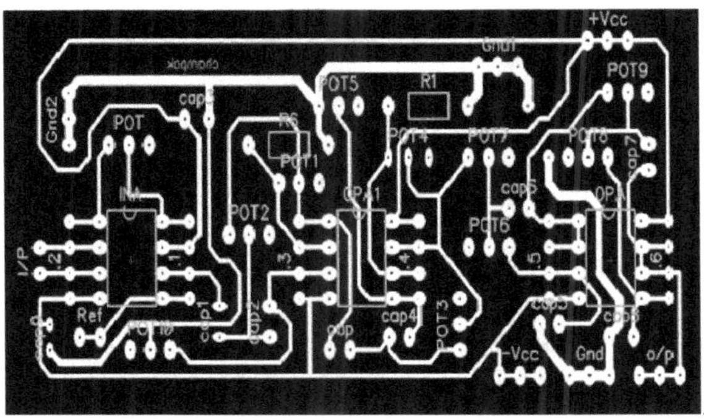

Fig. 2.20 CMAP acquisition circuit design in DIPTRACE software (copper side)

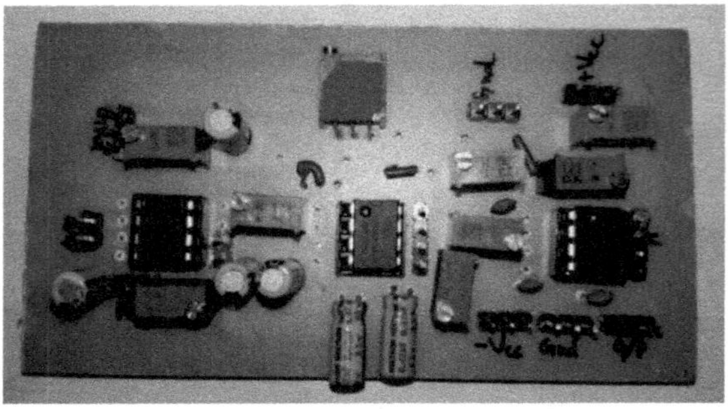

Fig. 2.21 CMAP acquisition circuit developed in hardware (top side)

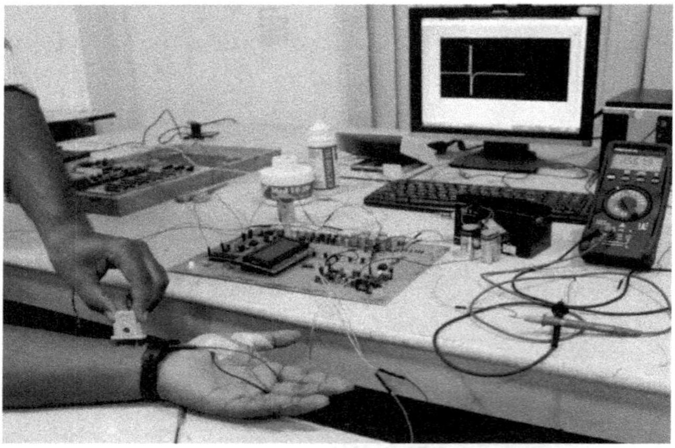

Fig. 2.22 Complete hardware based experimental Setup

2.4 Development of NCS Setup

2.4.1 Development of Circuits

The NCS system developed consists of several circuits i.e. mainly voltage controlled stimulating circuit, signal conditioning circuit, auto controlled stimulator circuit with respect to skin resistance etc., which are fabricated on one sided copper clad printed circuit board (PCB) sheet (1.6 mm, 305 g/m Cu). Dip trace with version of 2.4 is used to design the circuit schematic and layout. Print and press method of PCB design is used which consists of the following steps:

a) The designed circuit layout is printed on a photo paper using a laser printer.

b) The copper PCB board is cut according to the dimension of the printed circuit layout.

c) The cut PCB is then cleaned using sand paper to remove any oxide layer.

d) The circuit layout photo paper is placed in the PCB and electric cloth hot is done for about 10-15 minutes. Due to hot ironing the circuit layout gets imprinted on the PCB (circuit layout is under the black ink)

e) Etching solution is prepared by adding 120-150 g of ferric chloride ($FeCl_3$) powder in 300 ml of water in a plastic container.

f) The PCB is then immersed in the etching solution and rinsed for about 15-20 minutes. The copper layer of the PCB which does not contain the circuit layout gets directly exposed to the etchant and is slowly removed.

g) The PCB is then taken out to check if all unwanted copper is removed by the etchant. If not step 6 is repeated.

h) The PCB is taken out and the black ink of the circuit layout is removed using acetone.

i) The holes in the PCB as per the schematic design are made using a drill machine to hold the circuit components.

j) Finally the components are placed and soldered in the PCB as per the circuit schematic.

2.4.2 Data Acquisition Card

The process of recording responses of NCS signals from the recording electrodes as well as signal conditioning circuits in the form of electrical quantity at a predefined rate is known as data acquisition. The data acquisition and instrument control is attained through a NI USB-6351 DAQ card using Laboratory virtual instrument engineering workbench (LabVIEW) programming in a personal computer (Intel (R) Core (TM) i-3 processor 3.2 GHz and 2 GB of RAM). Unlike text based coding LabVIEW is a powerful graphic based dataflow programming language that uses icons for system-design. LabVIEW is a versatile tool as almost all the instruments physically available in the laboratory are accurately imitated by its program/ subroutines termed as virtual instruments (VI's) [40]

Moreover it is easy to create user defined VI's. Further external hardware or instruments can be smoothly connected using its predefined Vis for acquiring, analysing, displaying and storing data. LabVIEW consists of two panels: a) Front panel which is used to develop the user interface for VI's. It comprises of various controls, indicators, plotting tools etc. b) Block diagram for data transfer operation. It includes the graphical source code and connectivity between various icons through which the front panel objects are controlled.

The DAQ consists of 16 analog input channels, 2 digital output channels, 24 digital USB input output multifunction device, four 32-bit counters /timers, analog /digital ground pins and many special purposes pins. Fig.2.23 shows the NI USB-6351 DAQ card and Fig. 2.24 shows its pin configuration.

Fig. 2.23 NI DAQ USB-6351 card

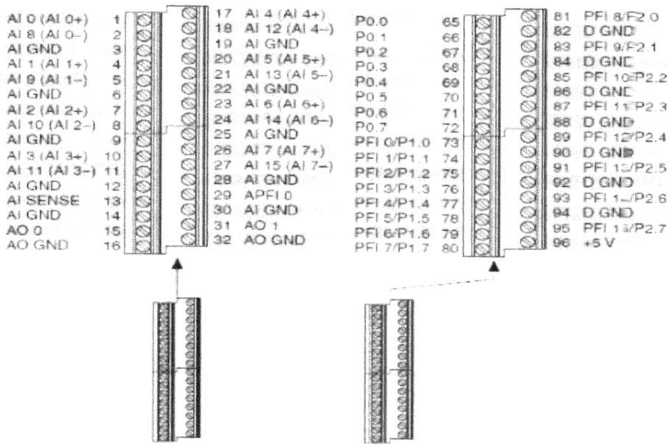

Fig. 2.24 Pin configuration of NI USB-6351 (Source: NI DAQ USB – 6351 datasheet)

2.4.2.1 Acquisition

The analog voltages from the recording electrodes and signal conditioning circuit of the NCS system are collected at a sampling rate of 1 kHz with RSE configuration as the system is connected to a common ground point. In RSE mode the analog voltage can be measured using any of the 16 analog input channels while the circuit ground is connected to any common analog ground pin.

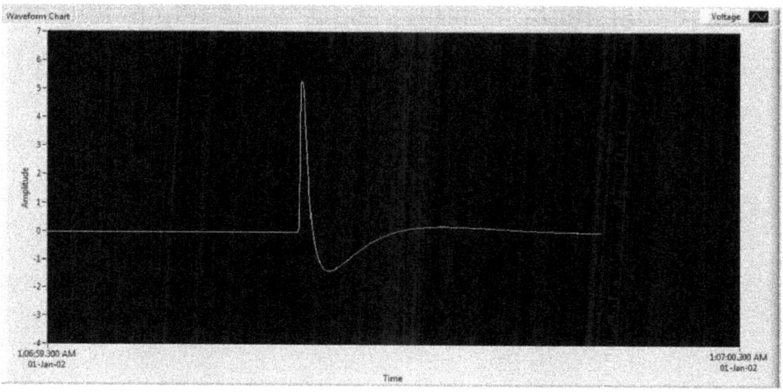

Fig. 2.25 CMAP response (amplified and filtered) of a subject displayed in LabVIEW front panel

This configuration provides a maximum of 16 channels. Data is stored as .lvm format in the PC. For visual interpretation, NCS signals e.g. CMAP response was displayed in a waveform chart in the front panel as shown in Fig.2.25.

2.5 Performance of the Voltage Controlled Stimulator

Initially the experiment was aimed to design a conventional voltage controlled neural stimulator to stimulus the nerve underlying the skin to acquire the NCS signal in the laboratory environment. During the experiment two 9 V Lithium-ion batteries (EBL6F22 9V 600 mAh) were used as source of power to the stimulator circuit instead of DC/AC power supply to avoid the system to be a bulky as well as considering the portability factor for the future applications. This design focuses on configuring a voltage multiplier circuit with conventional circuit in order to increase supply voltage range up to 70 V. The generated supply voltage was applied to a voltage divider circuit to control the voltage as per requirement. Furthermore a timer circuit is used to control the applied voltage duration from 10-110 ms across the electrodes. Finally the performance of the stimulator circuit was tested in terms of power consumption, voltage regulation and dynamic response of the stimulator pulses as well as accuracy of theoretical and experimental pulses duration generated by the stimulator circuit.

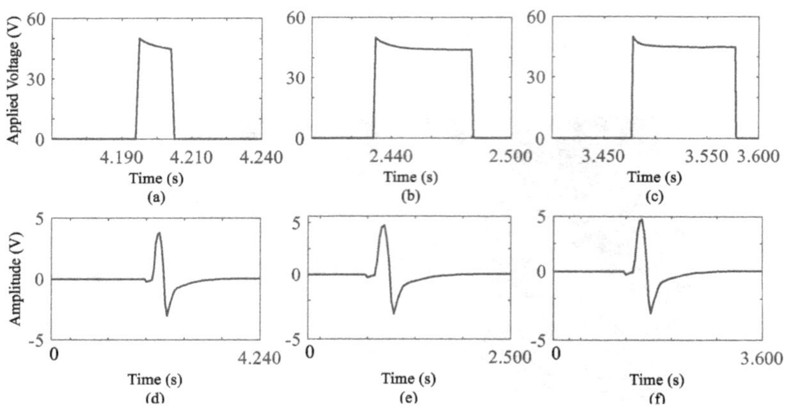

Fig. 2.26 Stimulating pulses of (a) 10 ms, (b) 50 ms and (c) 100 ms, and (d)-(f) are corresponding NCS amplified signals at amplifier gain of 330

The designed stimulator generates the pulses of different durations $\left(t_d = 1.1R_5C_7\right)$ by changing the various values of resistor and capacitor (R_5 and C_7) as outlined in Table

2.1. Before recording the signals, subjected are informed about the recording procedure and mild discomfort that may occur during electrical stimulation. Furthermore, it is carried out as per the protocols of institute Ethical Committee. Generated pulses are applied to median nerve of subject (male, age: 28 years weight: 65 kg) for acquiring the corresponding NCS signals as shown in Fig. 2.26.

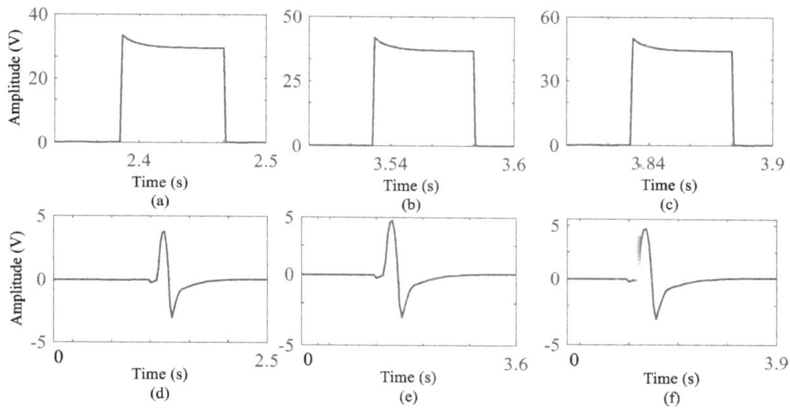

Fig. 2.27 Variation of pulse voltages (a)-(c) stimulating voltage of 30 V, 40 V and 50 V, and (d)-(e) corresponding NCS signals of (a)-(c).

Table 2.1 Theoretical and experimental values of pulse duration (Subject: male, age-28 years, weight-65 kg)

$[R_5; C_7]$ $[k\Omega; F]$	Theoretical/ Experimental Pulse duration, t_d (ms)	Error in %	Sensation [Yes/ No]
0.909, 10	10/ 11	10	Yes
4.54, 10	50/ 51	2.0	Yes
9.09, 10	100/ 102	2.0	Yes
22.72, 10	250/ 254	1.6	Yes
45.45, 10	500/ 508	1.6	Yes
90.9, 10	1000/ 1015	1.5	Yes

Table 2.2 Theoretical and experimental values of voltages of the stimulator (Subject: male, age-28 years, weight-65 kg)

$\left[R_9\left(R_X, R_Y\right)\right]$ $[k\Omega]$	Pulse amplitude [Theoretical/ Experimental, V]	Error [%]	Sensation [Yes/No]
10, 80	10/ 10.2	2.0	No
10, 35	20/ 20.5	2.5	Marginal
10, 20	30/ 30.8	2.6	Yes
10, 12.5	40/ 41	2.5	Yes
10, 8	50/ 53	6.0	Yes
10, 5	60/ 63	5.0	Yes
10. 2.85	70/ 72	2.8	Yes

Fig. 2.26 shows three pulses with constant amplitude of 50 V and varying pulse duration of 10 ms, 50 ms and 100 ms and accuracy of the pulse duration setting is outlined in Table 2.1. We have achieved minimum error of 2% in tuning the pulse duration. Furthermore, the pulse amplitude (i.e., voltage) are also varied as shown in Fig. 2.27 with a constant pulse duration of 100 ms. It is seen from Fig. 2.27 that with increase in pulse duration the CMAP amplitude gradually increases and its morphology looks similar to supramaximal NCS. On the other hand, too high duration pulse although suitable for acquiring for high amplitude CMAP, it may cause damage to nerve including high tingling. It is observed that the supramaximal NCS is obtained at 42 V for that subject. The accuracy of the pulse amplitude setting is shown in Table 2.2. The dynamics of the stimulating voltage also plays a vital role in attaining the supramaximal NCS signal for avoiding any misdiagnosis and discomfort. A delayed pulse may cause fatigue to the nerve under fat [8]. Therefore, we have measured the dynamic response of the stimulator output by analysing the rise and fall times of the stimulating pulse (Fig. 2.28) and found as 1 ms for a pulse width of 100 ms. Another important factor of the stimulator is its amplitude drift when stimulation is applied to a nerve. This implies the output impedance of the circuit. Moreover, voltage regulation (VR) is estimated by the Eq. (2.9)-

$$VR = \frac{V_{NL} - V_L}{V_{NL}} \tag{2.9}$$

where, V_{NL} and V_L are open circuit voltage (i.e., no-load voltage) and voltage when pulse applied to nerve (i.e., load voltage). The estimated voltage regulation is found to be 23.45% while the power consumption rate of the stimulating circuit is 17.18 mW.

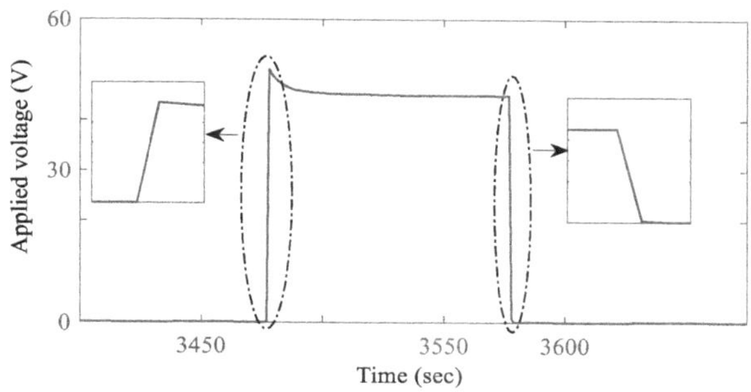

Fig. 2.28 Dynamic response: zoom views of raise and fall of stimulating pulses of 100 ms duration.

Furthermore, the ripple factor of the stimulator output pulse is calculated by dividing the RMS value of the a.c component of the output with the average value or d.c component of the output. The ripple factor of the stimulator output pulse is found to be 0.274.

2.6 Analysis of Noise in NCS Signal

2.6.1 Introduction

It is difficult to obtain high quality electrical NCS signals like all biomedical signals because noise suppresses the information by overlapping its profile. The noises occur due to low amplitude of the signal generated from biological sources. The signal is easily corrupted by capacitively or inductively coupled electrical noise One of the sources of such noise is low frequency power line interference (PLI) and its harmonics [5]. The PLI occurs due to the presence of multiple path in electrical devices from power lines in clinical environments because human body acts like an antenna [25]. Also the PLI is characterized by chronic sinusoidal 50/60 Hz element which is seen in raw biomedical signal and it usually occurs due to uses of the devices which employ alternating current as a source of power [1]. Due to movement of patient, loose electrode skin contact low frequency noises occurs.

An NCS signal is also corrupted with high frequency noises apart from PLI [4]. Electromagnetic interference from surroundings as well as electronic IC's and different components used in the circuits are the prime reason for the high frequency noises. Hence the elimination of PLI and other noises from NCS signal with low SNR is a challenging task that has been addressed by in different approaches. In this paper, 8th order analog high pass filter cascaded with a 4th order LPF using fully differential amplifier (LT1994) has been used to remove noise from sciatic nerve signal of rat. The filter was tested for simulated sinusoidal signals from 400Hz- 9KHz. The filter presents a maximum gain of 56dB in a BW of 800Hz- 3KHz [21]. In another work, tremor noise present in surface EMG acquired from essential tremor (ET) patients was filtered based on squared sine wave approximation [33]. In [3], an algorithm is developed for automated removal of stimulus artifact (SA) from NCS data. In this algorithm hardware-based model of the SA is used. The model can successfully remove the SA even it is overlapped with the nerve signal. In [1], a method is proposed by decomposing the recorded NCS data and extracted the power line noise via blind source separation and wavelet analysis. In [30], the researchers adopted a cascading of window based FIR filters are used to cancel out low frequency, mid frequency and high frequency noises from real ECG in single step performance. Satisfactory performance has been found by calculating SNR, Mean Square Error (MSE) and Power spectral Density (PSD) of the filtered ECG with comparison of the noisy ECG signal. In [19], a simulation based filter model was designed to remove PLI from ECG signal. In [32] an instrumentation amplifier cascaded with a 1st order passive high pass and 2nd order active low pass filter was used to reduce the noise from biomedical signals. In [25] an IIR Laguerre filter has been simulated to remove noise from EMG signal. In [31], wavelet based filtering techniques for real time QRS detection and denoising have been proposed and implemented in a 16 bit microcontroller.

From the above literature it is observed that biomedical signals including NCS signals are filtered to remove PLI and other artefacts using different techniques. However there is no attempt to reduce the noise immunity (both PLI and other noises) using battery operated stimulation, amplification and filtration. In this chapter, a novel battery operated system has been discussed that can considerably suppress PLI and other noises. The noise analysis has been performed on real NCS data acquired by the circuit powered by both DC power supply obtained from AC mains and battery as a power supply. Apart from statistical and frequency analysis, the noise voltage calculation has been performed from the spectral density spectrum.

2.6.2 Experimental Setup

As discussed earlier, we have developed a CMAP acquisition system operated by a rechargeable battery. The experiment has been performed in two different modes of power supplies separately- DC power supply (SCIENTECH multiple power supply ST4077) from AC mains and rechargeable battery (EBL 6F22 600 mAh, Lithium-ion) as power supply. The signals acquired by the developed PC based system have been stored in the PC and statistical and frequency analysis are carried out for verifying the noise performance of the developed technique. The experiment on CMAP acquisition has been performed under the supervision of a neurophysiologist, GNRC Hospitals, Guwahati, Assam.

2.6.3 Removal of Power line Interference

It has already been mentioned that CMAP acquisition system that gets supply from AC mains commonly produces a 50 Hz power line noise in the signal. The PLI is due to multiple paths which forms a ground loop picking stray currents through electromagnetic induction and propagates to the electrical appliances.

In this section we propose the battery operated stimulating and signal processing circuit which is free from the 50 Hz power line interference. The study was conducted on three healthy adult male subjects (Age 20-35) under the supervision of a neurophysiologist as mentioned above. The triggering pulse generated by the battery operated pulse generator was applied to the median nerve of the subject on the left hand. Before application of the pulse, skin preparation procedure was adopted as mentioned in the introduction section. As discussed, we have operated the experiment in two modes- first using battery operated power supply to the circuits, secondly using DC power supply acquired from AC mains. Both the signals were acquired through the DAQ card and stored in PC for frequency analysis. Fig. 2.29 shows the raw CMAP signals for the two cases-

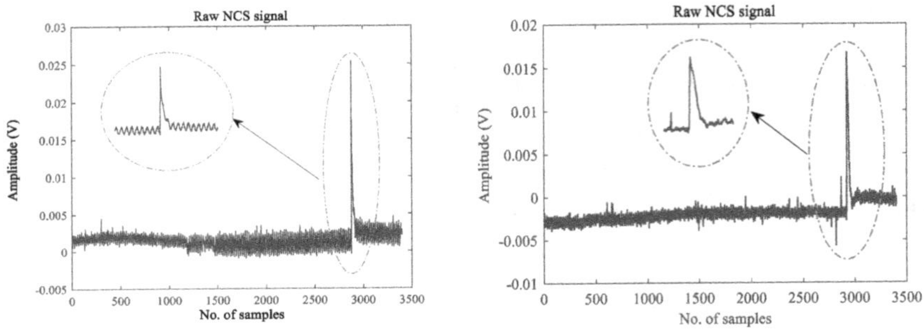

(a) (b)

Fig. 2.29 Raw CMAP signals of a healthy male subject (age: 27 years) by using (a) DC power supply (b) battery (zoomed of CMAP in inset)

From this figure it is evident that the DC power supply operated system produces more high frequency noise than the battery operated system.

To analyse the frequency spectrum of the signal, Fast Fourier Transform (FFT) was performed in MATLAB and Fig. 2.30 shows the FFT plots of the raw signals.

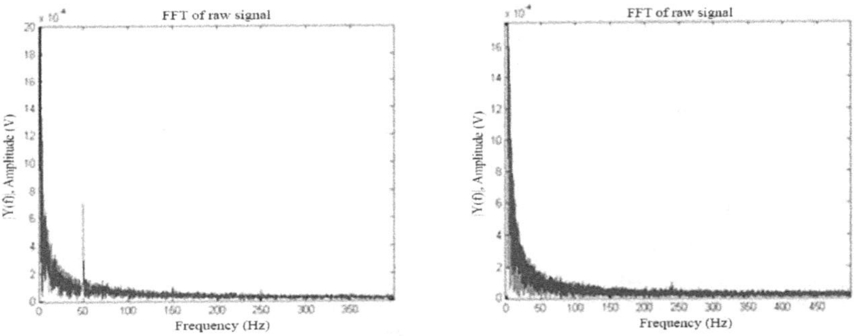

(a) (b)

Fig. 2.30 FFT of raw CMAP signals (a) DC power supply (b) battery

Fig. 2.30 (a) shows clearly that there is a distinct spectrum at 50 Hz indicating power line interference, while Fig. 2.30 (b) is free from the 50 Hz component. Further the frequency spectrum of the CMAP indicates that the signal is composed of noise mostly at low frequency. Therefore, FFT plot evidently shows that the noise is low frequency or $1/f$ noise.

2.6.4 Noise Voltage Calculation

The FFT gives the power spectral density (PSD) of the noise which follows a flat pattern at higher frequencies which is white noise while at low frequency the inversely proportional to the frequency. The frequency at which the noise becomes white s called 1/f corner frequency (f_c).The corner frequency of a $1/f$ noise spectrum is showr in Fig. 2.31-

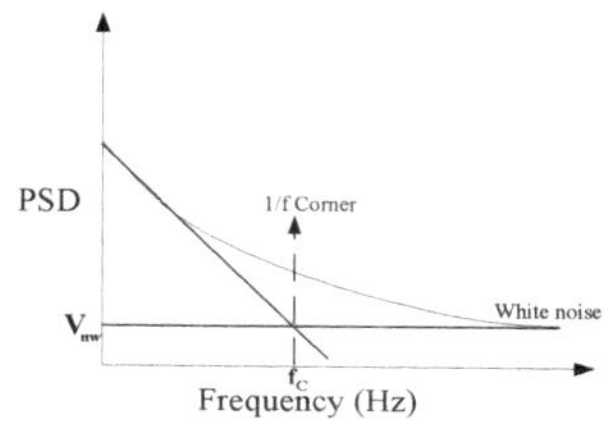

Fig. 2.31 Corner frequency of $1/f$ noise

The rms noise voltage for $1/f$ region in the bandwidth f_L to f_c is given by [29]-

$$V_{n,rms,\frac{1}{f}}(f_L, f_C) = V_{nw}\sqrt{f_C \ln\left[\frac{f_C}{f_L}\right]} \tag{2.10}$$

where, V_{nw} is the white noise voltage spectral density, f_L is the lowest frequency of interest and f_c is the corner frequency. The rms value of white noise voltage can be calculated from [29]-

$$V_{n,rms,white}(f_C, f_H) = V_{nw}\sqrt{f_H - f_C} \tag{2.11}$$

where, f_H is the highest frequency of interest.

$$V_{n,rms,total}(f_L, f_H) = V_{nw}\sqrt{f_C \ln\left[\frac{f_C}{f_L}\right] + (f_H - f_C)} \tag{2.12}$$

The peak to peak noise voltage is given by [29]-

$$V_{n,peak} = 6.6V_{n,rms,total} \tag{2.13}$$

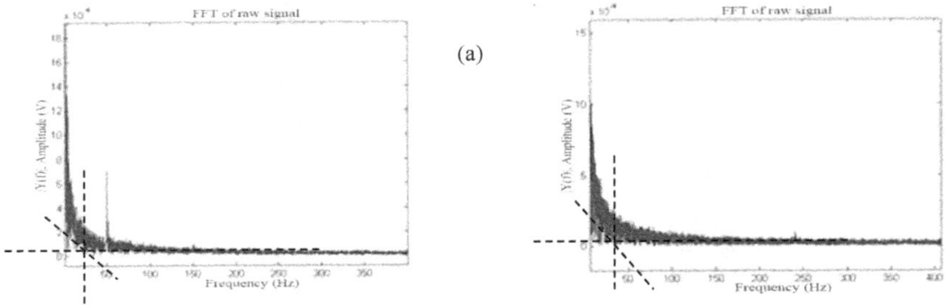

(b)

Fig. 2.32 Corner frequency of FFT signal using (a) DC power supply (b) battery

Let us consider a lowest frequency of interest as f_L = 10Hz

And higher frequency of interest as f_H = 400Hz

The different noises from the Fig. 2.32 (a) and Fig. 2.32 (b) were calculated by using equations (2.10)-(2.13) as shown in Table 2.3-

Table 2.3 Average noise values for the raw signals of 3 subjects

Power Supply	f_C (Hz)	V_{nw} (mV)	$V_{n,rms,\frac{1}{f}}$ (mV)	$V_{n,rms,white}$ (mV)	$V_{n,rms,total}$ (mV)	$V_{n,peak}$ (mV)
DC	24.66	0.071	0.3321	1.356	1.398	9.23
Battery	36.0	0.033	0.226	0.637	0.674	4.503

From Table 2.3 it is observed that the low frequency $1/f$ noise, white noise, total noise and peak noise are significantly less in case of battery compared to the DC power supply used as a source of power to the circuits.

2.6.5 Noise Removal

It has already discussed that the NCS signals, obtained from amplifier and filter circuit powered from DC power supply connected to AC mains, are composed by both PLI as well as high frequency noise. Although in battery power supply, the PLI is absent, however high frequency ripples are still present. Different batteries using different chemicals such as lithium ion or Lead acid etc. will have different spectrum of high frequency ripples. On the other hand, when the battery is recharged, the AC recharge sends noise to the battery bath. The system should not be used while charging. For comparison of the noise behaviour of the battery operated system, the signal was also acquired when the circuits are powered from a linear power supply system. Both raw and filtered signals were acquired using a DAQ card through Lab View software by using both DC power supply (AC/DC converter) and battery are shown in Fig 2.33 and Fig. 2 34 respectively.

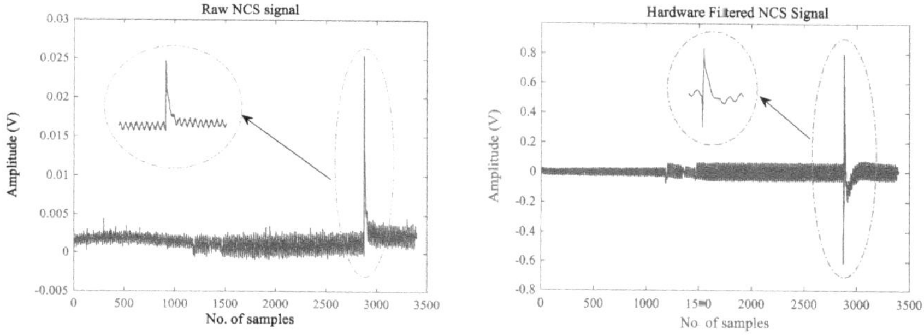

(a) (b)

Fig. 2.33 Signals with DC power supply (a) raw signal (b) filtered signal for a male subject of age 27 years (zoomed of CMAP in inset)

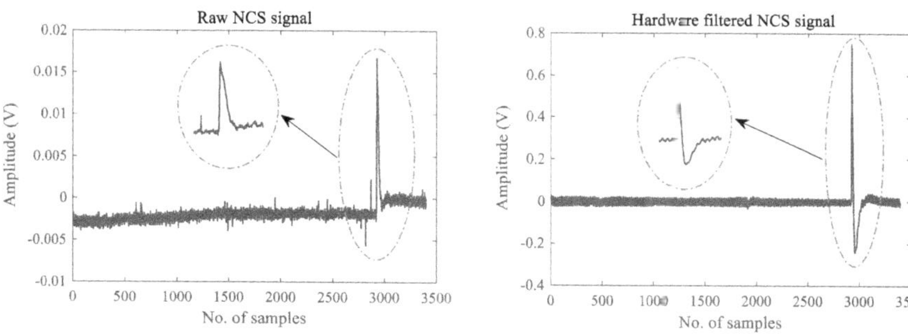

(a) (b)

Fig. 2.34 Signals with battery power supply (a) raw signal (b) filtered signal for a male subject of age 27 years (zoomed of CMAP in inset)

It is found that in case of DC power supply the raw signal is noisier (30.43 dB) than the battery operated signal (40.84 dB). The signal noise is filtered by the proposed filtering circuit which is evident from the increase in signal to noise ratio (SNR) from 30.43 dB to 56.62 dB (in case of DC power supply operated) and 40.84 dB to 71.53 dB (for battery operated).

However, average SNR of the signals for 3 subjects were computed for both raw and filtered signals and values are shown in the Table 2.4-

Table 2.4 Average SNR values of 3 subjects for the raw and filtered Signals

Power Supply	Raw Signal (dB)	Filtered Signal (dB)
AC/DC	32.41	57.12
Battery	41.54	69.43

Probability Density Function (PDF) of a signal signifies how much the signal fluctuations takes place which indicates the presence of noise. The PDF of the signals were calculated by using the following mathematical equation (2.14)-

$$f\left(x;\mu,\sigma^2\right)=\frac{1}{\sigma\sqrt{2\pi}}e^{-\frac{1}{2}\left(\frac{x-\mu}{\sigma}\right)^2} \tag{2.14}$$

$$\text{for } -\alpha\langle x\langle\alpha$$

Where, μ -is the mean distribution of the signal x

σ^2 -is the variance of the distribution of signal x

The PDF for the signals were estimated for a male subject (Age: 27 years) and shown in Fig. 2.35 and Fig. 2.36

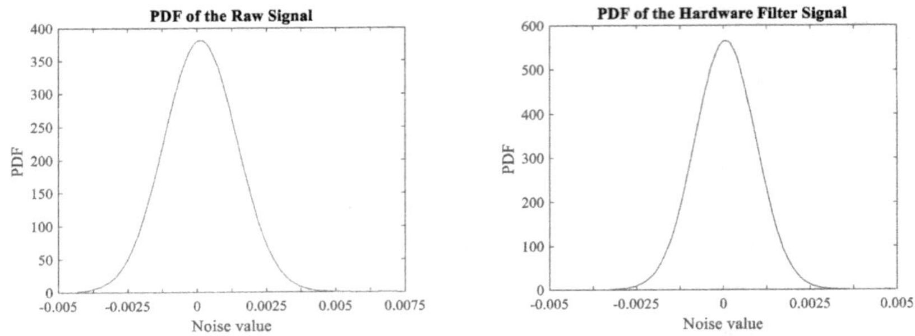

(a) (b)

Fig. 2.35 PDF of the NCS signals for DC power supply (a) raw signal (b) filtered signal

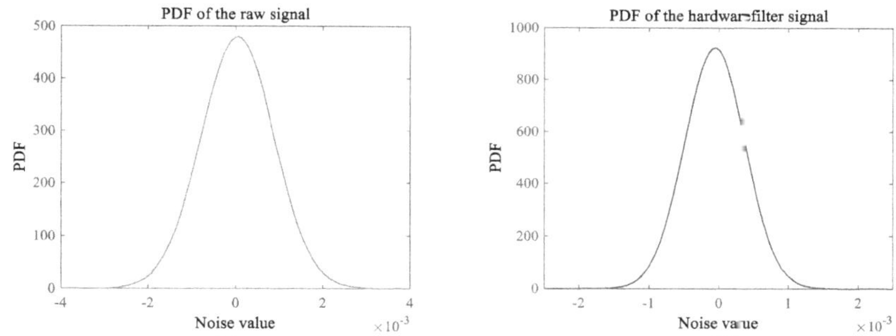

(a) (b)

Fig. 2.36 PDF of the NCS signals for battery power supply (a) raw signal (b) filtered signal

From the PDF of Fig. 2.35, it is observed that the raw signal has more signal spread of noise (-0.0039 to +0.0039) compared to filtered (-0.0027 to +0.0027) in case of the DC power supply based system. The noise per unit improvement (NUPI) can be calculated as follows-

NUPI= (Sum of raw range- Sum of filter range)/ Sum of raw range

= (0.0078-0.0054)/ 0.0078

= 0.307

Similarly in case of battery based system of Fig. 2.36, the signal spread of noise are (-0.0029 to +0.0029) and (-0.0015 to +0.0015) for raw and filtered signals respectively.

NUPI= (0.0058-0.0030)/ 0.0058 = 0.482

However, average per unit improvement in the PDF for the signals of three subjects are shown in Table 2.5-

Table 2.5 Average ccomparisons per unit improvement for 3 subjects

Power Supply	Per Unit Improvement
DC	0.318
Battery	0.487

2.7 Comparison of Custom made NCS Setup Vs Neuroperfect EMG -2000 Machine

To study the efficacy and validation of the designed NCS setup, we collected NCS signals of 10 healthy subjects with same environment conditions from both the systems. From these signals we had evaluated the NCS parameters like CMAP, latency and NCV and compared the values with error percentages. The comparison of NCS parameters acquired by developed custom made NCS setup with the Neuroperfect EMG-200 machine as shown in the Table 2.6 –

Table 2.6: Comparison of NCS parameters acquired through Neuroperfect EMG-2000 and custom made NCS Setup of 10 healthy subjects

Subjects, age (Y) and gender	Neuroperfect EMG-2000			Designed NCS setup			Errors in %		
	CMAP (mV)	Latency (ms)	NCV (m/sec)	CMAP (mV)	Latency (ms)	NCV (m/sec)	CMAP (mV)	Latency (ms)	NCV (m/sec)
S1, 25, F	15.15	4.12	58.73	14.50	4.05	59.25	4.29	1.69	0.88
S2, 28, F	18.36	3.88	61.85	17.65	3.98	60.30	3.86	2.57	2.50
S3, 30, M	14.45	3.88	64.43	13.55	3.71	67.38	6.22	4.38	4.57
S4, 25, M	13.95	3.63	65.56	12.80	3.80	62.63	8.24	4.68	4.46
S5, 26, M	13.12	4.63	53.99	13.75	4.75	52.63	4.80	2.59	2.51
S6, 24, F	15.98	3.92	61.22	15.15	4.10	58.53	5.19	4.59	4.39
S7, 29, M	14.88	4.05	58.76	14.10	3.95	60.25	5.24	2.46	2.53
S8, 26, F	14.50	4.64	48.49	15.25	4.72	47.66	5.17	1.72	1.71
S9, 31, M	13.08	3.98	60.30	12.35	3.75	64.00	5.58	5.77	6.13
S10, 23,F	16.50	3.63	65.56	17.15	3.81	62.46	3.93	4.95	4.72

2.8 Conclusion

A PC based NCS setup has been developed in the laboratory environment consisting of voltage controlled stimulator and signal conditioning circuit. The voltage controlled stimulator was tested and used with proper pulse duration and voltage setting, in acquiring signals in laboratory environment. In order to process and analyse the signals, signal condition circuit was designed that accurately amplifies and filters low level CMAP signal for analysis. Results and experimental demonstrations using real-time data collected reveal the practical necessity and efficiency of the developed NCS setup. Furthermore, we have analysed the noises present in the NCS signals acquired by the developed setup. For noise analysis, we have acquired the data in two modes of power supplies- D.C power supply from mains and battery as a source of power to the stimulating and signal processing circuits. It is seen that the PLI (50 Hz), low and high frequency noise are sufficiently reduced in battery operated system compared to the DC power supply operated system after FFT analysis of the raw signals. In addition other noise analyses like SNR, PDF and noise voltage calculation has been done on the data acquired by both conditions. The performance of noise cancellation is sufficiently higher in battery operated condition than DC power supply based condition.

Bibliography

[1] Akwei-Sekyere, S., Powerline noise elimination in biomedical signals via blind source separation and wavelet analysis. *PeerJ*, 3: 1086-1110, 2015.

[2] Banks, D. J., W. Balachandran, P. R. Richards, and D. Ewins Instrumentation to evaluate neural signal recording properties of micromachined microelectrodes inserted in invertebrate nerve. *Physiological measurement,* 23 (2), 437-448, 2002.

[3] B. H. Tracery and S. Krishnamachari. Automated removal of stimulus artifact in nerve conduction studies. *Annual International Conference on Engineering in Medicine and Biology Society,*USA, pages 6360-6363, Aug 30- Sept 3, 2006.

[4] Chang, C.H., Ko, H.J., and Chang, K.M. Cancellation of high-frequency noise in ECG signals using adaptive filter without external reference. In *2010 3rd International Conference on Biomedical Engineering and Informatics*, volume 2, pages 787-790, Yantai, China, 2010.

[5] D. T. Mewett, H. Nazeran and K. J. Reynolds,"Removing power line noise from recorded EMG," Engineering in Medicine and Biology Society. Turkey, vol. 3, pp. 2190-2193, October 2001.

[6] Dunseath, W.R., and Kelly, E.F. Multichannel PC-based data-acquisition system for high-resolution EEG. *IEEE Transactions on Biomedical Engineering*, 42(12): 1212-1217, 1995.

[7] Data manual, Neuroperfect plus EMG/NCV Test Machine (Model EMG-2000), Medicaid, India, 2008.

[8] Doucet, B.M., Lam, A., and Griffin, L. Neuromuscular electrical stimulation for skeletal muscle function. *The Yale journal of biology and medicine*, 85 (2): 201-215, 2012.

[9] Grinstead, B., and Parten, M.E. Biomedical signal acquisition using" Labview". In *Proceedings. 11th IEEE Symposium on Computer-Based Medical Systems*, pages 157-161, Lubbock, USA, 1998.

[10] Gupta, R., Bera, J. N., and Mitra, M. Development of an embedded system and MATLAB-based GUI for online acquisition and analysis of ECG signal. *Measurement*, 43 (9): 1119-1126, 2010.

[11] Gayakwad, R. A. *"Op-amps and linear integrated circuits"*.Prentice-Hall, 1988.

[12] Gozani, Shai N. "*Apparatus and methods for assessment of neuromuscular function.*" U.S. Patent 5,851,191, issued December 22, 1998.

[13] Hemmsen, M.C., Nikolov, S.I., Pedersen, M.M., Pihl, M.J., Enevoldsen, M.S., Hansen, J.M., and Jensen, J.A. Implementation of a versatile research data acquisition system using a commercially available medical ultrasound scanner. *IEEE transactions on ultrasonics, ferroelectrics, and frequency control*, 59 (7): 1487-1499, 2012.

[14] Harb, A., and Sawan, M. Low-power CMOS implantable nerve signal analog processing circuit. In *7th IEEE International Conference on Electronics, Circuits and Systems* (ICECS- 2000), volume 2, pages 911-914, Jounieh, Lebanon, 2000.

[15] INA128P IC Datasheet, Texas Instruments.

[16] Jamal, M.Z. Signal acquisition using surface EMG and circuit design considerations for robotic prosthesis. In *Computational Intelligence in Electromyography Analysis-A Perspective on Current Applications and Future Challenges*, volume 18, pages 427-448. InTech, 2012.

[17] Koo, Y.S., Cho, C.S. and Kim, B.J. Pitfalls in using electrophysiological studies to diagnose neuromuscular disorders. *Journal of Clinical Neurology*, *8* (1), 1-14, 2012.

[18] Kitchin, Charles, and Lew Counts. *"A designer's guide to instrumentation amplifiers"*.Analog Devices, 2006.

[19] Kim, K.J., Ku, J.H., Kim, I.Y., Kim, S.I., and Nam, S.W. Notch filter design using theα-scaled sampling kernel and its application to power line noise removal from ECG signals. In *2007 International Conference on Control, Automation and Systems*, pages 2415-2418, Seoul, South Korea , 2007.

[20] Luan, S. and Constandinou, T.G. A charge-metering method for voltage-mode neural stimulation. *Journal of neuroscience methods, 224*: 39-47, 2014.

[21] Loi, D., Carboni, C., Angius, G., Angotzi, G.N., Barbaro M., Raffo, L., Raspopovic, S., and Navarro, X. Peripheral neural activity recording and stimulation system. *IEEE transactions on biomedical circuits and systems*, 5 (4): 368-379, 2011.

[22] Massó, N., Rey, F., Romero, D., Gual, G., Costa, L., and Germán, A. Surface electromyography applications in the sport. *Apunts Med Esport*, 45 (165): 121-130, 2010.

[23] Mishra. U.K and Kalita. J. Clinical Neurophysiology, 3rd ed., Elsevier Health Sciences, India, 2014.

[24] Mallik, A and Weir, A. I.. Nerve conduction studies: essentials and pitfalls in practice. *J. Neurol. Neurosurg. Psychiatry*, 76 (2), 23-31, 2005.

[25] Malboubi, M., Razzazi, F., and Aliyari, S.M. Elimination of power line noise from EMG signals using an efficient adaptive Laguerre filter. In *ICSES 2010 International Conference on Signals and Electronic Circuits*, pages 49-52, Gliwice, Poland, 2010.

[26] Meister, M., Pine, J., and Baylor, D.A. Multi-neuronal signals from the retina: acquisition and analysis. *Journal of neuroscience methods* 51 (1): 95-106, 1994.

[27] Ng, K.A., Yuan, C., Rusly, A., Do, A.T., Zhao, B., Liu, S C., Peh, W.Y.X., Thow, X.Y., Voges, K., Lee, S., and Gammad, G.G.L. A wireless multi-channel peripheral nerve signal acquisition system-on-chip. *IEEE Journal of Solid-State Circuits*, 54 (8): 2266-2280, 2019.

[28] OPA2604AP datasheet, Texas Instruments.

[29] Opamp noise relationship : 1/f noise, rms noise and equivalent noise bandwidth, Analog Device Tutorial, MT-048, 1-6, October, 2008.

[30] Patro, K.K., and Kumar, P.R. De-noising of ECG raw signal by cascaded window based digital filters configuration. In *2015 IEEE Power, Communication and Information Technology Conference* (PCITC-2015), pages 120-124, Bhubaneswar, India, 2015.

[31] Stojanović, R., Knežević, S., Karadaglić, D., and Devedžić, G. Optimization and implementation of the wavelet based algorithms for embedded biomedical signal processing. *Computer Science and Information Systems*, 10 (1): 503-523, 2013.

[32] S. F. Pichorim, W. Vollmann, U. V. Pellanda and S. T. Malca. Nerve Conduction Velocity Measurement: A didactic example. *Congreso Argentino de Bioingeniaria*, 2009.

[33] Seki, M., Matsumoto, Y., Ando, T., Kobayashi, Y., Iijima, H., Nagaoka, M., and Fujie, M.G. Filtering Essential Tremor noise on surface EMG based on squared sine wave approximation. In *2011 Annual International Conference of the IEEE Engineering in Medicine and Biology Society*, pages 7487-7491, Boston, USA, 2011.

[34] Soulier, F., Rossel, O., Bernard, S., Cathébras, G., and Guiraud, D. Design of nerve signal biosensor. In *2009 Joint IEEE North-East Workshop on Circuits and Systems and TAISA Conference*, pages 1-4, Toulouse, France, 2009.

[35] Schuettler, M., Seetohul, V., Taylor, J., and Donaldson, N. Velocity-selective recording from frog nerve using a multi-contact cuff electrode. In *2006 International Conference of the IEEE Engineering in Medicine and Biology Society*, pages 2962-2965, New York, USA, 2006.

[36] Subasi, A. A decision support system for diagnosis of neuromuscular disorders using evolutionary support vector machines. *Signal, Image Video Process*, 9 (2): 399-408, 2015.

[37] Thie, J., Klistorner, A., and Graham, S.L. Biomedical signal acquisition with streaming wireless communication for recording evoked potentials. Documenta Ophthalmologica, 125 (2): 149-159, 2012.

[38] www. microchip.com.

[39] www. mikroelectronika.com.

[40] www.ni.com.

[41] Zefeng, Y., Fang, L., Yibiao, R., Yaowen, C., and Zhun, F. Design of a multichannel biomedical signal acquisition system based on Cortex-M4 processor. In *2015 IEEE International Conference on Cyber Technology in Automation, Control, and Intelligent Systems* (CYBER-2015), pages 1023-1027, Shenyang, China, 2015.

CHAPTER 3

Biofeedback Based Auto-Controlled Neurostimulator for NCS Testing

3.0 Introduction

Use of appropriate stimulator to be applied over the skin of underlying nerve is essential to acquire proper nerve conduction signal during nerve conduction study (NCS) [25]. There are two typical types of stimulators - current controlled and voltage controlled. However, current controlled stimulator design requires more numbers of circuit components that makes it more complex for laboratory usage and it is difficult task to control the amount of charge delivered [24]. Researchers have developed electrical stimulators for medical applications which are being improved and upgraded continuously.

It is to be mentioned that, the CMAP signal depends on the skin resistance of the subject which varies with various factors of the subjects [8, 33]. High resistance of the skin electrode interface reduces the current passing through the skin tissues resulting in ineffective nerve response [27, 26, 36]. Furthermore, the variations of skin-resistance alter the quality and quantitative values of NCS recordings [9]. Therefore, applying the stimulating pulse, one has to manually vary the stimulating current or voltage to obtain the ideal NCS response which is called supramaximal NCS signal, and the ideal stimulating pulse is called supramaximal stimulation. However, this is time consuming for doctors and irritating to the subjects. In that context, a stimulator that can measure the skin resistance of a subject and using it as a biofeedback parameter to find subject specific optimal stimulation could be an improvement.

Researchers have been working on auto-controlled biofeedback based system for biomedical applications since long time to abolish this kind of issues. Dorgan et al. [8] provided a theoretical human skin-impedance model for intelligent nerve activation with typically low frequency, high amplitudes and rectangular pulses to reduce pain. Zeng et al. [37] adopted a signal acquisition and a biofeedback system based on electrical muscle stimulation and surface EMG. It further fed signal features to classifier and finally controlled the stimulator based on results and levels of fatigue. Methods in [17] and [19] are biofeedback based approaches, where the former addressed decision making system based on features of galvanic skin response and EMG signals and the latter explored on the use of EMG feature based electrical biofeedback stimulation. However, inherent characteristics and objectives of [17] and [19] are different from our design approach that would be presented herein. In [1], Alejandro et al. proposed a biofeedback based system where electrical stimulation is used as biofeedback parameter for the EMG controlled prosthetic hand user to interact with the environment in order to develop an extended proprioception control. In [2], authors also developed a biofeedback based system by using functional electrical stimulation as biofeedback parameter in order to control prosthetic hand user movement. In this technique, the reaction to different kind of stimulations are measured and checked their effects on EMG acquisition process to evaluate the best approach to provide important feedback in the prosthetic application. Lee et al. [22] designed a foot pressure biofeedback neuromuscular system where electrical stimulation and visual auditory as biofeedback parameters to improve balance control and foot sensory compensation in below-knee amputees.

There is a considerable amount of work on biofeedback based auto-controlled stimulator based on different biofeedback parameters available in the literature, however, none of the literature explores skin resistance as biofeedback parameter to control the stimulating voltage or current though skin resistance is the highly influential marker for neurophysiologists that varies subject to subject. Therefore, motivated by this necessity, this research aims at development of an biofeedback based auto-controlled neurostimulator based on skin resistance of a subject as a biofeedback parameter in order to minimize unnecessary repeated trials avoiding nerve injury and wasted physician time to obtain supramaximal response.

3.1 Biofeedback Based Auto-controlled Neurostimulator Design

As stated earlier, the quality of signal recording depends on skin-electrode interface resistance [5] and the applied stimulation [21, 29, 6, 20]. The variations of skin-resistance alter the quality and quantitative values of NCS recordings [9]. Therefore proper stimulation using skin resistance of a subject as biofeedback is essential for NCS. The core focus of this study is to design an auto-controlled biofeedback based stimulator utilizing measured skin resistance of subjects for NCS acquisition. The novelty of the design lies on using skin resistance as biofeedback. This design steps are summarized as follows:

1. Acquisition of CMAP using the developed manual stimulator for multiple stimulations for experimentation. The NCS responses are compared with standard

NCS record in terms of CMAP amplitude i.e., supramaximal response (SR). The stimulation corresponding to this SR is termed supramaximal stimulus.

2. A skin resistance biofeedback model was developed based on the measurement method of [23]. A theoretical model was established for finding the relation between a measured load voltage and skin resistance. Then a technique was developed for automatic generation of the SS depending on the skin resistance.
3. Finally, a microcontroller based auto-controlled stimulator was developed. In this setup, the developed models were implemented for automatic evaluation of the SS for new subjects.

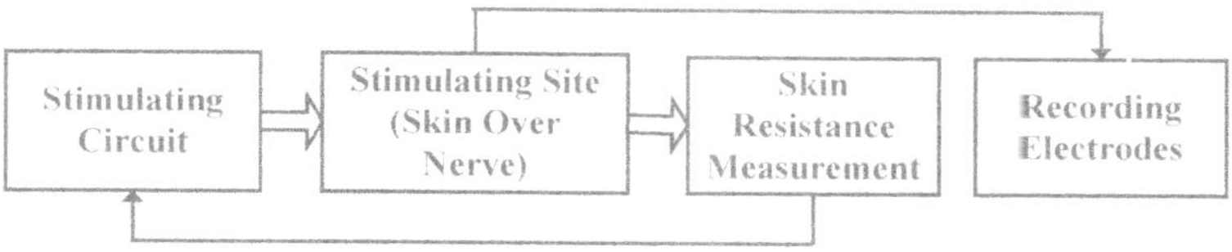

Fig.3.1 Proposed biofeedback based auto-controlled stimulation design

Conceptual block diagram of an auto-controlled stimulator using skin resistance as biofeedback is shown in Fig. 3.1.

This section first outlines the theoretical principle of using skin resistance as biofeedback and then focuses on measurement of skin resistance of subjects and its implementation.

3.1.1 Skin-electrode interface circuit

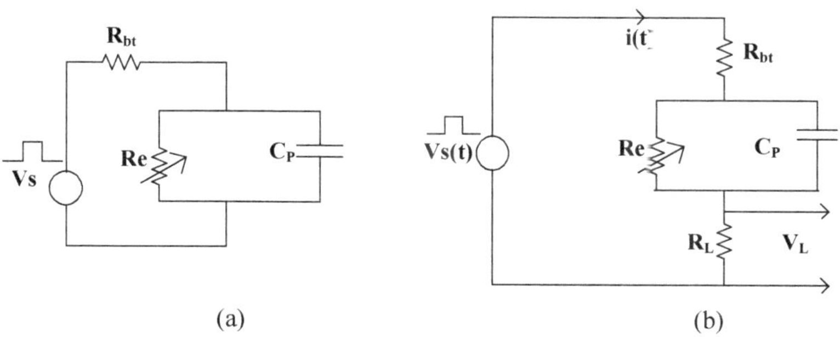

Fig. 3.2 Skin-electrode circuit (a) interface model [23], and (b) measurement circuit

Skin is composed of two layers - epidermis (outer) and dermis (inner). The total skin thickness varies from 0.5 mm at the eyelid to about 4 mm at the foot sole [23]. Tissues in the dermis contain more ions that provide low resistance; however, the epidermis layer provides maximum resistance to ionized-species at the skin electrode interface. During stimulation, the resistance often get changed due to structural changes of skin, either instantaneous change [7] or progressive change [14]. Instantaneous change causes increase in membrane permeability to ions to the electric field [18]. Fig. 3.2 (a) shows the skin-electrode interface model [23] based on which a measurement circuit is proposed. In Fig. 3.2 (a), R_{bt} indicates series combination of bulk of electrolyte resistance. The capacitor C_p is referred to as appendages of the skin and R_e is leakage resistance due to the lipid-corneocyte matrix for electroporation effect that varies with subjects. This is caused by activity of sweat glands, presence of other appendageal pathways, thickness and composition of stratum corneum and it also depends on age and sex [28], fat percentage and fat-free mass of body [16]. When the stimulator voltage (V_S) is applied, first C_p charges which then discharges through R_e and R_{bt}. The net current is given by-

$$i = \frac{V_S}{R_{bt} + R_e} = \frac{V_S}{R_S} \tag{3. 1}$$

where, $R_S = R_{bt} + R_e$ is the total skin resistance. Based on Fig. 3.2 (a), the proposed measurement circuit is shown in Fig. 3.2 (b) which includes a load resistance R_L across which the load voltage (V_L) is measured. The resistances of the circuitry are linearly dependent upon temperature ($R = R_0(1+\alpha dT)$), where α being a temperature coefficient. So, in order to avoid additional variations in measuring the skin resistance, the experiment was conducted at constant room temperature (25^0 C).

3.1.2 Skin-Resistance Measurement

In order to measure total skin resistance (R_S), a stimulating voltage $V_S(t)$ was applied to produce a voltage $V_L(t)$ across R_L. For monophasic, i.e., single phase voltage, R_S is given by:

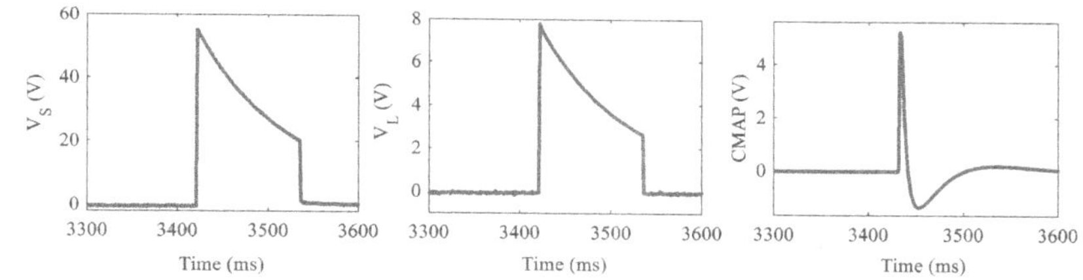

(a)

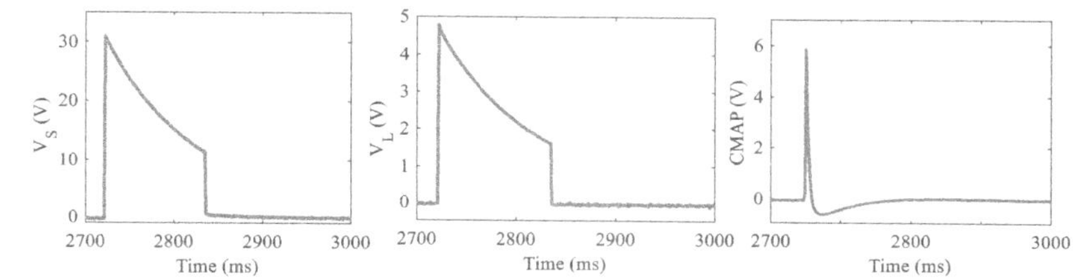

(b)

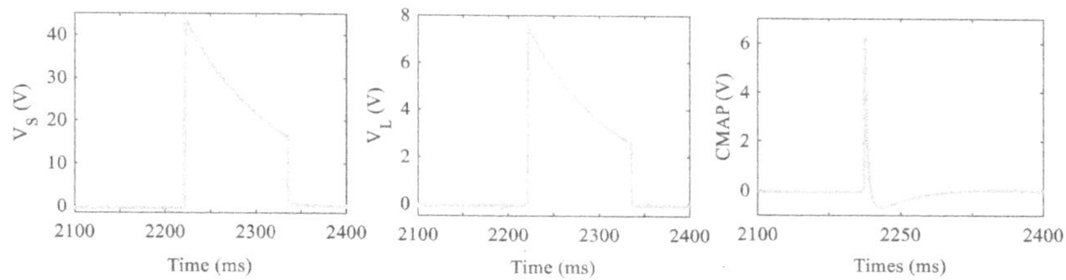

(c)

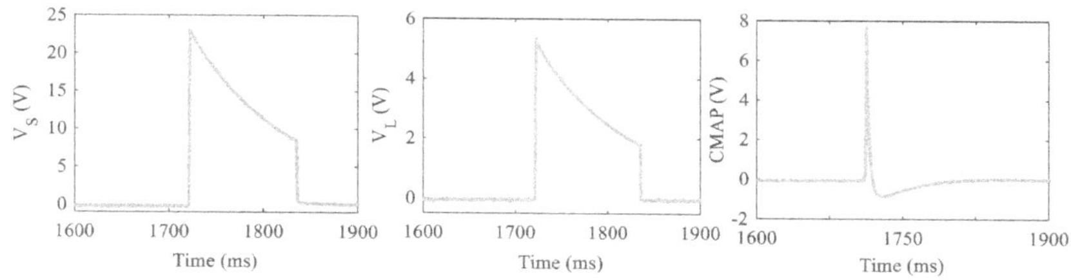

(d)

Fig. 3.5 Measured signals using custom made PC based NCS setup

(a) Male subject (110 kg): stimulating voltage (left), Load voltage (middle) and CMAP (right)

(b) Male subject (49 kg): stimulating voltage (left), Load voltage (middle) and CMAP (right)

(c) Female subject (75 kg): stimulating voltage (left), Load voltage (middle) and CMAP (right)
(d) Female subject (42 kg): stimulating voltage (left), Load voltage (middle) and CMAP (right)

To estimate the resistances using Eq. (3.2), $V_S(t)$ and $V_L(t)$ were acquired. This was done in order to derive model characteristics between R_S and supramaximal stimulating voltage (V_{SM}), at a stimulating voltage where best CMAP response was obtained. For modeling, stimulating voltages were applied and corresponding load voltages were obtained. Signals were acquired using DAQ with sampling frequency of 1 kHz and a set of typical signals is shown in Fig. 3.5. It is observed in Fig. 3.5 that the supramaximal CMAP is obtained at different triggering voltages for male and female subjects of different body weights. Taking these as basis, we propose two sets of models using dependable parameters for male and female subjects correlating stimulating voltage and load voltage for supramaximal conditions as-

$$E\left(V_{L,SM}\right)_m = f\left(V_L, \infty\right)_m \tag{3.3}$$

$$E\left(V_{SM}\right)_m = f\left(V_{L,SM}, \beta\right)_m \tag{3.4}$$

$$E\left(V_{L,SM}\right)_f = f\left(V_L, \gamma\right)_f \tag{3.5}$$

$$E\left(V_{SM}\right)_f = f\left(V_{L,SM}, \varphi\right)_f \tag{3.6}$$

where, subscript SM indicates supramaximal condition.
We set different parameter constants, $\infty = \{a, b, ...\}$; $\beta = \{c, d, ...\}$ for male subject (m) and $\gamma = \{p, q.......\}$; $\varphi = \{r, s.......\}$ for female subject (f) according to our formulation.

However, it is worth to be mention that, the resistance behaviour is more dominant than capacitive behaviour in skin modeling. Furthermore, to reduce complexity of the model we focused on resistance behaviour of skin instead of capacitive behaviour. Several researchers [19, 37, 17, 1, 2, 22] explored the auto-controlled neurostimulator by considering different biofeedback parameters mainly NCS and EMG responses i.e. by observing output responses. On the other hand, in our experiment we considered V_L as the representative marker of skin resistance R_S by applying first stimulation with the help of measuring circuit Fig. 3.2 (b) and from the equation (3.2). In this proposed framework V_S is mapped with the corresponding measured V_L which is fed to the stimulator circuit as biofeedback parameter to obtain supramaximal response in real time for the second stimulation.

3.1.4 Microcontroller Based Stimulator

As one of the objectives of the research, we have implemented the model equations as discussed in section 3.1.3 in a microcontroller to obtain the auto-controlled features in our neurostimulator which is based on skin resistance measurement. Fig. 3.6 shows the developed μC-based auto-controlled neurostimulator which is composed of five modules (a)-(e). The mathematical models according to the formulation described in Section 3.1.3, were analyzed by employing real-time data and the statistically optimal models were implemented in a μC for automatic generation of V_{SM}. The function of the circuit blocks a, b and c has already been explained in chapter 2.

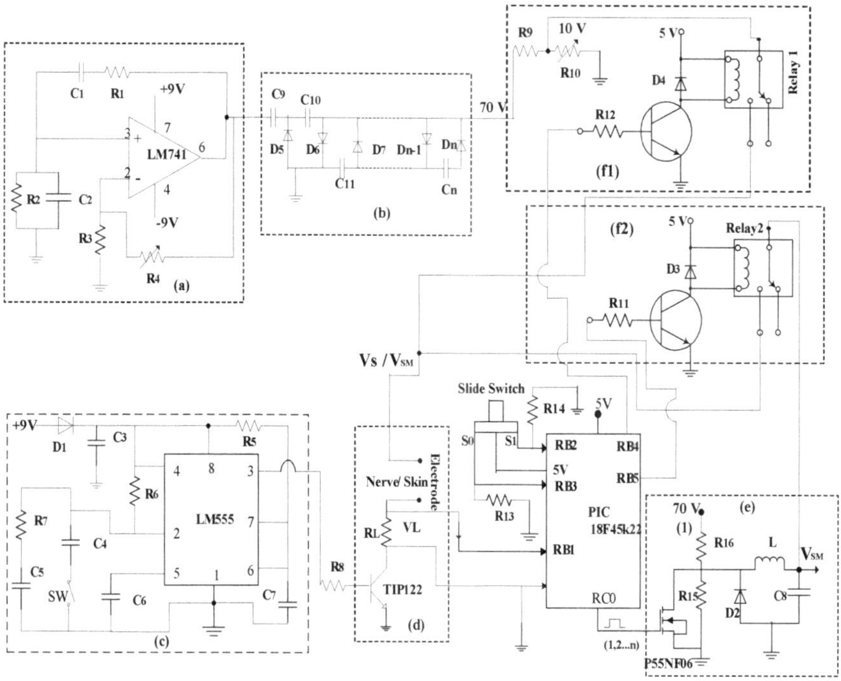

Fig. 3.6 μC-based auto-controlled stimulator circuit (a) oscillator (b) 8-stage voltage multiplier (VM) (c) timer circuit (d) electrode system with switching circuit (e) buck converter circuit (BC) (f) relay circuit. The oscillator circuit is powered by two 9 V lithium-ion batteries. It was designed to generate sustainable and stabilized sinusoidal oscillation and its oscillation frequency was 7.23 kHz. The output of the oscillator was fed to the VM that generates up to 70 V. The timer circuit was designed to generate pulse

duration of 110 ms [26]. Voltage divider unit (R_9 and R_{10}) of block (f) was adjusted to produce 10 V from 70 V. When SW is ON, V_L is obtained across R_L, which is connected to μC via port RB1. The pins S1 and S0 of the sliding switch were used to select female and male subject respectively, which were connected to the ports RB2 and RB3. Relays RLY1 and RLY2 were used to apply V_S of 10 V and V_{SM} respectively through RB4 and RB5. Initially, RB2-RB5 pins are in low state while μC power is on. When RB4 is high, RLY1 is ON and initial voltage V_S=10 V is applied to the subject via electrode by pressing the push button switch, SW for first time. This produces a pulse train of a specific duty cycle in RC0 corresponding to the V_{SM} calculated by μC so as to apply to the MOSFET of the BC in order to obtain V_{SM} at output. Now pin RB5 goes to high state so that RLY2 is on and simultaneously pin RB4 goes low state so as to make RLY1 OFF. This V_{SM} appears across the electrodes via RLY2 for final stimulation as soon as push button switch, SW is pressed for the second time.

For a given V_S (10 V) generated by block e, the programmed μC determines V_{SM} using V_L either for male and female subjects. The V_L produced in block d is applied to the μC to produce a train of pulse DC of which is calculated and produced by the μC based on the model equations. The DC represents the value of V_{SM}. This V_{SM} triggers a particular pulse train to be applied to the MOSFET of a buck converter (BC) in order to generate the supramaximal stimulus voltage. Prior to this, relation between duty cycle (DC) of pulse trains and output voltage of BC were calibrated, and implemented in μC for producing the estimated V_{SM}. The V_{SM} appears across the electrodes for final stimulation via relay 2. The μC generates a pulse train with amplitude of 0-5 V which is further adjusted to 0-1 V with a frequency of 10 kHz to ensure linear voltage variations of BC with the DC for finding the desired V_{SM} at the BC output. Therefore, we can relate the output of the BC (V_{BC}) i.e., V_{SM} proportionately with the DC of the pulse train-

$$V_{SM} = K \times DC \tag{3.7}$$

where K is a constant. The design employs an 8-bit PIC μC which has a RISC CPU and 10-bit ADC, and the program was coded in mikro C pro. The μC coded program size is of 2 kB and it uses 21% of ROM. The sampling frequency is 25 kHz. The values of V_S and V_{SM} are displayed in 20×4 alphanumeric LCD.

3.2 Results and Discussions

3.2.1 Results of Skin Resistance Measurement

A monophasic stimulating pulse with a pulse duration of 110 ms (f= 9.09 Hz) is used in the NCS. The estimation of R_S requires rising windows of both applied stimulating voltage V_S and measured load voltage V_L as discussed in section 3.1.2 and shown in Fig. 3.7. Using Eq. (3.2) the skin resistances are found as- for a male subject (weight: 80 kg) for a voltage level at t_1 (at 99 % peak levels), R_S as 15.2 kΩ for R_L = 1 kΩ. For a female subject (weight: 58 kg) for a voltage level at t_1 (at 99 % peak levels), R_S as 6.75 kΩ for R_L = 1 kΩ, which agrees with the prior findings [20].

According to [30], resistances decreases with high frequencies and they found the skin resistances within the ranges 10 kΩ- 1MΩ at 10 Hz frequency. However, it was unclear about the applied stimulating voltage or current which is also very important factor in the measurement of skin resistance.

The skin resistance also decreases with the applied stimulating voltages, more the applied voltages skin resistances decreases simultaneously [38]. In our experiment frequency of the stimulus impulses were fixed and amplitudes were varied and it was also found that skin resistances decrease with increase of applied stimulating voltages and it was found within the range of ~2-25 kΩ.

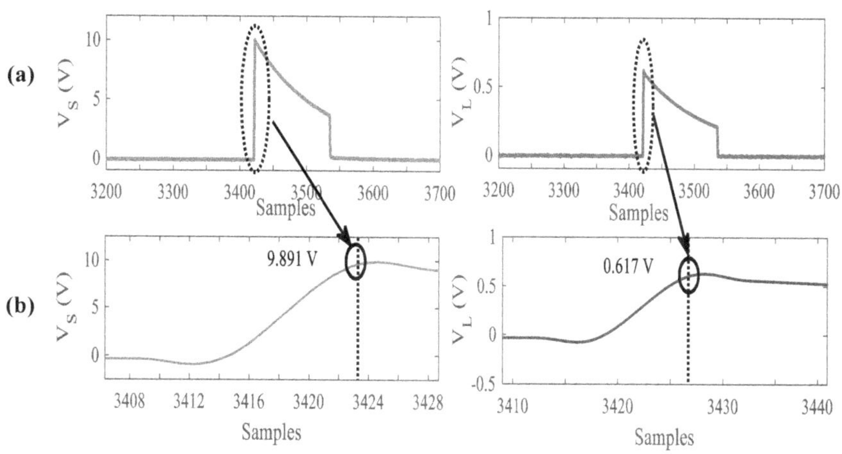

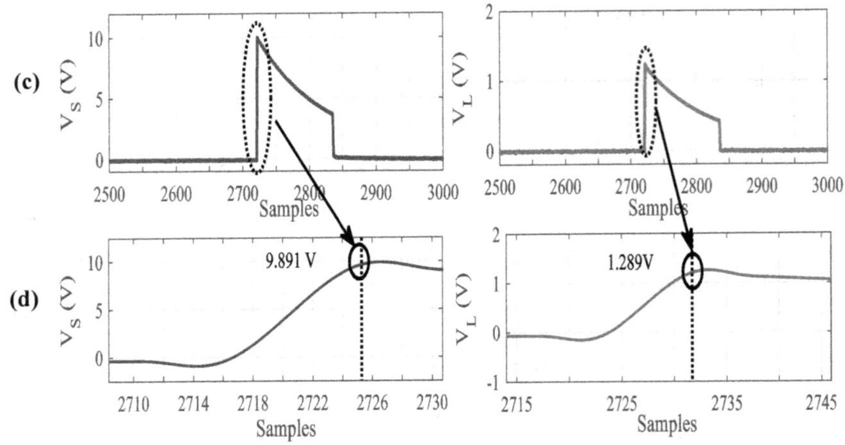

Fig. 3.7 Measured signals (a) applied stimulating voltage ($V_S = 10V$) and corresponding load voltage (V_L) for a male subject (80 kg). (b) zoomed versions of rising time of V_S and V_L of (a) at $t = t_1$. Similarly (c) applied stimulating voltage ($V_S = 10V$) and corresponding load voltage (V_L) for a female subject (58 kg). (d) zoomed versions of rising time of V_S and V_L of (c) at $t = t_1$

Table 3.1 Skin resistance measurements for wide applied voltages (V_S) over male subjects (weight range: 45-110 kg, mean: 74.2± 20.32 kg) (Part-I)

	Skin-resistance R_S (kΩ)± SD								
V_S (V)	[For S1] 49 kg	[For S2] 53 kg	[For S3] 57 kg	[For S4] 65 kg	[For S5] 72 kg]	[For S6] 80 kg	[For S7] 87 kg	[For S8] 93 kg	[For S9] 110 kg
10	8.074 ±2.10	9.611 ±2.25	10.570 ±2.55	12.473 ±2.66	12.94 ±2.92	14.634 ±3.21	16.780 ±3.20	19.316 ±3.23	24.920 ±3.25
15	6.804 ±1.98	8.282 ±2.12	9.0040 ±2.43	10.811 ±2.48	11.23 ±2.70	12.357 ±3.05	14.861 ±3.09	15.966 ±3.15	19.618 ±3.20
20	6.312 ±1.83	7.274 ±2.05	8.2890 ±2.24	9.111 ±2.35	10.63 ±2.65	11.150 ±2.89	12.431 ±2.92	13.347 ±2.97	16.490 ±3.01
25	6.014 ±1.72	6.880 ±1.94	7.2780 ±2.13	7.796 ±2.24	9.730 ±2.51	10.215 ±2.72	11.224 ±2.79	12.220 ±2.84	14.060 ±2.93
30	5.605 ±1.59	6.062 ±1.81	6.8570 ±2.02	7.045 ±2.11	7.520 ±2.39	9.200 ±2.61	10.025 ±2.65	11.024 ±2.71	12.800 ±2.78
35	5.159 ±1.50	5.321 ±1.68	6.2990 ± 1.77	6.641 ±1.94	7.239 ±2.26	8.600 ±2.48	8.929 ±2.57	9.297 ±2.62	10.164 ±2.69
40	4.841 ±1.36	5.015 ±1.55	5.7200 ±1.59	6.092 ±1.78	6.765 ±2.05	7.840 ±2.29	8.095 ±2.32	8.498 ±2.39	9.175 ±2.44
45	4.365 ±1.23	4.576 ±1.41	5.1110 ±1.43	5.806 ±1.65	5.997 ±1.83	6.270 ±1.98	6.486 ±2.11	6.813 ±2.23	7.685 ±2.29
50	3.782 ±1.04	4.086 ±1.19	4.6820 ±1.24	5.550 ±1.46	5.619 ±1.58	5.940 ±1.77	6.155 ±1.91	6.354 ±2.01	6.665 ±2.14
55	3.096 ±0.89	3.625 ±1.05	3.8970 ±1.12	4.809 ±1.28	4.826 ±1.33	5.029 ±1.71	5.259 ±1.76	5.429 ±1.80	6.046 ±1.83

Table 3.2 Skin resistance measurements for wide applied voltages (V_S) over female subjects (weight range: 40-75 kg, mean: 57.7 ±12.07 kg) (Part-II)

	Skin-resistance R_S (kΩ)± SD						
V_S (V)	[For S1] 42 kg	[For S2] 46 kg	[For S3] 51 kg	[For S4] 58 kg	[For S5] 64 kg]	[For S6] 68 kg	[For S7] 75 kg
10	4.945 ±1.89	5.459 ±1.87	5.988 ±1.72	6.757 ±1.60	7.460 ±1.46	8.363 ±1.34	10.15 ±1.25
15	4.512 ±1.93	5.172 ±1.75	5.678 ±1.58	5.996 ±1.52	6.739 ±1.31	7.542 ±1.27	8.469 ±1.18
20	4.006 ±1.84	4.197 ±1.62	4.768 ±1.43	5.644 ±1.38	6.142 ±1.23	6.448 ±1.15	7.658 ±1.06
25	3.454 ±1.71	3.616 ±1.53	3.744 ±1.32	5.044 ±1.29	5.522 ±1.17	6.058 ±1.07	7.033 ±0.97
30	2.977 ±1.59	3.354 ±1.44	3.430 ±1.26	4.626 ±1.18	5.082 ±1.11	5.458 ±0.96	6.610 ±0.86
35	2.705 ±1.48	2.979 ±1.31	3.167 ±1.12	4.112 ±1.07	4.263 ±1.04	4.916 ±0.88	5.789 ±0.79
40	2.337 ±1.39	2.809 ±1.23	3.002 ±1.08	3.721 ±0.95	3.899 ±0.92	4.361 ±0.79	5.463 ±0.71
45	2.030 ±1.26	2.529 ±1.16	2.584 ±0.99	3.524 ±0.89	3.502 ±0.78	3.869 ±0.73	4.664 ±0.65

Tables 3.1- 3.2 show the variation of R_S with weights for various subjects (male and female participants). Results are presented in terms of mean resistance with standard deviation as an error over five repeated measures at specific applied voltage for a given subject. The applied voltage ranges for male and female participants were kept at different levels by observing the optimal CMAP responses. A statistical test for optimal choice of voltage was also carried out which is statistically significant with $p < 0.005$. It is seen that the resistances are higher for subjects with higher body weight in both male and female subjects. However, the resistances for female subjects are smaller than that of male subjects for same weight and applied voltage. With increase in V_S, the resistance gradually decreases irrespective of gender. Therefore skin resistance profiles are different for male and female participants for the same range of applied voltage. The resistance profile for a given subject was found high initially and then decreased non-linearly with increase of applied stimulating voltage.

3.2.2 Modeling of Supramaximal Stimulation

Modeling of Supramaximal Stimulation requires measures of V_L and R_S for various applied voltages (V_S) as already discussed in section 3.1.3. This experiment was carried out for an applied voltage range of 10-55 V to achieve SS. However, measurement in case of female subjects was kept in the range of 10-45 V since for female subjects SS was achieved at a lower level of applied voltage as compared to male subjects. Fig. 3.8 shows the variation of V_L with V_S in steps of 5 V for male and female subjects. During measurement, optimum load voltages ($V_{L,SM}$) for each subject are noted down manually by observing signals in the DAQ. The $V_{L,SM}$ s are marked with A1,..,G1 for females and A2,..,I2 for males. The markers represent V_{SM} along V_S-axis and $V_{L,SM}$ along V_L-axis. For instance, D2 (42, 6.4) indicate V_{SM} at 42 V and $V_{L,SM}$ at 6.4 V as shown in Fig. 3.8 (b). It is seen that V_L with $V_{L,SM}$ and $V_{L,SM}$ with V_{SM} can be mapped for finding statistical model. This framework opens up a methodology to estimate the SS for a subject.

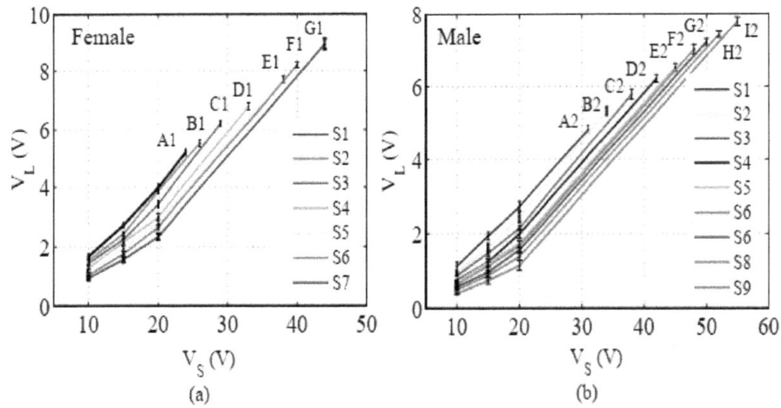

Fig. 3.8 Measured load voltages V_L for different applied voltages V_S. (a) female subjects S1-S7 and (b) male subjects S1-S9. For female subjects $V_{L,SM}$ were obtained at specific applied voltages, termed as V_{SM} (i.e., A1-G1) in the range of 20-45 V and for male $V_{L,SM}$ were obtained at various V_{SM} (i.e. A2-I2) in the range of 30-60 V.

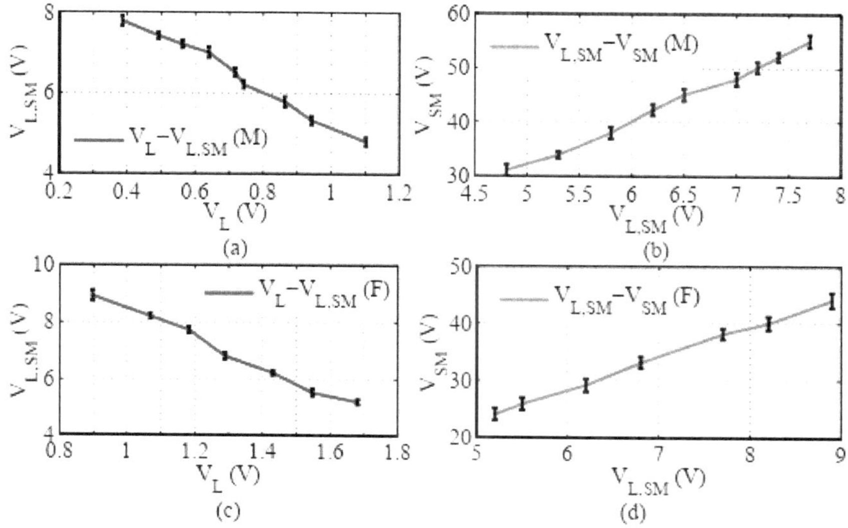

Fig. 3.9 Model characteristics of various subjects at V_S =15 V. (a) and (b) are for male, and (c) and (d) are for female subjects.

Table 3.3 Regression analysis with R^2 for $V_{L,SM}$ - V_L and V_{SM} - $V_{L,SM}$

Subject	Mathematical models	Model parameters	R^2
Male	**Eq.(10)** [V_S =10V]	a=-4.332, b=9.537	**0.9861**
	Eq.(10) [V_S =15V]	a=-2.576, b=9.634	0.9826
	Eq.(10) [V_S =20V]	a=-1.918, b=9.987	0.9791
	Eq.(11) [V_S = V_{SM} V]	c=8.041,d=-8.062	**0.9959**
Female	**Eq.(12)** [V_S =10V]	p=-5.032, q=13.47	**0.9841**
	Eq.(12) [V_S =15V]	p=-3.493, q=14.32	0.962
	Eq.(12) [V_S =20V]	p=-2.194, q=13.86	0.9698
	Eq.(13) [V_S = V_{SM} V]	r=5.667, s=-5.549	**0.9983**

The variation of V_L and $V_{L,SM}$ with V_S and V_{SM} respectively for both male and female subjects (Fig. 3.9) was used to fit to our model equations. In order to establish the mathematical relationships between the variables, a number of models were investigated. Subsequently, two sets of models for both male and female subjects were investigated based on a simple linear equation connecting two measurement points. These equations are simple and have less computational complexity for ease of implementation in MATLAB.

$$V_{L,SM,m} = aV_{L,m} + b \tag{3.8}$$

$$V_{SM,m} = cV_{L,SM,m} + d \tag{3.9}$$

$$V_{L,SM,f} = pV_{L,f} + q \tag{3.10}$$

$$V_{SM,f} = rV_{L,SM,f} + s \tag{3.11}$$

where *a, c, p, r* are model gains and *b, d, q, s* are model offsets. The subscripts *m* and *f* indicate male and female respectively.

Male: $V_{SM,m} = 8.041(-4.332 * V_L + 9.537) - 8.062 = -34.83 * V_L + 68.62$ (3.12)

Female: $V_{SM,f} = 5.667(-5.032 * V_L + 13.47) - 5.549 = -28.51 * V_L + 70.78$ (3.13)

Table 3.3 reports the best fits in terms of R^2 evaluated for V_S = 10 V, 15 V and 20 V. The best fit models for $V_{L,SM}$ - V_L and V_{SM} - $V_{L,SM}$ were found at V_S =10 V for both male and female subjects with R^2= 0.9861, 0.9959 and R^2= 0.9841, 0.9983 respectively. Furthermore, the best fit models are also statistically significant with $p < 0.001$ and $p < 0.005$. It is worth noting that some other mathematical models also showed good results with close proximity in R^2, however, in comparison with those models, aforementioned models showed slightly better results and were simpler. With optimal initial trigger voltage (V_{SO}) of 10 V, the V_{SM} could be accurately estimated in the very next triggering attempt. It was very close to the value obtained at V_S = 15 V. Due to high R^2 and in order to avoid tingling sensation to the subject, V_S = 10 V was selected for initial stimulation voltage. Therefore, we chose the following model equations for implementation in our auto-controlled system.

To test the validity of the modelled equations, we apply these equations to all the subjects and the model errors depicted in Table 3.4.

Table 3.4 Validation of modeled equations (3.12) and (3.13)

Sex	Subjects (S) & weights (kg)	Measured V_L (V)	Measured V_{SM} (V)	Modelled V_{SM} (V)	Percentage Error (%)
Male	S1, 49	1.102	31	30.2373	2.46
	S2, 53	0.9424	35	35.7962	2.27
	S3, 57	0.8643	38	38.5164	1.35
	S4, 65	0.7422	42	42.7692	1.83
	S5, 72	0.712	45	43.8210	2.62
	S6, 80	0.6396	48	46.3427	3.45
	S7, 87	0.5624	50	49.0316	1.93
	S8, 93	0.4922	52	51.4767	1.006
	S9, 110	0.3857	55	55.1861	0.338
Female	S1, 42	1.682	23	22.8262	0.75
	S2, 46	1.548	26	26.6465	2.48
	S3, 51	1.431	29	29.9822	3.38
	S4, 58	1.289	33	34.0306	3.12
	S5, 64	1.182	38	37.0812	2.41
	S6, 68	1.068	40	40.3313	0.82
	S7, 75	0.8968	44	45.2122	2.75

From Table 3.4 it is found that the maximum modeled percentage error for male is 3.45 % and for female is 3.38 %, which validates the correctness of the modeled equations.

3.2.3 Results of Microcontroller based Stimulator

Table 3.5 outlines the proposed algorithm for μC based measurement of V_L as a faithful representation of skin resistance, relate V_L to estimate $V_{L,SM}$ using Eq. (3.12), estimate V_{SM} using Eq. (3.13) and finally generate the V_{SM} via BC for automatic generation of supramaximal voltage for online measurements. The experimentation consists of two stages- offline and online stages as outlined in Table 3.5-

Table 3.5 Operation of the μC based auto-controlled neurostimulator

Step I: Model implementation (Offline measurement using LabView)
i. Apply V_S for study subjects (S)
ii. Find V_L s $\forall$ S
iii. Find model equations for V_{SM} and $V_{L,SM}$ using MATLAB
iv. Find optimum model using R^2 and initial triggering voltage
v. Embed program in μC for evaluation of V_{SM}
Step II: Buck converter (Offline measurement)
i. Find relation between input DC and output voltage of BC (V_{BC})
ii. Find DC for V_{SM} and embed program in μC
iii. Embed the program to trigger a pulse train with specific DC to generate corresponding V_{SM}
Step III: Evaluation of V_{SM} for Online measurement
i. Select subject (male/female) for recording using sliding switch S_0 / S_1
ii. Apply optimal trigger voltage to the nerve by setting the output voltage of voltage multiplier
iii. Generate V_L by block d
iv. Calculate $V_{L,SM}$ and V_{SM} for model equations by μC
v. Calculate DC using Eq.(7) by μC
vi. Output the pulse train with the calculated DC to BC
vii. Generate V_{SM} by the BC

The variations of V_{SM} generated by BC of block (e) with DC of pulse train for both 1 kHz and 10 kHz are shown in Fig. 3.11. The linearity of V_{SM} with DC is more prominent at 10 kHz than at 1 kHz. Furthermore, the dynamic responses of the conventional stimulator and buck converter (block (e) of Fig. 3.6) of auto-controlled stimulator are depicted in Fig. 3.12. The rise and fall time of both responses were found to be less than 1 ms. The ripple factors that measures the rms component contains in conventional stimulating pulse and BC output during the on-time were found to be 0.274 and 0.36 respectively. To exemplify the generation of pulse train in the μC and corresponding V_{SM} in the BC, the digital storage oscilloscope (DSO) display is shown in Fig. 3.13. The complete experimental is shown in Fig. 3.10.

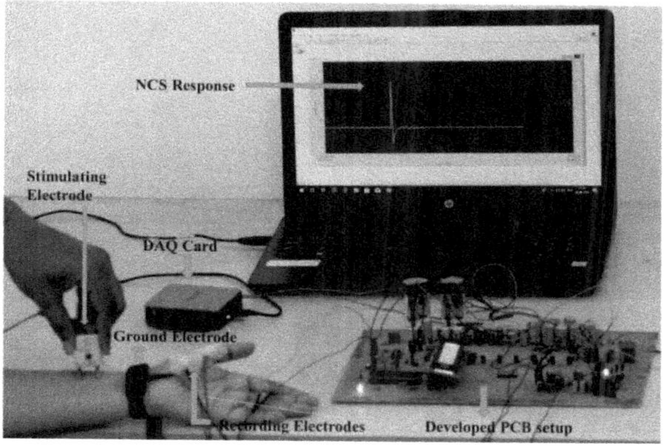

Fig. 3.10 Custom made NCS experimental setup with proposed μC-based auto-controlled stimulator.

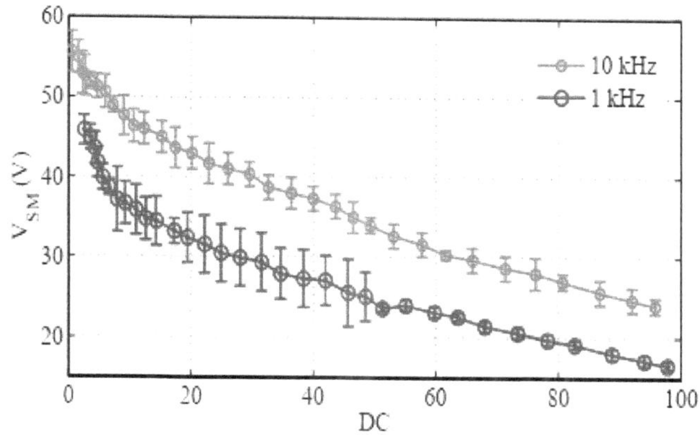

Fig. 3.11 The variation of V_{SM} with DC with a pulse train of frequency 10 kHz and 1 kHz generated by μC.

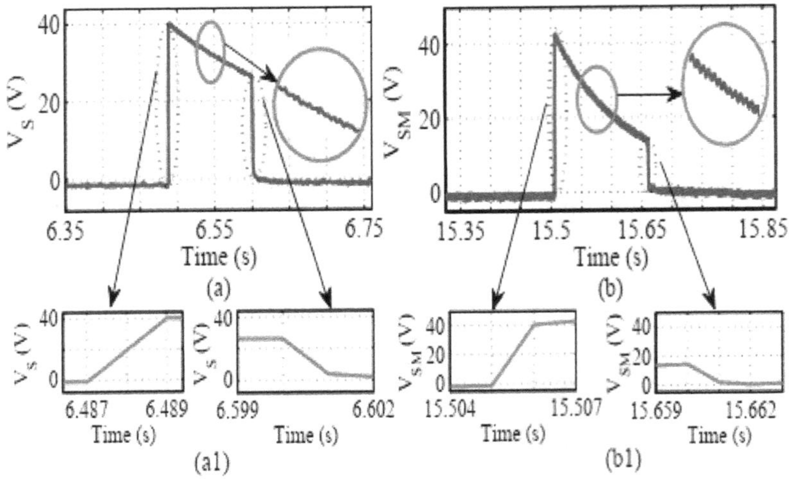

Fig. 3.12 Dynamic responses of stimulating pulse (a) conventional stimulator (b) buck converter.(a1) and (b1) are rise (left) and fall (right) time responses of (a) and (b) respectively.

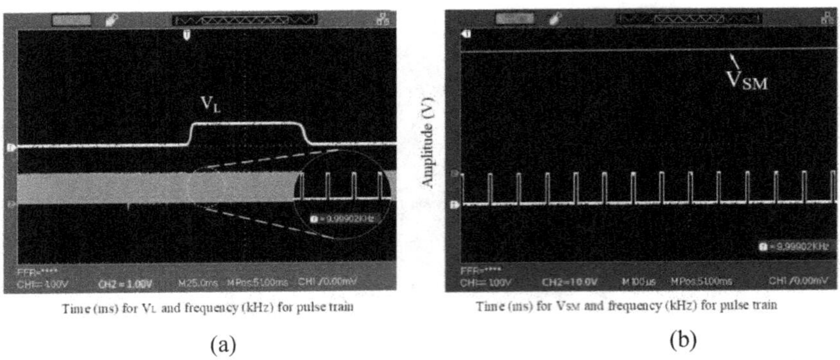

Fig. 3.13 DSO readings of pulse train for subject (S_4) with frequency 10 kHz (a) V_L and corresponding pulse train generated by the μC (b) V_{SM} output of the BC with applied pulse train from the μC. It is found that the zoomed output portion in Fig. 13 (a) indicates the pulse train with a specific duty cycle.

The experiment was carried out on the proposed μC based system for 20 new subjects (10 males and 10 females) who were not included in the modeling. The details of the subjects are shown in Table 3.6-

Table 3.6 The weights and heights of the new subjects

Male			Female		
Subjects (S)	**Age (years)**	**Weight (Kg)**	**Subjects (S)**	**Age (years)**	**Weight (Kg)**
S_1	23	48	S_{11}	22	40
S_2	26	54	S_{12}	25	43
S_3	27	59	S_{13}	24	48
S_4	30	66	S_{14}	24	53
S_5	27	73	S_{15}	27	60
S_6	28	82	S_{16}	25	63
S_7	32	86	S_{17}	26	70
S_8	29	90	S_{18}	29	76
S_9	31	103	S_{19}	28	81
S_{10}	33	114	S_{20}	30	86

The readings of V_L for male subject (S_4) of 66 kg weight and subsequently obtained V_{SM} at the BC output are shown in Fig. 3.13. Furthermore, V_L and CMAP at initial stimulating voltage V_S = 10 V and V_{SM} = 41.5 V (male, S_4) and 38.3 V (female, S_{16}) are depicted in Fig. 3.14.

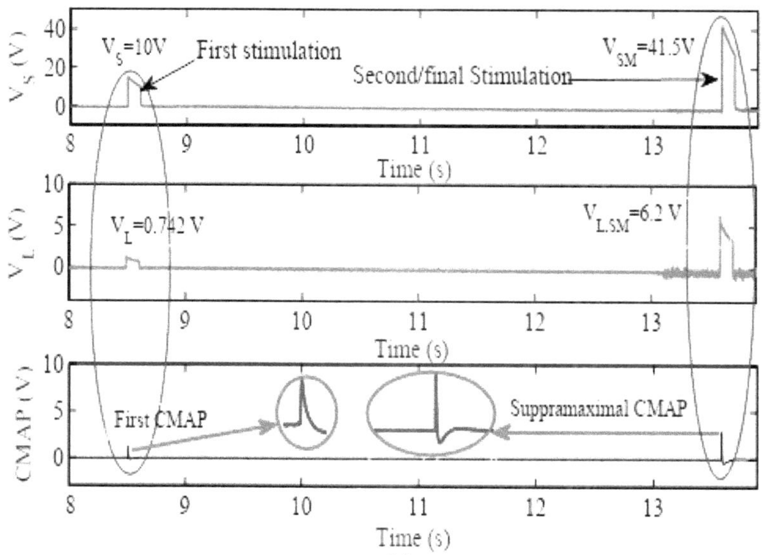

(a)

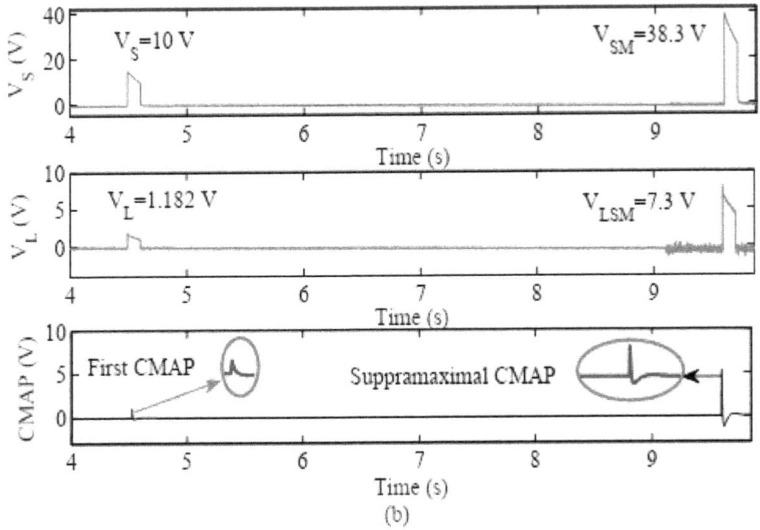

(b)

Fig. 3.14 Online measured signals for (a) male (age: 30 years, weight: 66 kg) and (b) female (age: 25 years, weight: 63 kg). Both subjects were excluded from the modeling data. (For each figure, top-stimulation, middle-load voltage and bottom-CMAP)

As is evident, the optimal CMAP, i.e., supramaximal response as indicated by circle in Fig. 3.14 (a) at final stimulation is far superior to that of initial stimulation for both the participants. For new subjects, the responses for second/final stimulations were found as supramaximal responses which were verified by a neurophysiologist.

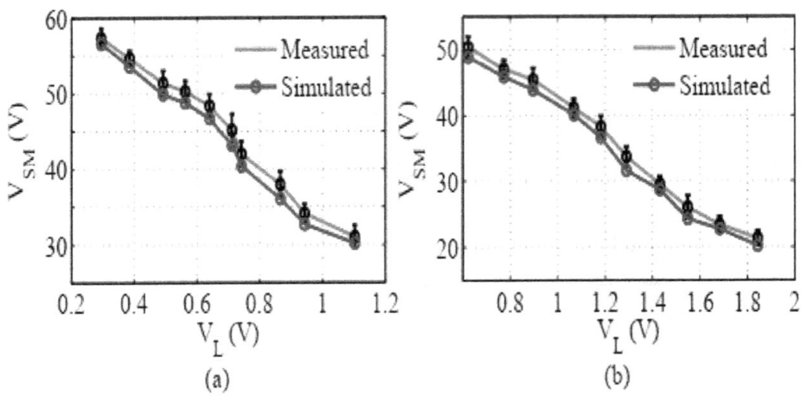

Fig. 3.15 Experimental values of V_{SM} vs. V_L for new subjects (a) males (b) females

The mean results of V_{SM} for different V_L over five repeated measurements on new subjects are shown in Fig. 3.15. It is seen that high V_L (i.e., low skin resistance) requires lower value of V_{SM} for final stimulation to achieve the supramaximal responses. Furthermore, the values of V_{SM} obtained at the buck converter output for new (excluded from modeling) subjects with five repeated trials in details with error in terms of mean, standard deviation, relative deviation and repeatability are shown in Table 3. 7. The quantitative difference of V_{SM} between theoretical and experimental are found 1.8 % (for male) and 2.31 % (for female) subjects respectively.

Table 3.7 Values of V_{SM} for five repeated trials for all new subjects

Sex	Subjects (S)	Trials (T) for V_{SM} (V)					Mean	S.D	R.D in %	Repeatability in %
		T_1	T_2	T_3	T_4	T_5				
Male	S_1	32.51	31.12	29.51	31.82	28.63	30.71	1.612	5.25	94.75
	S_2	35.32	34.22	32.52	33.34	32.13	33.50	1.293	3.86	96.14
	S_3	39.46	38.31	36.16	37.32	39.74	38.19	1.492	3.90	96.10
	S_4	43.46	42.46	40.16	41.43	43.26	42.15	1.371	3.25	96.75
	S_5	47.3	45.1	43.12	46.27	45.87	45.52	1.572	3.45	96.55
	S_6	49.9	48.32	46.91	47.65	46.52	47.85	1.335	2.79	97.21
	S_7	51.71	50.23	48.21	49.72	47.58	49.49	1.644	3.32	96.68
	S_8	52.95	51.54	49.65	52.45	48.73	51.06	1.813	3.55	96.45
	S_9	55.78	54.43	53.78	54.81	52.15	54.19	1.350	2.49	97.51
	S_{10}	58.62	57.32	55.12	57.98	60.23	57.85	1.871	3.23	96.77
Female	S_{11}	22.43	21.31	19.29	20.43	21.55	21.00	1.192	5.68	94.32
	S_{12}	21.81	24.35	22.12	23.25	24.82	23.27	1.325	5.69	94.31
	S_{13}	25.24	26.16	27.74	27.37	26.41	26.58	0.996	3.74	96.26
	S_{14}	30.72	29.46	28.42	30.69	29.33	29.72	0.981	3.30	96.70
	S_{15}	33.26	33.72	35.26	36.12	35.67	34.80	1.249	3.59	96.41
	S_{16}	39.93	38.25	36.73	37.38	38.55	38.16	1.219	3.19	96.81
	S_{17}	42.31	41.45	39.7	42.56	40.95	41.39	1.145	2.76	97.24
	S_{18}	47.12	45.56	43.75	44.42	45.76	45.32	1.300	2.86	97.14
	S_{19}	48.23	47.38	45.56	47.78	46.49	47.08	1.067	2.26	97.74
	S_{20}	51.91	50.45	48.75	47.31	50.56	49.79	1.785	3.58	96.42

The investigation and analysis thus reveal that the proposed auto-controlled stimulator accurately generates the V_{SM} for subjects not included in modeling. Our system provides supramaximal stimulus for proper NCS incorporating the skin-resistance as a comprehensive biofeedback parameter. This allows the proposed device to be used for stimulation of nerves in NCS/EMG applications without the need for repeated stimulation until supramaximal stimulus is obtained. Furthermore, Table 3.8 outlines comparison of many state-of-art methods with our method in terms of salient parameters, which also indicates the efficacy of our design.

Table.3. 8 Outlines of characteristics and limitations of various reported studies

Design system []	Biofeedback parameter	Characteristics/Limitations	Applications
EMG-biofeedback system [17]	zero-crossings and turns /second of EMG signal	Limited features. Use of EMG responses.	Muscle/fatigue analysis
64-channel neurostimulator [21]	No	Deep brain stimulation	neurological disorders
Programable neurostimulator [29]	No	Generate rectangular pulse (0-2.5 V).Model validated with rat only	Stimulation for rat
Current stimulator [6]	No	Complex design. High supply voltage (i.e., 15 V)	neurological disorders
CMOS-based neurostimulator [20]	No	Complex design	Seizure detection
Constant current-WNS [32]	No	100-channel design. Use biphasic constant current. Programmable system	motor fibers/muscle study
VLSI based stimulation [13]	No	Constant current source	visceral nerves study
Biofeedback therapy system [37]	Fatigue parameter based on sEMG	High processing steps Validation with limited datasets	nerve/muscle diagnosis
Biofeedback System [19]	Signal features. (EMG and galvanic skin response)	lack of stimulator design	diagnostic application
NeuroMetrix [4]	No	Stimulus duratiom 50-100 μS	DPN neuropathy
Apparatus and methods for assessment of neuromuscular	No	Stimulus duration less than 1 ms	CTS neuropathy

function [12]			
A handheld nerve conduction measuring device [34]	No	Stimulus duration 0.2 sec	CTS neuropathy
Digital electroneurometer [10]	No	Not mentioned about Triggering Pulse	CTS neuropathy
Automated hand-held nerve conduction devices [11]	No	Not mentioned about Triggering Pulse	CTS neuropathy
NC-stat automated device [3]	No	Not mentioned about Triggering Pulse	CTS and DPN neuropathy
portable electro-neurometer [35]	No	Not mentioned about Triggering Pulse	CTS and DPN neuropathy
Digital Electro - neurometer [31]	No	Stimulus duration less than 1 ms	CTS neuropathy
Proposed biofeedback stimulator	**Skin-resistance**	**Voltage controlled stimulator**	**Peripheral nerve analysis Low power system (i.e., 9 V). Portable and adaptable**

3.3 Conclusion

This study addresses the measurement of human skin-resistance and proposed a μC - based programmed biofeedback stimulator using skin-resistance as a representative marker to generate supramaximal stimulation in order to avoid repeated trials. First, a custom made NCS setup was designed to collect physiological data for theoretical modeling and for finding optimal statistical models using the regression R^2 analysis. Then, an algorithm was then developed and embedded in a μC for automatic generation of supramaximal stimulus voltage for online measurement. The programmed μC triggers the specific pulse train of duty cycle corresponding to the optimal voltage of the programmed μC. This pulse train was applied to the BC that produced the final stimulating voltage. The system was tested using new participants with the custom made NCS setup using the proposed stimulator and results were demonstrated. Furthermore, close agreement of results between optimal voltage of the μC and the output of the BC indicates the correctness of the biofeedback based stimulator design. The simulated and measured values are compared and show good agreement. Additionally, the proposed methodology was outlined in the context of many prior similar applications. Thus, this system is appropriate for stimulating nerves for getting NCS responses for real-time applications.

Bibliography

[1] Alejandro, H.A., Kato, R., Yokoi, H., Arai, T., and Ohnishi, T. An fMRI study on the effects of electrical stimulation as biofeedback. In *2006 IEEE/RSJ International Conference on Intelligent Robots and Systems*, pages 4336-4342, Beijing, China, 2006.

[2] Arieta, A.H., Yokoi, H., Arai, T., and Wenwei, Y. FES as biofeedback for an EMG controlled prosthetic hand. In *TENCON 2005-2005 IEEE Region 10 Conference*, pages 1-6, Melbourne, Australia, 2005.

[3] Armstrong, T.N., Dale, A.M., Al-Lozi, M.T., Franzblau, A. and Evanoff, B.A. Median and ulnar nerve conduction studies at the wrist: criterion validity of the NC-stat automated device. *Journal of occupational and environmental medicine*, 50 (7): 758-764, 2008.

[4] Boettcher, B., Cryan, M., Gozani, S.N., Herb, G., Kong, X., Williams, M. and Fendrock, C. NeuroMetrix Inc. *Apparatus and method for the automated measurement of sural nerve conduction velocity and amplitude*. U.S. Patent No. 9,173,581, 2015.

[5] Chi, Y.M., Jung, T.P., and Cauwenberghs, G. Dry-contact and noncontact biopotential electrodes: Methodological review. *IEEE reviews in biomedical engineering, 3*: 106-119, 2010.

[6] Charthad, J., Chang, T.C., Liu, Z., Sawaby, A., Weber, M.J., Baker, S., Gore, F., Felt, S.A., and Arbabian, A. A mm-sized wireless implantable device for electrical stimulation of peripheral nerves. *IEEE transactions on biomedical circuits and systems*, 12 (2): 257-270, 2018.

[7] Chizmadzhev, Y.A., Zarnitsin, V.G., Weaver, J.C., and Potts, R.O. Mechanism of electroinduced ionic species transport through a multilamellar lipid system. *Biophysical journal*, 68 (3): 749-765. 1995.

[8] Dorgan, S.J., and Reilly, R.B. A model for human skin impedance during surface functional neuromuscular stimulation. *IEEE transactions on rehabilitation engineering*, 7 (3): 341-348, 1999.

[9] de Talhouet, H., and Webster, J.G. The origin of skin-stretch-caused motion artifacts under electrodes. *Physiological Measurement*, 17 (2): 81-93, 1996.

[10] David, W.S., Chaudhry, V., Dubin, A.H. and Shields Jr, R.W. Literature review: Nervepace digital electroneurometer in the diagnosis of carpal tunnel syndrome. *Muscle & nerve*, 27 (3): 378-385, 2003.

[11] England, J.D. and Franklin, G.M. Automated hand-held nerve conduction devices: Raw data, raw interpretations. *Muscle & nerve*, 43 (1): 6-8, 2011.

[12] Gozani, S.N. NeuroMetrix Inc. *Apparatus and methods for assessment of neuromuscular function*. U.S. Patent No. 5,851,191, 1998.

[13] Greenwald, E., Wang, Q., and Thakor, N.V. VLSI circuits for bidirectional interface to peripheral and visceral nerves. In *2015 37th Annual International Conference of the IEEE Engineering in Medicine and Biology Society* (EMBC-2015), pages 2163-2166, Milan, Italy, 2015.

[14] Grimnes, S. Skin impedance and electro-osmosis in the human epidermis. *Medical and Biological Engineering and Computing*, 21 (6): 739-749, 1983.

[15] Gitter, A.J., and Stolov, W.C. AAEM Minimonograph# 16: Instrumentation and measurement in electrodiagnostic medicine–Part I. *Muscle & Nerve: Official Journal of the American Association of Electrodiagnostic Medicine*, 18 (8): 799-811, 1995.

[16] Hlubik, J., Lhotska, L., Hlubik, P., and Stritecka, H. Changes in bioimpedance and body composition parameters depending on measurement conditions. *Hygeia*, 48 (2): 181-184, 2013.

[17] Im, J.J., Rho, D.H., Jeon, Y.J., Lee, N.B., and Chung, J.I. Extraction of parameters from EMG signals for the biofeedback electrical stimulation. In *Proceedings of the Second Joint 24th Annual Conference and the Annual Fall Meeting of the Biomedical Engineering Society*, volume 1, pages 133-134, Houston, USA, 2002.

[18] Ivorra, A. Tissue electroporation as a bioelectric phenomenon: Basic concepts. In *Irreversible electroporation*, pages 23-61, Spriger, 2010.

[19] Jing, J., Zhang, W., Wang, Y., and Yuan, S. An intelligent biofeedback system based on pattern recognition and electroacupuncture imitating traditional Chinese

medical acupuncture. In *2006 6th World Congress on Intelligent Control and Automation*, pages 9454-9458, Dalian, China, 2006.

[20] Kassiri, H., Bagheri, A., Soltani, N., Abdelhalim, K., Jafari, H.M., Salam, M.T., Velazquez, J.L.P., and Genov, R. Battery-less tri-band-radio neuro-monitor and responsive neurostimulator for diagnostics and treatment of neurological disorders. *IEEE Journal of Solid-State Circuits*, 51 (5): 1274-1289, 2016.

[21] Lee, J., Rhew, H.G., Kipke, D.R., and Flynn, M.P. A 64 channel programmable closed-loop neurostimulator with 8 channel neural amplifier and logarithmic ADC. *IEEE Journal of Solid-State Circuits*, 45 (9): 1935-1945, 2010.

[22] Lee, M.Y., Lin, C.F., and Soon, K.S. Design of a new biofeedback proprioceptive neuromuscular facilitation system for below-knee amputees. *Biomedical Engineering: Applications. Basis and Communications*, 18 (4): 190-197, 2006.

[23] Luna, J.L.V., Krenn, M., Ramírez, J.A.C., and Mayr, W. Dynamic impedance model of the skin-electrode interface for transcutaneous electrical stimulation. *PloS one*, 10 (5): 1-15. 2015.

[24] Luan, S., and Constandinou, T. G. A charge-metering method for voltage-mode neural stimulation. *Journal of neuroscience methods*, 224 (1): 39-47, 2014.

[25] Mallik, A., and Weir, A.I. Nerve conduction studies: essentials and pitfalls in practice. *Journal of Neurology, Neurosurgery & Psychiatry*, 76 (2): 23-31, 2005

[26] Mishra, U. K., and Kalita, J. *Clinical Neurophysiology*. Elsevier Health Sciences, 3rd edition, India, 2014.

[27] Peckham, P.H., and Knutson, J.S. Functional electrical stimulation for neuromuscular applications. *Annu. Rev. Biomed. Eng.*, 7: 327-360, 2005.

[28] Prokhorov, E.F., González-Hernández, J., Vorobiev, Y.V., Morales-Sanchez, E., Prokhorova, T.E., and De Larrea, G.Z.L. In vivo electrical characteristics of human skin, including at biological active points. *Medical and Biological Engineering and Computing*, 38 (5): 507-511, 2000.

[29] Qian, X., Hao, H.W., Ma, B.Z., Wen, X.W., Hu, C.H., Li, L.M., Lau, R.Y.C., and Guo, X. Programmable and implantable neurostimulator with novel stimulus waveforms for rat models. *Electronics letters*, 48 (17): 1035-1036, 2012.

[30] Rosell, J., Colominas, J., Riu, P., Pallas-Areny, R., and Webster, J.G. Skin impedance from 1 Hz to 1 MHz. *IEEE Transactions on Biomedical Engineering*, 35 (8): 649-651, 1988.

[31] Rosier, R.N., University of Iowa Research Foundation (UIRF), *Digital electroneurometer*, U.S. Patent No. 4,807,643, 1989.

[32] Thurgood, B.K., Warren, D.J., Ledbetter, N.M., Clark, G.A., and Harrison, R.R. A wireless integrated circuit for 100-channel charge-balanced neural stimulation. *IEEE Transactions on Biomedical Circuits and Systems*, 3 (6): 405-414, 2009.

[33] Taji, B., Chan, A.D., and Shirmohammadi, S. Effect of pressure on skin-electrode impedance in wearable biomedical measurement devices. *IEEE Transactions on Instrumentation and Measurement*, 67 (8): 1900-1912, 2018.

[34] Tolonen, U., Kallio, M., Ryhänen, J., Raatikainen, T., Honkala, V., Lesonen, V. and Study Group, A handheld nerve conduction measuring device in carpal tunnel syndrome. *Acta neurologica scandinavica*, 115 (6): 390-397, 2007.

[35] Tanaka, H., Hashizume, H., McCown, C., Senda, M., Nishida, K. and Inoue, H. Accuracy of a portable electroneurometer for measuring distal motor latency. *Journal of Orthopaedic Science*, 10 (5): 445-450, 2005.

[36] Yang, B., and Dong, Y. A Portable Dual-Parameter Tester for Assessing Electrical Properties of Human Skin Surface. *IEEE Sensors Journal*, 16 (2): 426-435, 2015.

[37] Zeng, D., Hu, Y., He, Q., Leng, B., Wang, H., Zou, H., and Wu, W. Study of intelligent bio-feedback therapy system based on transcutaneous electrical nerve stimulation and surface EMG signals. In *2013 IEEE International Conference on Information and Automation* (ICIA-2013), pages 374-378, Yinchuan, China, 2013.

[38] Chizmadzhev, Y.A., Indenbom, A.V., Kuzmin, P.I., Galichenko, S.V., Weaver, J.C. and Potts, R.O. Electrical properties of skin at moderate voltages: contribution of appendageal macropores. *Biophysical Journal*, 74 (2): 843-856, 1998.

CHAPTER 4

Modeling and Impedance Analysis of NCS Signals by System Identification

4.0 Introduction

Peripheral nerves are immensely complex biological systems; therefore understanding of their response to stretch is pivotal to preferable recognition of physiological and pathological states [9]. Moreover, their mechanical reactions are deterministically related to the nature of the external stimulus for which theoretical and computational tools are used to explore the behaviour [9, 25]. Modeling of biomedical phenomena is an important tool for technological and clinical developments [13], furthermore, a well-organized statistical analysis is necessary to validate the models in order to obtain correct model for better prediction and accuracy as well as it helps to identify the problem from the collected data source [9, 12, 33]. A number of useful and productive modeling techniques of biomedical signals have been developed to study its behaviour and response [32, 2, 27, 28, 4, 22, 20]. Electrical stimulation that plays crucial role in NCS analysis is very essential in modeling nerve functioning and behavioural analysis [31, 7]. The NCS on a nerve determines the parameters that relates to the condition of the nerve such as- amplitude of action potential (mV), latency (ms) and nerve conduction velocity (m/sec). Quantitative and qualitative analysis of signal parameters help in finding the disorders of the nerves. Therefore, it is essential to model the nerve functioning in terms of electrical equivalent circuits that could replicate the behaviour of the nerves.

Various biomedical applications where electrical stimulation is applied and attempted modeling of problem specific phenomena are outlined herein. In [32] a study has been done on nerve blockage and computer based sinusoidal stimulation and in vivo trials. In [2] for auditory nerve fibres of cat, a stochastic single-pulse was modeled which can predict psychological measures of loudness in a better way than the equivalent deterministic model. In [27] impedance changes of unmyelinated nerve fibres have been studied by their developed models. They have analysed the changing behaviour of impedance by varying the parameters of the developed models. Developing a proper realistic model of unmyelinated nerve fibres allows the optimization of electrical impedance tomography parameters. In [28] the authors proposed a model based design which is adaptable to controlling modules for medical devices. The model framework is based on the classical PI controller. To analyse the behaviour of the device different control parameters are tested and validated. In [4] a predicting signal processing technique has been proposed to monitor heart activity through ECG signals by comparing universal reference model. During this process normal signals are processed via a personalized classifier to collect informative signal morphology distortions. In paper [22], a methodology has been developed to model the simulation of non-invasive biomedical signal acquisition devices. In this methodology they used colored petri nets modeling language to create formal models that integrated with MATLAB software to detect behaviours of digital filters used in the devices to make the system more effective and safe. In [20] a mathematical model was used to detect healthy and severed nerves of frogs by support vector machine (SVM). Here various stimulation pulses and corresponding responses were used as input and output for modeling which was further employed to investigate the model parameters for finding changes in parameters that indicate changes of nerve function or injury.

Moreover, modeling is a human activity consisting of representing, manipulating and communicating real-world daily life objects [19]. Mathematical and computational models are increasingly used to help interpret biomedical data produced by the biological systems. The availability of data representing various biological states, processes and their time dependencies enables the study of biological systems. Therefore, modeling is very useful to describe a system in terms of constitutive objects and relationships among them, where the description itself is, in general, decodable or interpretable by humans.

Since experimental output data in NCS test is very strongly correlated with the nerve conditions provided the input pulse is constant for a particular test, there is ample scope for exploring system identification to model the nerve. Several statistical based system identification algorithms are popular for modeling black box or grey box models. In this research we propose a technique to estimate the transfer function model of the nerve using measured input-output data. Furthermore, we foresee that there is a definite relationship between the model parameters i.e. electrical parameters (resistance and capacitance) with the NCS parameters such as CMAP, latency and conduction velocity of a subject. Therefore, we propose a technique for correlating the model with NCS parameters experimentally.

Motivated by the essence of modeling in biomedical application, in this thesis we address a human nerve modeling technique using input-output NCS data and analyze the functioning of the nerve. In order to establish the relation between stimulation and response, real time data of healthy subjects were collected using a custom made setup, which were stored in PC through a data acquisition card (DAQ-NI6001). The modeling technique adopts stimulus impulse as input and corresponding CMAP response as output and evaluated the transfer functions (*G(s)*) by using system identification technique (SIT) in the MATLAB environment to study nerve electrical model. Then, some approximate Randle's circuits were considered and manually evaluated the transfer functions for all those circuits. Moreover, similarity pattern was checked of the SIT generated transfer functions with the evaluated transfer functions of Randle's circuits on the basis of order of S-domain and R-C coefficients to select the adequate R-C model. In the next step, by solving the transfer functions by using Eq. (4.21), a data set of R-C values are obtained for each subject as discussed in section 4.3.1.

In the analysis, evaluated R-C values are considered as training data set which is independent variables and NCS parameters are considered as target data set which is dependent variables. For clinical perspective, the NCS parameters can be classified as 'Normal' and 'Abnormal' class. By analysing the range of NCS parameters the nerve status of a particular subject can be evaluated. The clinical data complements biological data, enabling detailed descriptions of both healthy and diseased states, as well as disease progression and response to therapies.

Furthermore, the complexities of modern biomedical technologies are rapidly increasing. Therefore modeling and simulation have become increasingly important as a strategy to understand and predict the trajectory of diseases in support of clinical and policy decisions.

Then statistical models are employed for establishing the proper mathematical guidelines in order to find NCS parameters that closely match with that of the derived values of electrical parameters of RC circuits. The statistical analysis includes linear and support vector regressions that mainly employ statistical markers, namely root mean square error (RMSE) and R^2 for quality prediction of the relation. This analysis finally concludes with best fit nerve model equations for different subjects.

4.1 Experimental Method

Modeling using system identification technique requires measured input-output data. The acquisition of data and method of estimation of models are described in subsequent sections. The experimental setup is shown using a block diagram in Fig. 4.1. As mentioned in Chapter 2, the setup includes stimulator, electrode system, switching circuit, signal conditioning circuit and a DAQ followed by PC. In the stimulator circuit, oscillator employs an OPAMP with Lithium-ion battery (9 V) to generate sustainable sinusoidal oscillation frequency. The output of the oscillator is fed to the voltage multiplier to generate up to 70 V. The designed stimulator circuit generates pulse duration of 110 ms [18]. The voltage divider unit is used to adjust the supply voltage 70 V. The proposed design avoids circuit complexity due to simple circuit components and tunes easily to obtain nerve response of the subjects.

Raw NCS signals are noisy as well as very small to detect, that usually falls in the range of mV. Therefore, a signal conditioning circuit is used that consists of an instrumentation amplifier to amplify the raw signal and a band pass filter circuit to minimize the noise profiles from it.

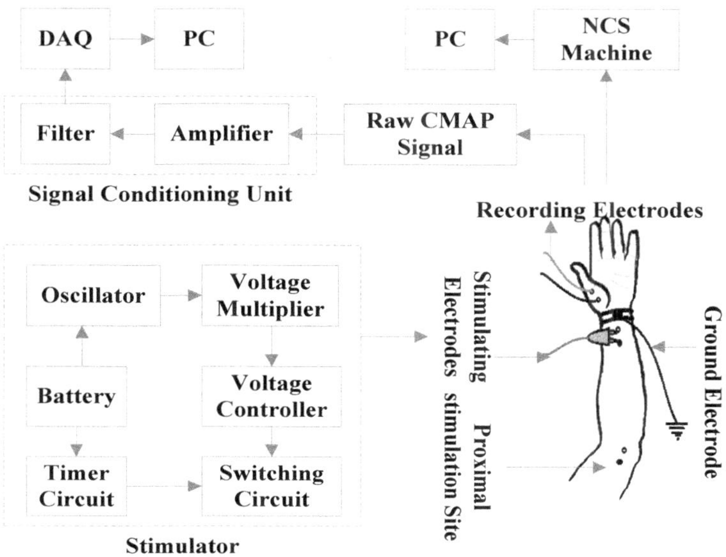

Fig. 4.1 Block diagram of experimental setup

As discussed in the Chapter 2, the stimulating circuit produces unipolar rectangular pulses with variable amplitudes of range 20-70 V for duration of 110ms. Instrumentation amplifier amplifies the low amplitude signal (CMAP), so as to detect by DAQ interfaced with the PC. Raw CMAP contains both low and high frequency components for which a band pass filter is implemented with cut off frequency of 2 Hz- 10 kHz. Frequency range is selected based on the analysis of raw signal spectrum prior to the signal acquisition as discussed in chapter 2.

4.1.1 Acquisition of Data

The experimental setup for acquisition of real time data is depicted in Fig. 4.2 It is worth mentioning that acquisition of signals from subjects are performed following the guidelines of the standard NCS protocol under the supervision of a neurophysiologist, GNRC Hospitals, Guwahati, Assam and with permission from ethical committee of the university. While collecting the input-output data using our custom made setup the NCS parameters are simultaneously collected using a commercial NCS machine (Neuroperfect-2).

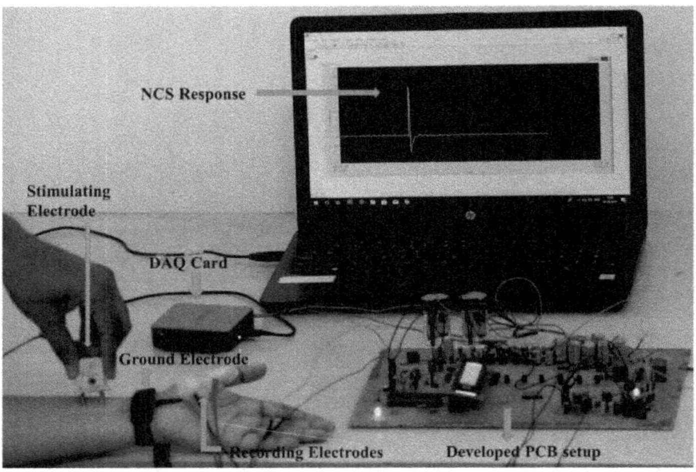

Fig.4.2 Experimental setup of NCS that includes mainly stimulator, signal conditioning circuit and electrodes

Data was collected from 44 healthy subjects of different ages (21-35 years) and weights (45-110 kg) including male and females, to ensure diversity of data patterns that will be suitable for robust modeling. Subjects were asked to lay on bed for few minutes for relaxation and as per protocol the skin was prepared to apply stimulation so as to acquire quality signals using electrodes. Stimulating electrode is of 5 mm diameter with inter-electrode gap of 1.5 cm whereas the recording electrode is of 10 mm diameter (Medicaid Neuroperfect). Ag/AgCl electrode is typically used for stable electrode polarization [18] and impedance of electrode is less than 5-10 kΩ for acceptable recording [8]. The left upper limb median nerve under the *abductor pollicis brevis* muscle is taken for stimulation. The active and reference electrodes were placed over the underlying locations of median nerve and the ground electrode was placed on the wrist between stimulating and recording electrodes to avoid electrical shock and unwanted noise. The signals acquired for 44 healthy subjects, were stored in PC for modeling and validation as described in subsequent sections.

4.2 Modeling Technique

Modeling of the nerve aims to find the RC circuit parameters using system identification techniques employing measured input-output data as shown in Fig. 4.3. In our experimental method, we use the NCS data to form two sets of data vector as-

$$V_i(k)=\left[V_i(k-1),V_i(k-2),........V_i(k-n)\right] \tag{4.1}$$

$$V_O(k)=\left[V_O(k-1),V_O(k-2),........V_O(k-n)\right] \tag{4.2}$$

where, V_i is the input pulse, V_O is the output CMAP, n is the total numbers of data and k is the sampling instants. The data set is used to estimate the Laplace transfer function given by-

$$G(s)=\frac{V_O(s)}{V_i(s)} \tag{4.3}$$

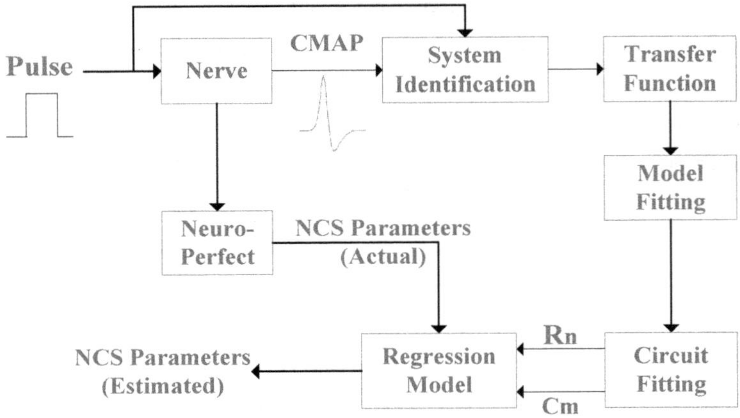

Fig. 4.3 Modeling block diagram with stimulation impulse and CMAP (n and m are the numbers of resistances and capacitances)

4.2.1 ARMAX Modeling

We have used Autoregressive moving average model with exogenous inputs (ARMAX) modeling technique in MATLAB using system identification tool in order to find the models with typical circuit parameters that could replicate the NCS parameters. ARMAX model is based on a time series input-output data of a linear time invariant (LTI) system given by-

$$\sum_{k=0}^{n_a} a_k y(n-k) = \sum_{k=0}^{n_b} b_k x(n-k) + e(n-k) \tag{4.4}$$

where, $e(n-k)$ is the moving average error, n_a is the number of poles, n_b is the number of zeroes and k is the moving average delay.

It is worth noting that the nerve conduction is adequately represented by RC circuit [16] with the help of cable theory [21]. According to cable theory, the membrane of the neuron represents capacitor due to its ability to store and separate the charges and ion channels represents resistor in passive transport [23]. In the neuron, the flow of current of the cell occurs through the ion channels and more the ion cells open more the ions are able to flow i.e. increase in conductance which leads to decrease in resistance. In a battery the RC equivalent circuit expresses the potential differences in the ion concentration between inside and outside of the cell [15]. Various modified Randle's RC circuits are considered for modeling as shown in Fig. 4.4-

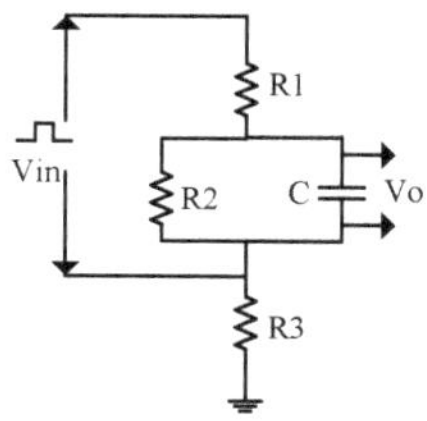

(A) 3R-1C model

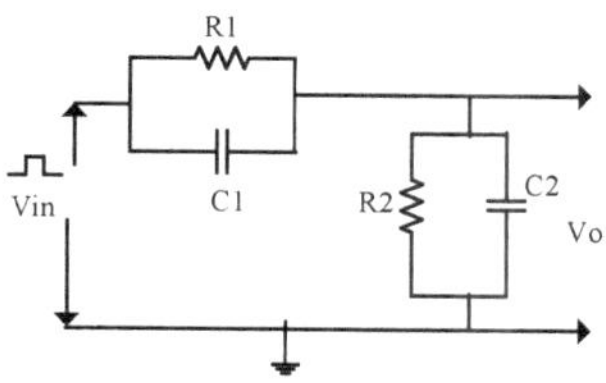

(B) 2R-2C model

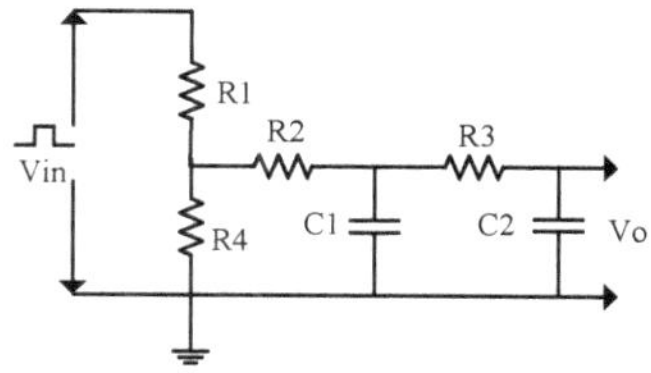

(C) 4R-2C model

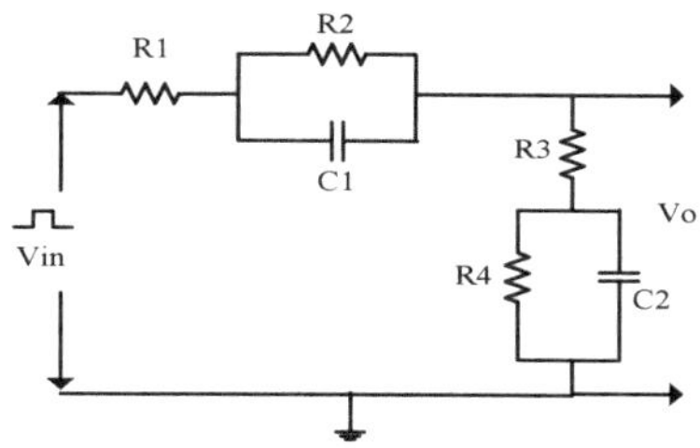

(D) 4R-2C model

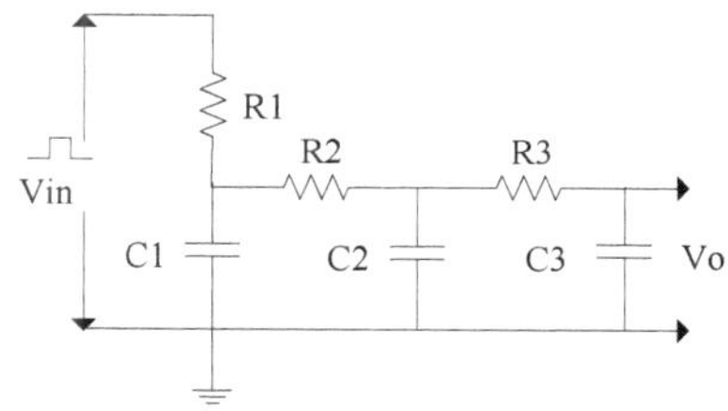

(E) 3R-3C model

Fig. 4.4 Different combination of series/ parallel modified Randle's circuits

4.2.2 Model Validation by Regression Analysis

Regression analysis employs a mathematical model that describes the relationships between dependent and independent variables in a simplified form [26]. Statistical regression is another method of model validation discussed in [14]. It predicts the output response of the dependent variables from the independent variables, given by-

$$Y = f\left(x_n, \beta\right) \tag{4.5}$$

where, Y and x are dependent and independent variables respectively and β is unknown parameter to be estimated from the measurement.

In regression analysis, the performance of the model is primarily checked based on coefficient of determination i.e. R^2 value as given by [26]-

$$R^2 = \frac{\sum_{i=1}^{n}\left(y_i - \bar{y}\right)^2}{\sum_{i=1}^{n}\left(y_i - \bar{y}\right)^2} \tag{4.6}$$

where, n- number of observations, y_i - estimated value of dependent variables for i[th] observation, y_i - observed value of the dependent variables for i[th] observation and $\bar{y}$ - mean of all n observations of the dependent variables.

4.2.2.1 Linear Regression

Linear regression is the simplest out of all regression methods, though it is an incredibly powerful tool for analyzing data [29]. In simple linear regression there are only two variables of interest, however, for multiple linear regression there are more variables. Multivariate linear regression determines a linear function so that best fits of data can be observed [6]. Furthermore, linear regression is widely used modeling technique to predict the dependent variables based on the independent variables. Linear predictive model is the simplest one to identify the relationship between the variables. Multiple linear regressions employ two or more independent variables for one output variables. The dependent variable can be either univariate or multivariate in regression. In multivariate cases-

$$Y = \beta_0 + \beta_1 x_1 + \beta_2 x_2 \ldots\ldots\ldots + \beta_n x_n + \varepsilon \tag{4.7}$$

where, ε is the measurement error.

In this analysis we considered the values of independent variables resistances (R) and capacitances (C) as input features for training the regression model while the dependent variables CMAP, latency and NCV are set as target parameters.

We have used two sets of parameters for training the regression models for 30 subjects as-

$$\text{Input:}\, \theta_i = \left[R_1\ R_2\ R_3\ R_4\ \ldots. R_n\ ; C_1\ C_2\ C_3\ \ldots. C_m\right] \tag{4.8}$$

$$\text{Target:}\, \theta_2 = \begin{bmatrix} v_0 & \Delta T & v \end{bmatrix} \tag{4.9}$$

where, v_0 is the amplitude of the CMAP, ΔT is the latency and v is the nerve conduction velocity.

4.2.2.2 Support Vector Regression

Support vector machine (SVM) is a supervised learning model for classification and regression, and for regression it is termed as support vector regression (SVR) [24]. The SVR can be either linear or nonlinear based on its respective used kernel functions. The SVR is an effective tool in real value function estimation since its computational complexity does not depend on the dimensionality of the input space and with high prediction accuracy [1].

In case of linear support vector regression, let the training data are -

$$\{(x_1, y_1), \ldots, (x_i, y_i)\} \subset \chi \times \mathbb{R} \tag{4.10}$$

where, χ -space of the input pattern.

The function f can be expressed as [3]-

$$f(x) = \langle w, x \rangle + b \text{ with } w \in \chi,\ b \in \mathbb{R} \tag{4.11}$$

where, $\langle ., . \rangle$ means the dot product in χ. The small w can be obtained by minimizing the norm i.e. $|w| = \langle w, w \rangle$.

This problem can be expressed as a convex optimization as follows-

$$\text{Minimize} \frac{1}{2}|w|^2 \tag{4.12}$$

$$\text{Subject to} \begin{cases} y_i - \langle w.x_i \rangle - b \le \in \\ \langle w.x_i \rangle + b - y_i \le \in \end{cases} \tag{4.13}$$

After employing the slack variables to Eq. 4.13, a Lagrange function can be derived from the objective function. To evaluate w, the expression will be-

$$w = \sum_{i=1}^{\ell} \left(\alpha_i - \alpha_i^*\right) x_i \tag{4.14}$$

And the function, *f* can be expressed as-

$$f(x) = \sum_{i=1}^{\ell} \left(\alpha_i - \alpha_i^*\right) \langle x_i, x \rangle + b \tag{4.15}$$

By computing the process of b and developing the regression model, the non-vanishing coefficients are called support vectors, accuracy of the model increases as number of support vector increases.

However, in our analysis, SVR is employed with different kernel functions by considering R_n and C_m values as training data set and NCS parameters are target data set of 30 subjects to estimate the models and remaining data of 14 subjects are used for validation of the models.

4.2.2.2.1 Kernel Functions

SVM or SVR algorithms use a group of mathematical functions that are known as Kernels. Kernel plays a vital role in classification and is used to analyse some patterns in the given dataset. They are very helpful in solving a no-linear problem by using a linear classifier. The SVR algorithm uses kernel-trick for transforming the data points and creating an optimal decision boundary. Kernels help to deal with high dimensional data in a very efficient manner [10].

There are different kernel functions generally used in SVR. The details of some of used kernels are given as follows [5]-

(i) Linear Kernel

It is the most basic type of kernel which is one dimensional in nature and it is very useful when there are lots of features. Linear kernel functions are faster than other functions. It can be represented by the following equation-

$$F(x, xj) = sum(x.xj) \tag{4.16}$$

Where, x, xj represents the data

(ii) Polynomial kernel

It is more generalized representation of the linear kernel. It is not as preferred as other kernel functions as it is less efficient and accurate. It can be represented by the following equation-

$$F(x, xj) = (x.xj + 1)^d \tag{4.17}$$

Here, '.' shows the dot product of both the values

d- denotes the degree

F(x, xj) representing the decision boundary to separate the given classes.

(iii) Gaussian kernel

It is commonly used kernel when there is no prior knowledge of a given dataset.

It can be expressed by the following equation-

$$k(x, y) = \exp\left(-\frac{\|x - y\|^2}{2\sigma^2}\right) \tag{4.18}$$

Here, σ - is the kernel width parameter that controls variation between data points

4.3 Results and Discussion

Using the stimulation impulse as input and corresponding CMAP response as output data, we have estimated the ARMAX model transfer functions with different numbers of poles and zeroes. Table 4.2 shows the model transfer functions with five different circuits with poles (P) and zeroes (Z) and the performance of the models in terms of fit and MSE. Table 4.2 shows that the maximum fit percentage of 75.69% is found for a transfer function of circuit 4R-2C with P=2 and Z=2 while lowest fit is 6.943% for transfer function for circuit 2R-2C with P=1 and Z=1.

4.3.1 Estimation of RC parameters

In this analysis, parameters *R* and *C* are estimated by comparing the derived transfer functions (Table 4.1) with that of the estimated functions (Table 4.2) according to the order of the transfer functions. Nonetheless, the comparison is made as per the order of poles and zeroes with special emphasis on the best fit shown in Table 4.2 so as to get approximate model. As is evident, $G_D(s)$ outlined in Table 4.2 corresponding to the 4R-2C model (Fig.4.4 D) is found to be suitable for this modeling depending on performance markers, i.e. fit percentage (75.69 %) and RMSE (0.5576).

The fit of the estimated models as well as MSE are evaluated using the mathematical functions as follows:

$$\text{Fit Percentage: } F_1(y) = \left(1 - \left|\frac{y - \hat{y}}{y - \bar{y}}\right|\right) \times 100 \tag{4.19}$$

$$\text{MSE: } F_2(y) = \frac{1}{n}\sum_{i=1}^{n}\left(y_i - \hat{y}_i\right)^2 \tag{4.20}$$

Here, y is the measured output, $\hat{y}$ is the simulated or estimated model output and $\bar{y}$ is the mean of y.

Table 4.1 Evaluated transfer functions $G(s)$ of the Randle's circuits shown in Fig.4.4 [A to E]

$G_A(s) = \frac{C}{As + B}$	$A = CR_1R_3 + CR_1R_2 + CR_2R_3$ $\quad B = R_1R_2 + R_2R_3 + R_1R_3$ $C = R_2R_3$
$G_B(s) = \frac{Cs + D}{As + B}$	$A = R_1R_2C_1 + R_1R_2C_2$ $\quad B = R_1 + R_2$ $\quad C = C_1R_1R_2$ $\quad D = R_2$
$G_C(s) = \frac{C}{s^2 + Bs + D}$	$A = C_1C_2R_2^2R_3^2R_4 + C_1C_2R_2^2R_3^2R_1 + C_1C_2R_2R_3^2R_4$ $B = C_2R_2R_3^2R_4 + C_1R_3R_1^2R_4 + C_2R_3R_2^2R_4 + C_2R_1R_3^2R_2 + C_1R_3R_2^2R_4$ $+C_2R_1R_2^2R_3 + C_2R_1R_3^2R_4 + C_1R_1R_2R_3R_4 + C_2R_1R_2R_3R_4$ $C = R_1R_3R_4$ $\quad D = R_2R_3R_1 + R_2R_3R_4 + R_1R_3R_4$
$G_D(s) = \frac{s^2D + sE + F}{s^2A + sB + C}$	$A = C_1C_2R_1R_2R_4 + C_1C_2R_2R_3R_4$ $B = R_1R_4C_2 + R_3R_4C_2 + R_2R_3C_1 + R_2R_4C_2 + R_2R_4C_1 + R_1R_2C_1$ $C = R_1 + R_2 + R_3 + R_4$ $\quad D = C_1C_2R_2R_3R_4$ $E = C_1R_2R_4 + C_2R_3R_4 + C_1R_2R_3$ $\quad F = R_3 + R_4$
$G_E(s) = \frac{D}{s^3 + As^2 + Bs + C}$	$A = 1/C_1R_1 + 1/C_1R_2 + 1/C_2R_2 + 1/C_2R_3 + 1/C_3R_3$

$$B = 1/C_2C_1R_2R_1 + 1/C_2C_1R_3R_1 + 1/C_2C_1R_2R_3 + 1/C_3C_1R_3R_1 + 1/C_3C_1R_3R_2 + 1/C_3C_2R_2R_3$$

$$C = 1/C_1C_2C_3R_1R_2R_3 \qquad D = 1/C_1C_2C_3R_1R_2R_3$$

Table 4.2 ARMAX transfer functions with different poles (*P*) and zeros (*Z*) for circuits (A)-(E)

Transfer Functions $G(s)$	***Z***	***P***	**Fit [%]**	**MSE [x 10^{-6}]**
$G_A(s) = \frac{0.05911}{s+167.3}$	0	1	27.31	2.503
$G_B(s) = \frac{0.000119s + 6.38\times10^{-5}}{s+2.678}$	1	1	6.943	4.102
$G_C(s) = \frac{-7.795}{s^2 + 60.92S + 1784}$	0	2	51.46	1.116
$G_D(s) = \frac{-0.00007s^2 + 0.05556s + 0.4503}{s^2 + 105.7s + 1775}$	**2**	**2**	**75.69**	**0.5576**
$G_E(s) = \frac{-60.29}{s^3 + 124.6s^2 + 6196s + 1.106\times10^5}$	0	3	39.77	1.780

The individual electrical parameters (4R-2C) corresponding to $G_D(s)$ and circuit of Fig. 4.4 (E) are obtained by the following analysis. For example in case of subject 1, comparing estimated and derived transfer functions calculation is shown as-

$$G_D(s) = \frac{s^2D + sE + F}{s^2A + sB + C} = \frac{-0.00007s^2 + 0.05556s + 0.4503}{s^2 + 105.7s + 1775} \qquad (4.21)$$

where,

$$A = C_1C_2R_1R_2R_4 + C_1C_2R_2R_3R_4 = 1$$
$$B = R_1R_4C_2 + R_3R_4C_2 + R_2R_3C_1 + R_2R_4C_2 + R_2R_4C_1 + R_1R_2C_1 = 105.7$$
$$C = R_1 + R_2 + R_3 + R_4 = 1775$$
$$D = C_1C_2R_2R_3R_4 = -0.00007$$
$$E = C_1R_2R_4 + C_2R_3R_4 + C_1R_2R_3 = 0.05556$$
$$F = R_3 + R_4 = 0.4503$$

The corresponding ARMAX polynomial coefficients (A, B, C, D, E and F) are used for solving in MATLAB to obtain the electrical parameters (4R-2C).

$$R_1 = 0.679k\Omega;\ R_2 = 1.095k\Omega;\ R_3 = -0.047\Omega;\ R_4 = 0.497\Omega;\ C_1 = 11.381\mu F;\ C_2 = 0.023F$$

Afterwards, the R and C values of the best fit models $G_D(s)$ as outlined in Table 4.3 are evaluated for 44 different subjects. As already mentioned, we simultaneously acquired the NCS parameters (CMAP, latency and NCV) for all 44 subjects while acquiring the input-output data using our custom made NCS setup. However, it is observed that value of R_3 is found to be negative, for the models to be applied for electrochemical systems with bulk electrolytes and interfacial electrodes [25], furthermore negative resistance generally occurs in establishing the dynamic models of electrochemical systems [17, 11, 30].

Table 4.3 Estimated RC parameter values and NCS responses for 44 subjects

Subjects	Custom Made Setup						Neuroperfect-2		
	R_1 $(k\Omega)$	R_2 $(k\Omega)$	R_3 (Ω)	R_4 (Ω)	C_1 (μF)	C_2 (F)	CMAP (mV)	Latency (ms)	NCV (m/sec)
S_1	0.679	1.095	-0.047	0.497	11.381	0.0230	14.3	4.12	58.25
S_2	0.509	1.041	-0.044	1.206	51.975	0.0160	15.3	3.92	61.22
S_3	0.569	1.127	-0.078	0.932	58.539	0.0240	14.9	4.00	59.50
S_4	0.594	1.065	-0.041	1.021	53.853	0.0213	14.7	4.05	59.25
S_5	0.530	2.144	-0.023	1.227	27.377	0.0260	15.2	3.95	60.75
S_6	0.949	1.369	-0.069	1.312	45.417	0.0123	10.2	4.75	46.31
S_7	0.622	1.630	-0.035	0.964	37.946	0.0260	14.4	4.15	57.83
S_8	0.764	1.359	-0.051	1.162	43.834	0.0180	12.8	4.40	53.40
S_9	0.604	1.217	-0.056	1.271	41.932	0.0140	14.4	4.12	58.73
S_{10}	0.421	1.316	-0.010	0.204	19.864	0.0440	16.5	3.63	65.56
S_{11}	0.537	1.170	-0.022	0.245	17.359	0.0370	15.1	3.98	60.30
S_{12}	0.915	1.234	-0.020	1.175	52.740	0.0142	10.5	4.73	47.56
S_{13}	0.545	1.192	-0.037	0.868	18.210	0.0379	15.0	4.00	60.0
S_{14}	0.805	1.562	-0.021	0.771	73.688	0.0395	11.2	4.64	48.49
S_{15}	0.504	1.858	-0.011	1.263	10.182	0.0328	15.5	3.90	61.53
S_{16}	0.460	1.471	-0.021	1.430	16.889	0.0258	16.1	3.71	64.15
S_{17}	0.549	1.136	-0.033	0.955	65.728	0.0254	15.0	4.00	58.75
S_{18}	0.600	1.564	-0.012	1.181	12.704	0.0398	14.4	4.13	58.11

S_{19}	0.432	1.225	-0.073	1.660	89.861	0.0931	16.4	3.68	64.67
S_{20}	0.456	1.114	-0.013	1.631	20.875	0.0177	16.2	3.70	63.51
S_{21}	0.539	1.272	-0.045	0.852	18.825	0.0423	15.2	3.95	60.25
S_{22}	0.760	1.302	-0.016	0.972	49.873	0.0988	12.8	4.40	54.09
S_{23}	0.339	1.562	-0.045	1.363	12.097	0.0594	16.9	3.60	65.27
S_{24}	0.982	1.458	-0.077	1.570	28.831	0.0260	10.1	4.80	45.83
S_{25}	0.665	1.720	-0.042	1.193	13.135	0.0600	14.2	4.20	57.14
S_{26}	0.511	1.452	-0.015	1.400	82.808	0.0309	15.2	3.94	60.91
S_{27}	0.383	1.341	-0.013	1.284	99.496	0.0600	16.6	3.64	64.56
S_{28}	0.455	1.629	-0.034	1.143	80.180	0.0529	16.2	3.75	63.46
S_{29}	0.534	1.144	-0.022	1.390	15.128	0.0826	15.2	3.90	61.02
S_{30}	0.755	1.391	-0.040	1.429	58.426	0.0126	12.8	4.45	52.80
S_{31}	0.772	1.710	-0.075	1.670	37.341	0.0650	12.7	4.42	53.16
S_{32}	0.791	1.204	-0.079	0.904	33.239	0.0100	12.5	4.50	51.11
S_{33}	0.418	1.365	-0.010	1.116	13.487	0.0363	16.5	3.68	64.67
S_{34}	0.659	1.248	-0.036	1.063	73.044	0.0160	14.2	4.30	55.34
S_{35}	0.585	1.533	-0.025	0.874	30.222	0.0974	14.8	4.05	58.76
S_{36}	0.661	1.071	-0.012	0.920	23.847	0.0295	14.2	4.15	57.34
S_{37}	0.943	1.723	-0.067	1.371	19.811	0.0727	10.2	4.75	47.36
S_{38}	0.826	1.676	-0.029	1.737	26.336	0.0932	11.0	4.65	48.38
S_{39}	0.672	1.287	-0.024	0.905	61.371	0.0275	14.1	4.17	55.54
S_{40}	0.554	1.418	-0.038	0.678	61.700	0.0258	15.0	4.01	59.85
S_{41}	0.871	1.367	-0.012	1.290	15.165	0.0597	10.8	4.69	47.97
S_{42}	0.626	1.175	-0.060	1.409	17.011	0.0619	14.4	4.12	58.25
S_{43}	0.545	1.287	-0.041	1.383	14.584	0.0619	15.0	4.05	58.76
S_{44}	0.709	1.668	-0.042	1.615	18.570	0.0831	13.8	4.20	57.61

4.3.2 Regression Analysis

As mentioned earlier, two types of regressions, namely, linear and SVR are adopted for statistical validation of the estimated models. Fig. 4.5- Fig. 4.6 shows the linear and stepwise linear regression analysis in terms of R^2 and RMSE.

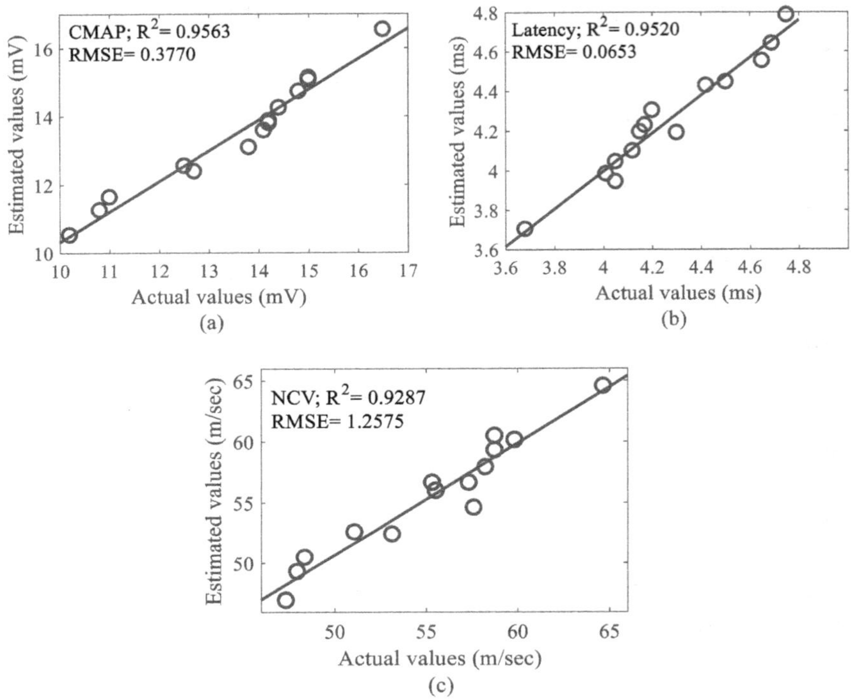

Fig. 4.5 Linear regression in terms of R^2 and RMSE for (a) CMAP (b) latency and (c) NCV

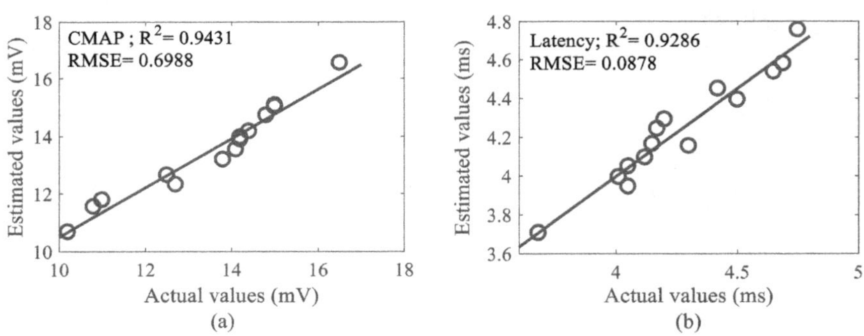

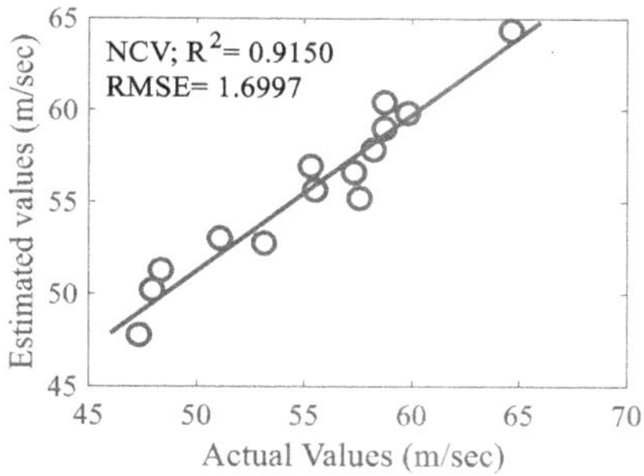

(c)

Fig. 4.6 Stepwise linear regression in terms of R^2 and RMSE for (a) CMAP (b) latency and (c) NCV

Fig. 4.7 to Fig. 4.10 shows the linear, cubic, Gaussian and quadratic support vector regression analysis along with R^2 and RMSE.

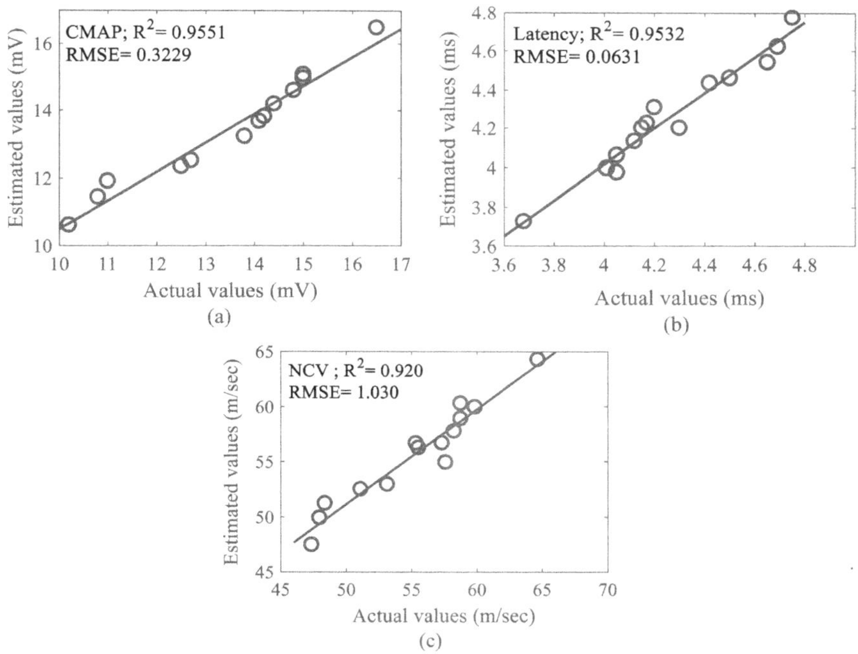

Fig. 4.7 Linear SVR in terms of R^2 and RMSE for (a) CMAP (b) latency and (c) NCV

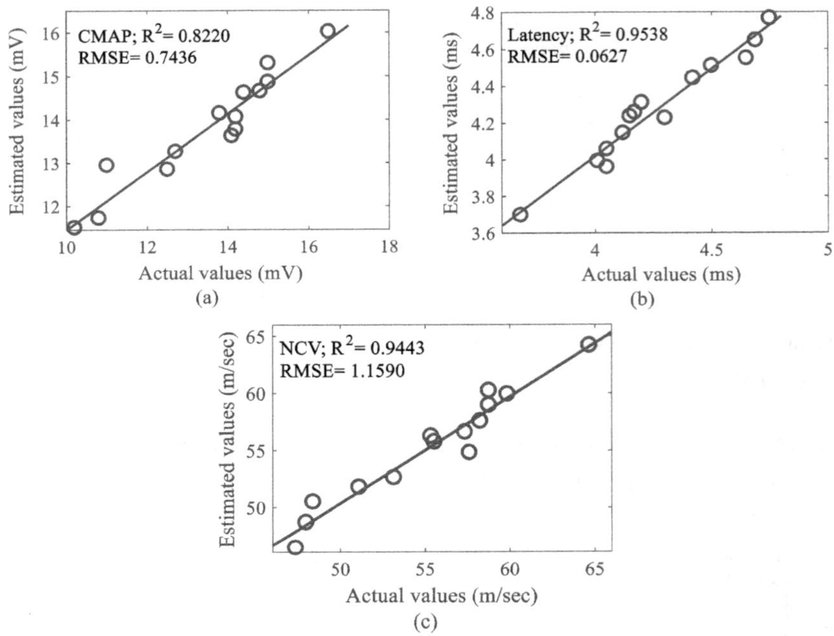

Fig. 4.8 Cubic SVR in terms of R^2 and RMSE for (a) CMAP (b) latency and (c) NCV

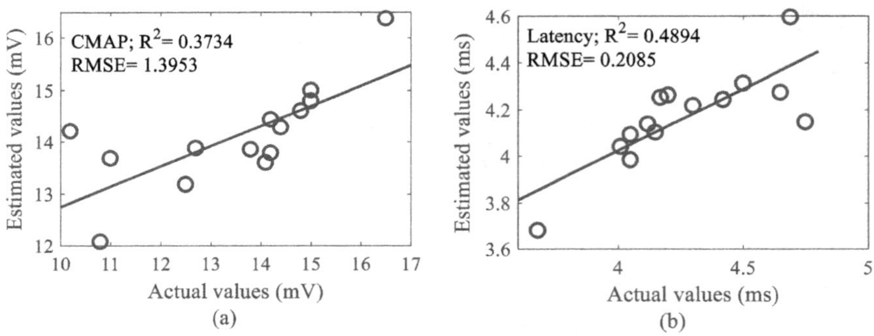

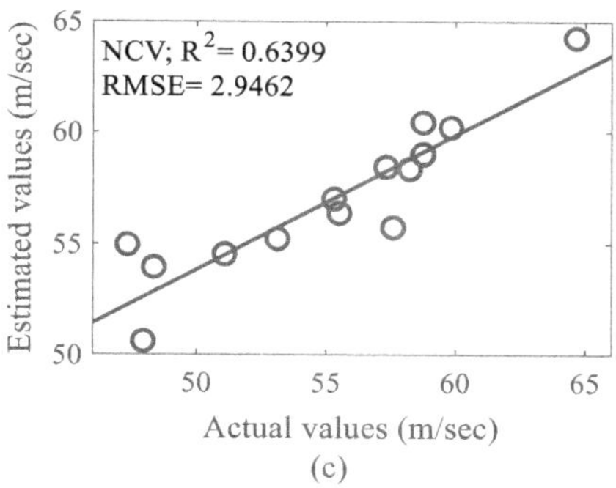

Fig. 4.9 Gaussian SVR in terms of R^2 and RMSE for (a) CMAP (b) latency and (c) NCV

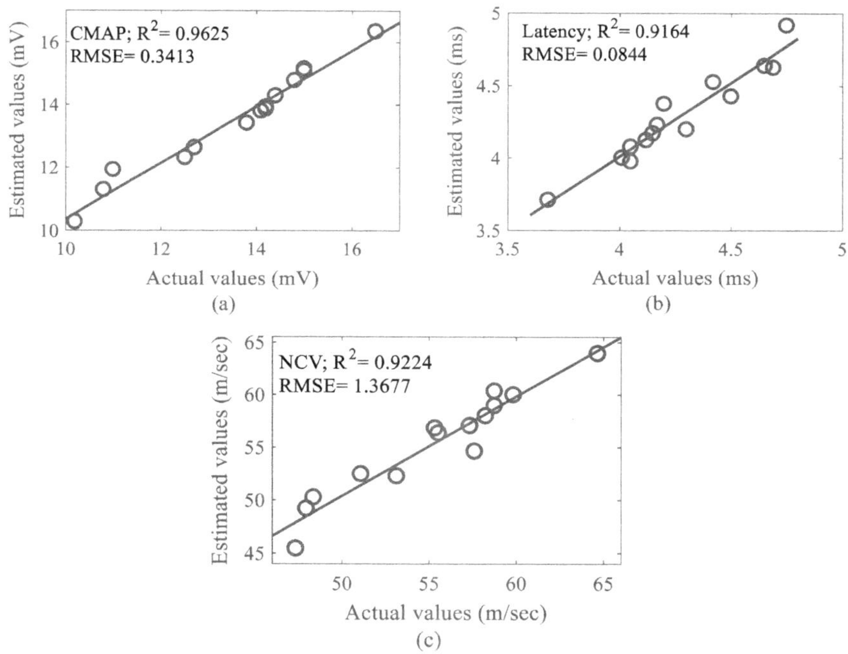

Fig. 4.10 Quadratic SVR in terms of R^2 and RMSE for (a) CMAP (b) latency and (c) NCV

Whereas, the model performances of all mentioned regression methods are outlined in the Table 4.4 based on testing data acquired from the remaining 14 subjects of Table 4.3.

Table 4.4 Actual and estimated NCS parameters for 14 subjects by the following six regression methods

Subject	Regression Methods	Actual values CMAP (mV)	Estimated values CMAP (mV)	Actual values Latency (ms)	Estimated values Latency (ms)	Actual values NCV (m/sec)	Estimated values NCV (m/sec)
	Linear		12.39		4.42		52.42
	Stepwise linear		12.31		4.44		52.70
S_1	Linear SVR	12.7	12.51	4.42	4.43	53.16	52.50
	Cubic SVR		13.28		4.38		53.56
	Gaussian SVR		13.80		4.28		56.99
	Quadratic SVR		12.65		4.50		52.12
	Linear		12.55		4.44		52.60
	Stepwise linear		12.65		4.39		52.96
S_2	Linear SVR	12.5	12.35	4.50	4.45	51.11	52.05
	Cubic SVR		12.84		4.28		54.84
	Gaussian SVR		13.14		4.33		56.05
	Quadratic SVR		12.30		4.43		52.50
	Linear		16.53		3.70		64.54
	Stepwise linear		16.54		3.70		64.31
S_3	Linear SVR	16.5	16.48	3.68	3.72	64.67	64.50
	Cubic SVR		16.01		3.76		62.95
	Gaussian SVR		16.36		3.68		64.20
	Quadratic SVR		16.35		3.70		63.95
	Linear		13.86		4.19		56.64
	Stepwise linear		13.98		4.15		56.90
S_4	Linear SVR	14.2	13.81	4.30	4.19	55.34	56.46
	Cubic SVR		14.04		4.15		57.79
	Gaussian SVR		13.80		4.20		57.19
	Quadratic SVR		13.93		4.19		56.84
	Linear		14.72		4.04		59.29
	Stepwise linear		14.73		4.05		58.96
S_5	Linear SVR	14.8	14.61	4.05	4.06	58.76	58.83
	Cubic SVR		14.65		4.05		59.15
	Gaussian SVR		14.60		4.08		58.81
	Quadratic SVR		14.79		4.07		58.94

	Linear		13.80		4.19		56.62
	Stepwise linear		13.89		4.16		56.57
S_6	Linear SVR	14.2	13.81	4.15	4.19	57.34	56.46
	Cubic SVR		13.79		4.17		56.79
	Gaussian SVR		14.38		4.11		58.42
	Quadratic SVR		13.85		4.17		57.10
	Linear		10.53		4.78		46.93
	Stepwise linear		10.67		4.75		47.70
S_7	Linear SVR	10.2	10.60	4.75	4.77	47.36	46.73
	Cubic SVR		11.56		4.68		48.54
	Gaussian SVR		14.09		4.22		58.32
	Quadratic SVR		10.29		4.88		45.12
	Linear		11.64		4.55		50.47
	Stepwise linear		11.78		4.53		51.23
S_8	Linear SVR	11.0	11.91	4.65	4.53	48.38	50.69
	Cubic SVR		12.99		4.48		52.99
	Gaussian SVR		13.57		4.34		56.65
	Quadratic SVR		11.94		4.61		50.07
	Linear		13.58		4.22		55.98
	Stepwise linear		13.53		4.24		55.61
S_9	Linear SVR	14.1	13.67	4.17	4.22	55.54	56.02
	Cubic SVR		13.63		4.26		55.53
	Gaussian SVR		13.62		4.23		56.46
	Quadratic SVR		13.79		4.22		56.36
	Linear		15.06		3.98		60.12
	Stepwise linear		15.02		3.99		59.79
S_{10}	Linear SVR	15.0	14.97	4.01	3.99	59.85	59.93
	Cubic SVR		14.85		4.06		58.87
	Gaussian SVR		14.83		3.99		59.46
	Quadratic SVR		15.10		3.99		60.00
	Linear		11.25		4.64		49.29
	Stepwise linear		11.55		4.57		50.15
S_{11}	Linear SVR	10.8	11.44	4.69	4.61	47.97	49.31
	Cubic SVR		11.75		4.58		50.78
	Gaussian SVR		12.00		4.62		51.73
	Quadratic SVR		11.27		4.62		49.12

	Linear		14.24		4.09		57.89
	Stepwise linear		14.17		4.09		57.80
S_{12}	Linear SVR	14.4	14.19	4.12	4.13	58.25	57.61
	Cubic SVR		14.61		4.04		59.29
	Gaussian SVR		14.27		4.12		58.14
	Quadratic SVR		14.29		4.12		58.01
	Linear		15.12		3.94		60.46
	Stepwise linear		15.08		3.94		60.37
S_{13}	Linear SVR	15.0	15.08	4.05	3.97	58.76	60.29
	Cubic SVR		15.29		3.93		60.86
	Gaussian SVR		15.04		3.96		60.28
	Quadratic SVR		15.17		3.97		60.34
	Linear		13.09		4.30		54.58
	Stepwise linear		13.19		4.29		55.16
S_{14}	Linear SVR	13.8	13.21	4.20	4.30	57.61	54.62
	Cubic SVR		14.16		4.22		56.68
	Gaussian SVR		13.81		4.28		56.53
	Quadratic SVR		13.42		4.35		54.54

Table 4.4 shows the both estimated and measured NCS parameters of 14 healthy subjects; however a composite analysis only can indicate the effectiveness of the regression analysis. We have further determined the closeness of the results in terms of RMSE and R^2 as shown in Table 4.5 for all the regression methods. As is evident, the linear SVR is found to be superior in the context of RMSE comparison to the other models for analysis of CMAP, Latency and NCV. However, Quadratic SVR outperforms over others for analyzing of CMAP and Cubic SVR shows better results than others for Latency and NCV in the context of R^2.

Table 4.5 Statistical analysis results of all regression methods in terms of RMSE and R^2

Regression Methods	**RMSE**			R^2		
	CMAP	**Latency**	**NCV**	**CMAP**	**Latency**	**NCV**
Linear regression	0.3770	0.0653	1.2575	**0.9563**	0.9520	0.9287
Stepwise Linear regression	0.6988	0.0878	1.6997	0.9431	0.9286	0.9150
Linear SVR	**0.320**	**0.060**	**1.030**	0.9551	0.9532	0.920
Cubic SVR	0.7436	0.0627	1.1590	0.8220	**0.9538**	**0.9443**
Gaussian SVR	1.3953	0.2085	2.9462	0.3734	0.4894	0.6399
Quadratic SVR	0.3413	0.0844	1.3677	**0.9625**	0.9164	0.9224

4.4 Conclusion

This study addresses the modeling of the human nerve based on impedance analysis. First, a custom made NCS setup was designed to collect the real time signals for theoretical modeling using regression analysis as well as performances of the models was also validated. In the modeling, stimulus impulse was applied as input and corresponding responses was used as output in the system identification technique to find the transfer functions in MATLAB tool by which nerve function is studied. Afterwards some RC Randle's circuits was considered and its transfer functions were evaluated and check the similarity pattern with respect to the order of S and R-C coefficients with the SIT generated transfer functions to find as well as study the nerve electrical model. Then equating both the transfer functions we get some nonlinear equations, by solving the equations we got the R-C values of the equivalent nerve electrical circuit model. Furthermore a dataset was arranged with the R-C values as well as the corresponding responses in terms of CMAP, latency and NCV for 44 subjects. Then different models were estimated using regression analysis by considering R-C values as input parameters and response parameters as output parameters employing the 30 subject's data out of 44 subjects. The remaining 14 subject's data were used to validate the performances of the models.

Bibliography

[1] Awad, M., and Khanna, R. Support vector regression. In *Efficient learning machines*, pages 67-80, Apress, Berkeley, Springer, 2015.

[2] Bruce, I.C., Irlicht, L.S., White, M.W., O'Leary, S.J., Dynes, S., Javel, E., and Clark, G.M. A stochastic model of the electrically stimulated auditory nerve: pulse-train response. *IEEE Transactions on Biomedical Engineering*, 46 (6): 630-637, 1999.

[3] Clarke, S.M., Griebsch, J.H. and Simpson, T.W. Analysis of support vector regression for approximation of complex engineering analyses. *Journal of Mechanical Design*, 127 (6): 1077-1087, 2005.

[4] Chen, J., Valehi, A., and Razi, A. Predictive modeling of biomedical signals using controlled spatial transformation. *arXiv preprint arXiv:1811.00079*, 2018.

[5] Cristianini, N. and Shawe-Taylor, J. An introduction to support vector machines and other kernel-based learning methods. Cambridge university press, 2000.

[6] Du, W., Han, Y.S. and Chen, S. Privacy-preserving multivariate statistical analysis: Linear regression and classification. In *Proceedings of the 2004 SIAM international conference on data mining* Society for Industrial and Applied Mathematics, pages 222-233, 2004.

[7] Einziger, P.D., Livshitz, L.M., and Mizrahi, J. Generalized cable equation model for myelinated nerve fiber. *IEEE transactions on biomedical engineering,* 52 (10): 1632-1642, 2005.

[8] Gitter, A.J., and Stolov, W.C. AAEM Minimonograph# 16: Instrumentation and measurement in electrodiagnostic medicine–Part I. *Muscle & Nerve: Official Journal of the American Association of Electrodiagnostic Medicine*, 18 (8): 799-811, 1995.

[9] Giannessi, E., Stornelli, M.R., and Sergi, P.N. A unified approach to model peripheral nerves across different animal species. *PeerJ,* 5: 1-22, 2017.

[10] Genton, M.G. Classes of kernels for machine learning: a statistics perspective. *Journal of machine learning research*, 2, 299-312, 2001.

[11] Hsing, I.M., Wang, X., and Leng, Y.J. Electrochemical impedance studies of methanol electro-oxidation on Pt/C thin film electrode. *Journal of the Electrochemical Society*, 149 (5): 615-621, 2002.

[12] Harimurti, R., Yamasari, Y., and Asto, B.I.G.P. Predicting student's psychomotor domain on the vocational senior high school using linear regression. In *2018 International Conference on Information and Communications Technology* (ICOIACT-2018), pages 448-453, Yogyakarta, Indonesia, 2018.

[13] Hope, J., Vanholsbeeck, F., and McDaid, A. A model of electrical impedance tomography on peripheral nerves for a neural-prosthetic control interface. *Physiological Measurement*, 1-17, 2018.

[14] Kavitha, S., Varuna, S., and Ramya, R. A comparative analysis on linear regression and support vector regression. In *2016 Online International Conference on Green Engineering and Technologies* (IC-GET-2016), pages 1-5, Coimbatore, India, 2016.

[15] Kandel, E.R., Schwartz, J.H., and Jessell, T.M. *Principles of neural science*, McGraw-hill, New York, 2000.

[16] Koch, Christof. *Biophysics of computation: information processing in single neurons*. Oxford university press, New York, 2004.

[17] Melnick, R.E., and Palmore, G.T.R. Impedance spectroscopy of the electro-oxidation of methanol on polished polycrystalline platinum. *The Journal of Physical Chemistry B*, 105 (5): 1012-1025, 2001.

[18] Mishra, U. K., and Kalita, J. *Clinical Neurophysiology*. Elsevier Health Sciences, 3rd edition, India, 2014.

[19] Motta, S. and Pappalardo, F. Mathematical modeling of biological systems. *Briefings in Bioinformatics*, 14 (4), 411-422, 2013

[20] Puanhvuan, D., Chumnanvej, S., and Wongsawat, Y. Peripheral nerve function estimation by linear model of multi-CMAP responses for surgical intervention in acoustic neuroma surgery. *Physiological Reports*, 5 (23): 1-10, 2017.

[21] Rall, W. Membrane potential transients and membrane time constant of motoneurons. *Experimental neurology*, 2 (5): 503-532, 1960.

[22] Sobrinho, Á., Cunha, P., da Silva, L.D., Perkusich, A., Cordeiro, T., and Rêgo, J. A methodology for modeling and simulation of biomedical signal acquisition devices. In *2015 17th International Conference on E-health Networking, Application & Services* (HealthCom), pages 227-231, Boston, USA, 2015.

[23] Squire, L., Berg, D., Bloom, F.E., Du Lac, S., Ghosh, A., and Spitzer, N.C. *Fundamental neuroscience*. Academic Press, 4th edition, 2012.

[24] Smola, A.J., and Schölkopf, B. A tutorial on support vector regression. Statistics and computing, 14 (3): 199-222, 2004.

[25] Sadkowski, A. Unusual electrochemical immittance spectra with negative resistance and their validation by Kramers–Kronig transformation. *Solid State Ionics,* 176 (25-28): 1987-1996, 2005.

[26] Schneider, A., Hommel, G. and Blettner, M. Linear regression analysis: part 14 of a series on evaluation of scientific publications. *Deutsches Ärzteblatt International*, 107 (44): 776-782, 2010.

[27] Tarotin, I., Aristovich, K., and Holder, D. Model of impedance changes in unmyelinated nerve fibers. *IEEE Transactions on Biomedical Engineering*, 66 (2): 471-484, 2018.

[28] Ugalde, H.M.R., Ojeda, D., Le Rolle, V., Andreu, D., Guiraud, D., Bonnet, J.L., Henry, C., Karam, N., Hagege, A., Mabo, P., and Carrault, G. Model-based design and experimental validation of control modules for neuromodulation devices. *IEEE Transactions on Biomedical Engineering*, 63 (7): 1551-1558, 2015.

[29] www.mit.edu

[30] Wang, Z.B., Yin, G.P., Shao, Y.Y., Yang, B.Q., Shi, P.F., and Feng, P.X. Electrochemical impedance studies on carbon supported PtRuNi and PtRu anode catalysts in acid medium for direct methanol fuel cell. *Journal of power sources*, 165 (1): 9-15, 2007.

[31] Wesselink, W.A., Holsheimer, J., and Boom, H.B.K. A model of the electrical behaviour of myelinated sensory nerve fibres based on human data. *Medical & biological engineering & computing*, 37 (2): 228-235, 1999

[32] Williamson, R.P., and Andrews, B.J. Localized electrical nerve blocking. *IEEE Transactions on Biomedical Engineering*, 52 (3): 362-370, 2005.

[33] Yang, Y. Prediction and analysis of aero-material consumption based on multivariate linear regression model. In *2018 IEEE 3rd International Conference on Cloud Computing and Big Data Analysis* (ICCCBDA-2018), pages 628-632, Chengdu, China, 2018

CPSIA information can be obtained
at www.ICGtesting.com
Printed in the USA
LVHW031159310123
738241LV00013B/1446

9 781805 455264